AMERICAN CATHOLIC SOCIAL TEACHING

edited by

Thomas J. Massaro, s.j.

and

Thomas A. Shannon

A Michael Glazier Book

THE LITURGICAL PRESS
Collegeville, Minnesota

www.litpress.org

Cover design by Greg Becker

1   2   3   4   5   6   7

0-8146-5105-4

Contents

ACKNOWLEDGMENTS

The articles in Volume II of this work are reprinted from the following sources:

Archbishop William H. O'Connell, "The Church—The Strong Safeguard of the Republic," *The Catholic Mind* 6 (1908) 275–93.

Bishop John G. Dunn, "Is Catholic Education a Waste of Time and Money?" *The Catholic Mind* 10 (1912) 331–44.

Bishop John Ireland, "Catholicism and Americanism," *The Catholic Mind* 11 (1913) 237–57.

Richard H. Tierney, s.j., "The Needy Family and Institutions," *The Catholic Mind* 12 (1914) 659–65.

Joseph Husslein, s.j., "The Eight-Hour Day," *The Homiletic and Pastoral Review* 21:10 (July 1921) 926–30.

John A. Ryan, "A Living Wage," *The Church and Labor*, ed. John A. Ryan and Joseph Husslein, s.j., 259–71. New York: MacMillan Co., 1924.

George G. Higgins, "What Is Social Justice?" *The Yardstick: Catholic Tests of a Social Order*, 5 May 1947. Department of Archives and Manuscripts. The Catholic University of America, Washington, D.C.

George G. Higgins, "Catholic Union Theory," *The Yardstick: Catholic Tests of a Social Order*, 19 February 1951. Department of Archives and Manuscripts. The Catholic University of America, Washington, D.C.

"This Matter of Religious Freedom," by John Courtney Murray, s.j., was originally published in *America*, 9 January 1965, and is reprinted with permission of America Press, Inc. Copyright © 1965. All rights reserved. www.americapress.org.

Francis L. Broderick, "The Encyclicals and Social Action: Is John A. Ryan Typical?" *The Catholic Historical Review* 55:1 (April 1969) 1–5.

Introduction

The phrase "Catholic social teaching" is usually applied to a set of approximately a dozen documents from Vatican sources—popes, councils, and synods of bishops. What makes these documents "social" is that, among all the numerous examples of encyclicals, apostolic exhortations, instructions, constitutions, and other genres, these documents deal primarily with issues of life in modern society, including economic and political realities facing all people. These were originally addressed to members of the Catholic Church, but are now typically addressed to "all people of good will." Collections of the most important of these Vatican social teaching documents, beginning with Pope Leo XIII's 1891 encyclical *Rerum Novarum* ("On the Condition of Workers"), are widely available.[1]

A more expansive understanding of Catholic social teaching would extend the conventional definition of the phrase in three ways. First, we might wish to extend the phrase backward in time, to consider how Church leaders and theologians addressed social realities in eras prior to the advent of modern social teaching. Here we might include the social theories and teachings implicit and/or explicit in the writings and sermons of patristic figures, medieval popes and bishops, and theologians of the scholastic and early modern eras. Second, we might expand the definition to include developments on the more local level, including statements by individual bishops in their dioceses and regional groupings of bishops such as national episcopal conferences. Third, we might extend the definition to include various types of "applied Catholic social teaching." This category includes the least official but perhaps the most effective vehicles for disseminating the Church's message of our social responsibility for advancing peace and justice. Whenever a particularly strong sermon about justice and charity is

---

1. See, for example, Thomas A. Shannon and David J. O'Brien, *Catholic Social Thought: The Documentary Heritage* (Maryknoll, N.Y.: Orbis Books, 1992), which contains English translations of the twelve most important Vatican social teaching documents, as well as two from U.S. Catholic bishops. Many of these documents can also be found online by searching the home page of the United States Conference of Catholic Bishops.

preached, whenever a union leader or politician inspired by papal pronouncements about just wages stands up for policies to help a group of
poorly paid workers, whenever a lay contributor to a diocesan newspaper publishes an article advocating creative ways to battle injustices
of any sort, these are the ways Catholic social teachings are incarnated
in the everyday world. In many ways, the Dorothy Days and Lech
Walesas of our world are just as effective advocates of social responsibility as any pope or bishop. If Catholic social teaching is to change
the world, then it will be largely through the efforts of lay adherents
who daily take up the challenge of working for justice and peace.

The primary focus of this two-volume work concerns the second
definition listed above—efforts at the local level—although we will
have occasion to push back the time line of the usual understanding
of Catholic social teaching by about a century (thus addressing the
first item above) and will also address the role of the laity and the
concrete application of social teachings on the part of laity (the third
item above). Volume I (which appears in CD-ROM form) contains
twenty-three documents of social teaching that come from bishops of
the Catholic Church in the United States. This list does not aspire to
be exhaustive—a much larger collection of bishops' statements on social issues could be compiled—but does attempt to provide a representative sampling of the most important stances taken by American
Catholic bishops on issues of social import in various eras of U.S. history. The first four of the documents included here, dating from 1792,
1829, 1866, and 1884, were written before the American bishops formally established a national episcopal conference that would meet on
a regular basis. The remaining nineteen documents date from the twentieth century and reflect the bishops' collective efforts to address social
issues, particularly those of a political and economic nature. Here the
bishops attempt to offer ethical guidance on such matters as racism,
the mass media, economic justice, war and peace, social policy, the
environment, and the role of women in society, among other topics.

Volume II, which consists of the twenty contributions contained in
this printed volume, presents a selection of representative discussions of
the same social issues addressed by the bishops' statements in Volume I.
In some cases, these articles apply teachings contained in the bishops'
social documents. Others provide the reader with more theoretical discussions of the methodologies and approaches taken by the bishops.

Even the most cursory survey of the early documents contained in
Volume I reveals that bishops in previous eras utilized a style of writing and discussion that is quite foreign to our contemporary usage.

Additionally, the topics discussed are much more frequently focused on the internal life of the Church—urging, for example, attendance at Mass and frequent confession, the orderly structuring of parish life, the preeminence of the role of the clergy, and relations with Roman authorities. While this may make reading these documents somewhat onerous, exposure to these perspectives is important in tracing how the Church in the United States came to understand itself in its formative years. The casual reader will find the phraseology quaint and perhaps at times off-putting. Nonetheless, the documents highlight a developing vision of justice, charity, and the demands of the common good particular to the American scene. It is valuable to comprehend how these concepts were articulated in an earlier age so that we can learn from this history how to make the appropriate application of these same realities to our time and situation.

Additionally, these bishops' statements also document the social concerns of Catholics at the time of their authorship. For example, they frequently deal with the question of how to respond to the growing and differing waves of immigrants into American society. The bishops reflect upon national events and traumas, such as racial and regional reconciliation after the Civil War. For the Catholic laity, industrialization raised new and challenging questions regarding social justice, questions that were addressed by a variety of Church teachings. Education of the young (particularly questions pertaining to the procurement of public funding for the growing system of Catholic schools and to appropriate ways for Catholics to relate to the public school system) was of particular importance and became the subject of strenuous debates within intellectual circles of the hierarchy and laity. In spite of this excellent record of addressing the critical social issues of the day, a variety of issues remained largely neglected or addressed only inadequately. Among these topics are Reconstruction, the treatment of Native Americans, racism, ecumenism, and the status of women in the Church and society. Overall, however, this body of early teachings shows a Church beginning to find its own footing in a democratic and religiously pluralistic society and a Church that is beginning to articulate its own distinctive vision of social life and appropriate responses to it.

Interspersed with these efforts were articulations of fears about anti-Catholic sentiment. As Catholics and the Church were forging their way into American society, they experienced discrimination, violence, and suspicion. The primary reasons for this were their different ethnic roots as well as their allegiance to the pope, which rendered them suspicious in the eyes of those who feared the effects of divided loyalties on the part of American Catholics. Such fears were not figments of the imagination. For example, an Ursuline convent was burned in Charleston, Massachusetts, in 1831. Irish-Catholics quickly learned that small signs in places of potential employment reading "NINA" meant "No Irish Need Apply." The Ku Klux Klan was yet another visible reminder that the Catholic presence in the United States was by no means universally welcomed. When coupled with the nativist movement, discrimination and violence against Catholics escalated greatly. All of this found culmination in the 1924 presidential campaign of Al Smith, the Tammany Hall Democrat who, as the first Catholic to receive a major party nomination for president, was reviled as much for his religion as for his politics, as evidenced by the revival of the old saw that the Democrats had once again become the party of "Rum, Romanism, and Rebellion."

The Catholic reaction to this was, on the one hand, a degree of hostility to the larger Protestant-dominated culture, and, on the other hand, an uncritical hyper-patriotism, which reached its nadir in the statement of Francis Cardinal Spellman during the Vietnam War, "My country, right or wrong." Each of these responses is problematic and has led to a variety of entanglements of Catholics with both the culture and the Church. The distinctive bind in which Catholics found themselves caught involved proving their patriotism while simultaneously maintaining allegiance to Rome—a Rome which already harbored suspicions about the orthodoxy of the American Church because of the previous experience of trusteeism that resulted in the condemnation of what is usually referred to as the "Americanist heresy."

Nonetheless, emerging out of this complex history is a pervading consensus that the American Catholic Church has much to offer the wider American society. A major contributing factor to this positive perception was the election of Pope John XXIII, whose personality revealed the warm and gracious side of Catholicism. This was coupled with the pope's own liberal openness to embracing contemporary trends in both Church and modern society. This recognition of the positive aspects of Catholicism was illustrated by the election of John F. Kennedy as the first Catholic president of the United States. While Kennedy was still pressed to demonstrate his allegiance to the constitution, he nonetheless was able publicly to profess his Catholicism. The releases of *The Challenge of Peace* (1983) and *Economic Justice for All* (1986) by the American bishops were seen by most as positive contributions to significant public policy issues in our nation, marking a "coming of age" for Catholicism as fully a "public church." Neither would have been possible without the pioneering efforts of bishops and laity who sacrificed deeply to create propitious conditions for the eventual flowering of subsequent generations of Catholic Americans.

Such positive efforts have been redescribed by some in the triumphalistic notion of "the Catholic Moment." Certain commentators have interpreted elements of the distinctive Catholic patrimony (such as natural law approaches to morality) as not only an appropriate contribution to life in a pluralistic society, but, in a heavy-handedly doctrinaire and objectionable way, as normative for all. At root, such a viewpoint is at variance with the most constructive elements in the history of the Catholic Church in America. Catholics have benefited from striking a pose of modesty and avoiding any pretense that could be interpreted as arrogance and a failure to respect the legitimate plurality of viewpoints in our country. Such a perspective makes the additional error of granting primacy to impersonal rules rather than respecting the conscience of the person as the proximate source of moral obligations. Since the Second Vatican Council (1962–65), Catholicism has unambiguously emphasized the dignity of the human person, a major aspect of which entails respecting the inviolability of the individual conscience that is formed through dialogue within the overlapping communities of Church, culture, and interpersonal relations.

Other commentators promote the term "counter-cultural Catholicism." One source of inspiration for this position comes from Pope John Paul II who, in his 1995 encyclical *Evangelium Vitae*, highlighted the destructive aspects of what he called a "culture of death." Some American Catholics turned to this phrase as a way not only to critique American culture, but more importantly to suggest a stance of the church vis-à-vis the larger culture. This stance suggests that the values promoted by Catholicism stand in direct opposition to the dominant practices of mainstream American life. Examples of such perspectives would include Catholic teachings on marriage and family life, the role of women, and respect for life at its beginning and end. A key problem with this stance is its tendency to set the Church and its members outside the culture in which both live and to have them speak only with a prophetic voice of condemnation and judgmentalism. If one insists on such a strident prophetic style, one may find only a single opportunity to make that statement of principles. If one speaks from within the culture and in dialogue with the culture, then one enjoys frequent opportunities to comment upon problems within the culture and to make constructive suggestions for the resolution of public policy issues.

The history of the Church has emphasized speaking to cultures from within them, highlighting their best values, and seeking to encourage and inspire participants of these cultures to an ever-higher standard of morality. While the counter-cultural model has the benefit of moral clarity and the strength associated with single-issue politics, it has the concomitant danger of simplistic analysis and cultural disengagement—something which is at variance with the mainstream of the Catholic tradition. However, this mainstream tradition, while it possesses the benefit of recognizing the complexity of the context in which it lives, also stands in danger of being co-opted by that very culture—a reality to which the Church has frequently fallen victim, as history attests. Arguably, the problems associated with speaking from within the culture are preferable to the problems associated with removing oneself from the culture in an uncompromisingly prophetic and counter-cultural fashion.

Responses focusing on the counter-cultural stances (such as the "Catholic moment" commentators mentioned above) may not be formed out of a motive of sheer malevolence, for we must consider that the issues facing both the larger culture and the Catholic Church specifically are quite complex. One critical issue is the appropriate competence of individuals in addressing particular questions. In composing their pastoral letters on peace and the economy during the 1980s, the Bishops' Conference proposed a noteworthy model for responding to such issues through a broad process of consultation of Catholic, other religious, as well as secular experts in specific policy areas. The bishops recognized the need for the best possible understanding of the social and technical aspects of public policy questions before they could even begin addressing their moral dimensions. This method respects the distinction between the technical and moral dimensions of a public policy debate, and seeks to offer ethical judgments whenever possible, but only within the context of a well-informed technical analysis of the relevant question. Such a method recognizes the need for caution and modesty in assessing the status of a particular question, but also affirms the necessity of a moral judgment based upon one's best formulation of the problem. Thus under the leadership of the bishops, American Catholics have come to a greater appreciation of the value of pluralism and public policy debate informing a moral judgment addressed to a particular set of historical circumstances, a judgment that is provisional yet authoritative.

The documents in Volume I of this work as well as the articles in Volume II, reflect a variety of stances toward these and other problems the Church has experienced during its over two centuries in the United States. Each document is of course shaped by the distinctive context in which it was authored. For example, "Human Life in Our Day" (November 1968) was an application to the American scene of the ideas contained in the papal encyclical *Humanae Vitae* (published earlier that same year). The see-judge-act schema adopted by John XXIII in his 1961 encyclical *Mater et Magistra* (pars. 237–41) is employed by the bishops of the Appalachian region in their 1975 pastoral letter "This Land Is Home to Me"—a ground-breaking document which has the added and intriguing feature of appearing in poetic verse format. Other documents, of course, are responses to unique American situations such as the economic challenges that are addressed in the 1919 "Bishops' Program of Social Reconstruction," as well as the 1933 letter "Present Crisis."

In recent decades, other letters mark special anniversaries of previous statements or call attention to specific issues raised in the American electoral cycle, such as the quadrennial statements on political responsibility published a full year before each presidential election (included in this collection is the 1999 letter "Faithful Citizenship"). Another entire class of documents is exemplified by regularly occurring statements, such as the Labor Day statements from the Bishops' Conference (included here is the 1996 Labor Day statement of Bishop William Skylstad). Important to note especially in the latter documents is that they are addressed both to members of the Church as well as to other members of society, thus continuing the later papal tradition of addressing encyclicals to "all people of good will." The genre of these letters is not that of a theological treatise but rather a practical application of foundational Catholic social principles to a range of very practical issues, from family life to foreign policy to principles such as progressive taxation.

We intend the articles we have selected to model the broader public discussion of issues raised by the bishops' social teaching documents. In many cases, these articles make direct reference to papal and/or episcopal teachings. In other cases, the articles discuss general themes or specific issues of relevance to the social teaching. Represented among the articles are some of the twentieth-century giants who have contributed to the practical articulation of Catholic social teaching in the American context, such as Msgr. John A. Ryan, John Courtney Murray, s.j., Msgr. George Higgins, as well as the Catholic Worker tradition. The reader will note that most of the articles are actually authored by bishops, religious, and clerics, rather than laity. Part of the reason for this is that in the early eras of Catholic Church life in the United States, few lay Catholics wrote on such issues. Additionally, in recent years the Church has been blessed with several extraordinary commentators on social issues who also happen to hold church office —Joseph Cardinal Bernardin, Archbishop Rembert Weakland, and Bishop James Griffin come to mind immediately—and some of their most noteworthy contributions are included in this collection. Our selection of authors was further guided by our editorial bias that favored articles offering specific commentary upon themes in the bishops' social teaching statements. Our hope is that future collections of commentary on Catholic social teaching will include expanded representation of lay voices analyzing the social issues of the day.

Neither in this brief introduction nor in the documents or articles themselves will the reader encounter an over-arching schema for the automatic application of teaching to practical life in American society. One will find, however, a number of suggestions, perspectives, and guiding principles for approaching these problems. The reader will note that the Catholic tradition is successful in avoiding either of two extremes. The first of these would be the extreme privatization of religious convictions that effectively removes faith-based contributions from the political discourse within our national public life. The other extreme would be a stance of didactic or overly dogmatic resolutions of extremely complex social problems. Although religious people should never refrain or be restrained from articulating a well-reasoned response to particular issues, they need to remember that such a resolution is dependent upon a particular reading of empirical data, as well as highlighting one set of themes within a broad tradition. The best of the Catholic tradition has recognized the difference between general principles, middle axioms, and specific solutions to problems. As the tradition develops, particular solutions will be abandoned and the middle axioms modified, but the general principles will remain fairly constant. Such methodology results in a felicitous modesty in engaging in public dialogue and making policy recommendations, while never compromising the tradition's commitment to the core of its social teaching.

We conclude by highlighting potential agenda items for the future of American Catholic social teaching. It is clear that the issue of the public responsibility of the Catholic citizen will come much more to the fore. One indication of this is the explicit courting of the Catholic vote in the Clinton administration; this has been continued in an even more explicit way by the George W. Bush administration as it seeks support for its social agenda. American Catholic social teaching as well as public policy efforts of the hierarchy surely point us in the direction of a much more actively engaged life of citizenship, but not for the opportunistic motives suggested by partisan politics.

Whatever approaches emerge within the Catholic community must be informed by an understanding of the history of the Catholic Church in U.S. public life. David J. O'Brien, astute historian of American Catholicism, has identified three historical stances taken by the American Catholic community as it takes up the task of engaging public life in our nation and culture. He identifies the first of these as a "republican style" that consists of an awareness of the dualism of citizenship and discipleship and calls Catholics to an explicit separation of both tasks. It tends to emphasize a style of lay trusteeship. Its "shadow side" includes the danger of an exaggerated secularism. The second is termed the "interest group" or "immigrant" style that emerged in the nineteenth century as an attractive option for a church that consisted largely of newly arrived immigrants facing a hostile social environment. Its "shadow side" included the danger of being too selfish, seeking its own advantages even if this merely consisted of securing an equal place at the table of our public life. The third is the more recently prominent "evangelical" style, one that O'Brien notes is the least distinctively Catholic, although arguably the most clearly "Christian" of the styles. This post-ethnic piety, perhaps best captured in the activism of the Catholic Worker and similar social movements, tends to affirm American individualism and personal freedom while engaging in counter-cultural acts of resistance.[2] As the Catholic community continues to grapple with current issues, we need to be informed by these responses as we seek to forge a new and creative stance toward emerging contemporary issues.

We call attention in particular to the following seven problems as significant challenges to the process just discussed. The first is the challenge presented by calls for a counter-cultural Catholicism. Such a brand of Catholicism would be primarily prophetic, with the concomitant danger of losing a social base for engaging in constructive leverage of the political process through the well-established routes of compromise and responsible give-and-take in the ordinary workings of the political arena. The second is the danger of partisan captivity to a particular political party or ideology. While frequent and public association with political leaders may be personally gratifying

2. See David J. O'Brien, *Public Catholicism*, 2d ed. (Maryknoll, N.Y.: Orbis Books, 1996).

for Catholic leaders, such associations may ultimately compromise the ability to provide a necessary critical response of the Catholic community; this is a temptation to be avoided at all costs. The third is constructing constituencies around single-issue politics. While such movements are easy to understand because of the clarity with which they isolate one issue from all others, nonetheless such strategies make it impossible to recognize both the complexity of social analysis as well as the moral linkage between seemingly disparate social problems. Fourth is the privatization of religion and the contemporary tendency to redefine religion as merely spirituality. While it is clear that religion without grounding in personal engagement is reduced to a mere formalism, nonetheless exclusive focus on personal spirituality leads to an abandonment of the public dimension of religion and its potential to influence the public sphere. Fifth is a narrow understanding of economic and social issues that results in the exclusion from public debate of substantive social issues such as racism, sexism, xenophobia, and other barriers to social mobility. While it is true that specific economic problems commend themselves most urgently to our attention, nonetheless we must not forget the frequently skewed social and institutional structures that provide the overarching frameworks for their resolution and must be addressed prior to resolving specific issues. Sixth, while Catholic social teaching is eager to highlight the legitimate role of religion in addressing social issues, such teaching does not suggest (as other current commentators often seek to do) that religion is a substitute for legitimate government intervention into the social problems of our age. While there is a consensus that government funding to supplement a variety of religious initiatives such as Catholic and other religious colleges, hospitals, and social service programs is not inappropriate, Catholic social teaching urges that government has an independent obligation in justice to respond to the needs of its citizens. How this is worked out in practice is a function of the traditional principle of subsidiarity that offers guidance regarding the division of responsibility among national and local government entities as well as private and voluntary sectors. Seventh and finally, the locus of authority for Catholic social teaching needs to be expanded from a vision that emphasizes hierarchical authority only to an enlarged vision that includes a place for a wider variety of agents, including religious and secular experts in various disciplines, both technical and ethical. While bishops clearly hold a legitimate teaching office, the two major pastoral letters of the bishops (*Economic Justice for All* and *The Challenge of Peace*) afford excellent models of how such authority can be shared in creative and productive fashion.

There are several important signs of hope regarding these challenges that the authors find particularly noteworthy. One of these is the Common Ground Initiative founded by the late Joseph Cardinal Bernardin and emerging from the moral vision of the "consistent ethic of life" which he articulated and championed. This process of dialogue seeks to engage a broad spectrum of opinions within the Catholic community in order to address in a constructive fashion the differing social agenda brought to public policy debates by a variety of Catholic voices. A second sign of hope is the ever-increasing number of volunteer programs and service-learning opportunities, both religious and secular, situated in colleges and high schools that draw students into active and practical participation in the social problems of a variety of peoples and communities. These programs not only account for much constructive work on behalf of needy peoples and communities, but also provide for invaluable exposure of young Americans to social problems faced by segments of the population whom they may seldom otherwise encounter. A third and related sign of hope is the recent explosion of interest in the study of social justice in Catholic schools at all levels. Through curricular, co-curricular, and extra-curricular programs and activities that introduce students to social justice in both its theoretical and practical aspects, many Catholic elementary schools, high schools, and colleges encourage their students to explore the tradition of Catholic social teaching in creative and thoughtful ways. Ultimately, this is the most encouraging sign that Catholic social teaching, as it has developed at both the universal and local levels, will be transmitted to future generations with a sense of its innate vitality and potential.

Thomas J. Massaro, s.j.
Thomas A. Shannon
Eagles Mere, Pennsylvania
July 19, 2001

FOREWORD

INSTRUCTIONS FOR USING THE CD-ROM

The CD-ROM portion of this publication is designed to be completely self-contained. Nothing will be loaded onto your computer system; everything needed to run the application software is on the CD-ROM. The CD is an "autoload" CD.* Insert the CD into your CD reader and Adobe Acrobat Reader will start and display the "title page." Click anywhere on the title page to access the Contents of the CD.

From the Contents page, click on the name of the chapter to be accessed. Where applicable, footnote numbers within chapters are linked to the footnote at the end of the document. Each file offers a fully linked list of bookmarks to navigate to other chapters from within any given chapter (click the Bookmark tab on the left side of the screen to access bookmarks).

The entire CD-ROM is indexed and searchable across documents. To enable the index, click the Search button (*not* the Find button). In the Adobe Acrobat Search dialog box, click the Indexes button. Click Add, direct the computer to the CD drive, double-click the ACST folder, and open the index file. The ACST index will then appear in the Available Indexes box; check the box in front of ACST index and choose OK. Once the index is enabled, enter the search term and click Search to generate a list of Search results.

*Some computer users disable the Windows autorun feature. If the Adobe Acrobat Reader does not start automatically:
- Double-click on the My Computer icon to display icons for your configuration.
- Locate the icon for your CD Reader (usually the D drive) identified by the name "ACST" and an Acrobat PDF icon.
- Click on the CD Reader icon and the Acrobat Reader will start.

Volume 1:

The Documents

See CD-ROM for these texts.

Volume II:

Analysis of the Tradition

1

THE CHURCH — THE STRONG SAFEGUARD OF THE REPUBLIC[1]

Archbishop William H. O'Connell

Undoubtedly one of the things which drew the hearts of men towards our Blessed Lord was the gentle human sympathy which pervaded His whole life and manifested itself in all His dealings with men. At times, indeed, He showed Himself to be the lion of the tribe of Juda. Again and again He withstood the great ones of the world to their very faces. He lashed the venders from the temple gates, and more mercilessly still He lashed with the scorn of derision and contempt the haughty Pharisee and the proud hypocrites who lorded it over the people. When the honor of the Father's house demanded cleansing and defence He rose in righteous anger and His very countenance struck terror to the hearts of those who beheld Him.

But such moments were rare, and in his terrifying mood He showed Himself only to the imposter and the hypocrite, the very sight of whom moved Him to lofty scorn. But to the people He was never thus. They knew Him only as a compassionate friend and a gentle benefactor. Upon them His face beamed with sympathy and love. When they suffered He was sad, and He bore their importunities and even their fickleness with an unruffled patience. At times as He looked over the land, whose soil His sacred feet were sanctifying, a deep and tender melancholy took possession of His soul, seeing, as He did, the aridness which it seemed no heavenly dew could soften. In such a mood

---

1. Sermon preached at the opening of the Seventh Annual Convention of the American Federation of Catholic Societies, Boston, Mass., August 9, 1908.

3

His sadness was as deep and touching as, when before the mighty ones of Judea, His bearing was awe-inspiring.

To-day's gospel pictures Him in one of those touching moments. Seated upon the hills which overlooked the Sacred City, he gazed upon it long and wistfully. For Christ loved not only mankind in general, but He loved His own people as brother loves brother. With all their faults, and He knew them all profoundly, they were His people, His Mother's people, and they were dear to Him as the blood which ran in His veins, and this city, Jerusalem, God's own city, wherein were the temple built by God's command and the ark, the table of God's law, how precious they were to Him.

Over the whole world His vision ranged, and before His vision rose the proud citadels of other lands, castles and palaces, powerful and rich and fair to behold. Other temples, too, raised their splendid walls, their white marble turrets glittering in the sunlight and their gilded domes glinting like mirrors of gold. But within them were the abomination of desolation and the worship of false gods and foolish idols. Once more He looked down upon the Holy City. In that Holy of Holies the name of the true God was spoken. Upon those altars sacrifice was offered daily to Jehovah, to His own Father. There, alone, in all the world, was God known and worshipped, and yet as He looked He drooped His head, His face betrayed the awful sadness of His soul, the tears sprang to His eyes and coursed down His sacred cheeks and Jesus wept.

When at another time, standing near the grave of His beloved friend, Lazarus, the great sorrow that filled His soul showed itself in tears, those who stood by Him said one to another: "See how He loved him." His tears were the marks of His love. And now as He sits solitary on the mount, His love for Jerusalem is attested by the same witnesses. Christ was a true patriot. The love of His fatherland with Him was deep and true and strong. For it doubtless He would have died, indeed He did die for it, and the cause of His weeping now is the thought that even His death will profit it so little, and amid His tears He raises His voice in this lamentation: "Ah, Jerusalem, Jerusalem, if thou didst but know the things which are for thy peace!"

To establish peace in the world Christ had come among men. "Peace to men of good will,"—that was the burden of the angel's song when in Bethlehem the Prince of Peace was born into the world. The pagan nations, ignorant as they were, of the true God and of His law, had long since lost the secret of that harmony of human and divine rights and duties which is the very groundwork of Peace. There was no law but the law of force. Might alone prevailed. The weak had long since ceased to look for justice; the poor and the little ones of earth had long since accepted degradation, and the voice of complaining had long since been stifled. Tyranny reigned supreme, and among the thousand gods to whom they offered incense and sacrifice, there was not one with power enough to aid the weak. There was a God of Riches, and a God of War, and a God of Beauty, and a God of Pleasure; there was no God of poverty, of humility and of pain. The rich sacrificed to wealth, that they might obtain even greater riches and they went out from its temple to plunder the defenceless. The slaves dragged from their burning hamlets were whipped into the wine vats and their aching feet trod the purple grapes into the rich wine which their drunken and pampered masters were to offer to the Wine God.

There was no law but the law of force; and hatred of man to man, of tribe to tribe, of nation to nation, was the logical and natural consequence. Justice and equity are founded not upon force, but upon the eternal principles which emanate from the God Who established His universe. And when He is banished from the nation's heart, justice and equity vanish with Him.

What a garden of weeds God's beautiful world had become— weeds, poisonous and loathsome, that grew out of the fetid swamps, and which, climbing as they grew, reached even now to where He was sitting on the mountain, and whose tendrils had already gripped the Land of Promise over which God's representatives had so long reigned. Already, within the gates of the Holy City, disorder had raised its shrill voice. The atmosphere of paganism all around it had begun to do its work.

The egotism, the selfishness and the heartlessness of wealth had entered through the gates with the merchandise which Jerusalem had brought from Tyre and Sidon. The gap between the rich and poor was ever widening. The luxury of the farther Orient was fast sapping the moral vigor of the Israelite. The tablets of the law were still revered, but the law itself was fast losing its power over the nation; and secretly, step by step, the vices of paganism had crept up the Mount of Zion into the very sanctuary of the Lord. The cankerworm of irreligion and infidelity was gnawing at the very vitals of faith in God and in His law. And the thin veil of hypocrisy barely covered the hollowness and the sham with which the Pharisee and Sadducee strove to hide by empty ceremonial the lack of true observance of God's commands.

As Christ looked, from the high place where He sat, over Jerusalem and Palestine, it seemed as if the sacred cause of God was all but lost. The very citadel of God was now the center of attack. There was force enough and more still within that citadel to rout the whole assembled army of infidelity and idolatry now gathered in battle array up to its very walls. The power of God, the infinite and all-powerful, was there in their midst. A hundred times before He had rescued them, when the faith of the people was strong and all that faith was in God. They had but to rise from the lethargy which their indifference and hypocrisy had brought down upon them, to fling off the selfishness which luxury was weaving about them, and to stretch out their hands in sincerity toward the Son of God, there seated upon the mountain above them, to accept His sweet yoke of humility and His gentle burden of charity, and once more the reign of Jehovah would return, bringing in its train justice and righteousness and the tranquility of order which is blessed peace.

But alas! pride blinded their eyes and selfishness had hardened their hearts. The humility of the carpenter's son was foolishness to their proud minds, and the law of His fraternal love was folly to their selfish and greedy hearts. And He Who had come to save them from themselves, He Who had brought with Him the power of Heaven to make them again a great nation upon the earth, He Who had brought the reality of God's presence instead of the figure and the shadow which they had possessed, He Who was their God and their King, was out there on the hills weeping for the blindness which hid Him from their eyes, a blindness which even He could not heal because they did not wish to see. Christ weeping over Jerusalem will remain as long as the world lasts a picture of that true patriotism of love of home and country, which every follower of Christ should feel—a picture, not of the false and flattering love which cries, "Peace, peace," when there is no peace, which signals, "All is well," even when the enemy is at the gates, which lulls the dozing citizens to sleep with lullabys fit only for babes. There are plenty such now being sung—sweet meaningless messages of false optimism telling the world how good it is and that it is constantly growing better.

Not such was Christ's patriotism, not such may be ours, as we prize at their true value the prosperity and the real happiness of the land we love with truly Christian patriotism. Our duty it is rather to see, as if with His vision, what are the foes which silently and stealthily tend to undermine the strength of our beloved nation; and to raise our voices incessantly against them, not with the wail of pessimism, but with the voice of affectionate warning.

For this land has been given over by God's providence to the rule of all the people, and every citizen must in accepting its benefits accept also the responsibility of guarding its welfare and helping on its prosperity. And first ever in its defence, as first in every civic duty, should be the Catholic Christian; for the Church of Christ has much to be grateful for here, where its liberty is guaranteed, and its precious freedom protected; and the Catholic has always shown his gratitude on every field where his country's honor demanded it.

To-day thousands of her children from every part of this vast land are gathered in this historic city to give new proof of their fidelity to their country's interests; to sit for a while with Christ upon the mountain, and to see as with His eyes what things are for the nation's peace; and then to go forward and strive as He did to diminish as far as we can the false principles which threaten her very vitality, and to make known the doctrine of Christ, in which alone there is life and strength, not only for the individual, but for the whole nation.

This in brief is the primary motive and reason for the Federation of Catholic Societies—namely, to safeguard the best interests of the nation by endeavoring to bring out into the actual and throbbing life of the people those vivifying principles of Christian civilization upon which Christian society is built; and secondly by denouncing fearlessly whatever endangers the public moral welfare, and by agitating prudently to bring about a healthy public sentiment.

No one who knows, even superficially, the national life can doubt for an instant that there is great and crying need for activity on the part of all men of good will. And, since the impending ills of the body corporate are not physical but moral in their nature, the Church whose field is the moral world must confront them now as she has done in all the ages since the days when Peter and Linus, Cletus and Clement, faced them in the Roman Empire, and by the power of the cross defeated them in their very stronghold. And I dare say that the Catholic Church alone must soon be recognized not merely as the strongest but as the only bulwark against the prevalent social evils which seem even now to threaten not only the prosperity, but the very life of the nation. For she is to-day the only moral body which gives indication of growing vitality and increasing vigor. She has grown in these fifty years past by leaps and bounds, while all around her are strewn the wrecks of what once appeared to be flourishing sects. The Catholic Church has but just begun to manifest in this young land the undying vitality with which Christ endowed her, while on every side are heard the cries of dissolution and dismemberment of what but a few brief years ago seemed energetic religious organizations. It is not we who now say this, but their own leaders who can no longer deceive themselves when the evidences are so palpable.

I used to wonder, as a boy, beholding our own small number and negligible influence, when I read that Protestantism contained in itself the germ of dissolution and decay, for facts around me seemed to offer little proof of the truth of that assertion; but to-day more rapidly than one could ever imagine the proofs have come to hand in the facts under our eyes, and it is the leaders of Protestantism, again I repeat, who are now proclaiming it to the world that, unless all signs fail, their churches may soon close their doors. Step by step the principle of private judgment and the so-called "higher criticism" have done their havoc. The Bible which half a century ago was a fetich is to-day a fable, and whatever there was of simple faith in the supernatural is fast being dried up in the hearts of those whose ancestors made faith alone the only condition of eternal salvation. Lutheranism and Anglicanism, as they were a century ago, have disappeared from the face of the earth. All the other "isms," which followed quickly, one upon the other, have reduced themselves at last to "nothingism." No faith, no church, no fixed moral law; nothing, in fine, of all that can not be touched with the hands and seen with the eyes; even God Himself is no longer God, but a first cause, or an unseen power, or anything but that Eternal Father Whose beloved Son was Christ, the Redeemer of the world.

A few earnest souls outside of the Church already recognize the writing on the wall. They behold with dismay the disintegration of societies, congregations and parishes. They are raising their voices now against the debacle, but it is like building a wall of sand against an incoming tide—the tide which, four centuries ago, started with the rebellion of Luther against his ecclesiastical superiors; and now, by the force of its own logic, that wave has gone on mounting until, rebellion succeeding rebellion in increasing proportions, it has submerged those who caused it and has left in its wake the utter ruin of the supernatural, and, scarce a vestige of a revealed religion remains. And with its advance in sympathetic progress the seeds of civic rebellion have been sown, and that, too, was a logical consequence. The king rebelled against Papal supremacy and made himself Pope in his own domain; the people rebelled against the king with perfect logic, and assumed to themselves both papacy and royalty; and now, as the gaunt forms of anarchy and communism stalk abroad, the process goes further, and wealth and power wherever they exist are assailed. If the first rebellion was justifiable, so is the last. If no rights are sacred, then every revolution is justified. The Church is the only moral body in the whole world, which has remained consistent and sternly logical. Whole nations have risen up against her, her rebellious children have often offered her violence, but she has remained ever the same, serene in the midst of revolutions, confident of the promises of Christ; and she has beheld the dissolution and decay of all that threatened her, while she, ever youthful, ever more vigorous, still flourishes, still teaches the truths which save society and the world.

Christ warned His Church of the battle and the warfare through which she was to march to her eternal triumph. Each century has verified His prophecy. A century ago Protestantism was in the field against her, and the ground of warfare was a few texts of Scripture. To-day Protestantism has thrown Scripture to the winds, and with Protestantism there is no longer any struggle. It has vanished from the field self-destroyed. But a new foe faces the Church, or rather its most ancient enemy in a new armor. It is paganism, the paganism of Rome and Greece marching under a standard woven from the last shreds of those Christian principles which have been saved from the ruins. It knows no Christ, no dogma, no leader, no time but the present, no place but the earth. It sneers at all revelation, and scoffs at the supernatural. And yet it hails as a new salvation the ravings of half-demented prophets, and grovels in the stupidity of Oriental superstition.

And leagued with this foe who fights with lazy indifference, there is another which is neither lazy nor indifferent, but, with a virulence of antipathy and a tireless activity all its own, wields in season and out of season its sharp weapon, with a hate that is almost blind, at everything that is left of the Christian name. The aggressiveness of this enemy of Christ is the aggressiveness of the evil one himself. And its cunning is the cunning of him who is the father of lies. It disdains no means, it scorns no assistance, that will produce desired results. The press, the stage, the platform, however and wherever it can catch the public ear and the public eye, serve its purposes. In France it worked for half a century without showing its true hand; and when at last it was caught red-handed, no lie was too gross, no calumny too vile, to cloak its own trickery and deception.

And so the two foes which face to-day the cross of Christ, still raised aloft by His Church as the tree of eternal life and the banner of salvation, are first, the last remnants of that negation once called Protestantism and now styling itself queerly enough "The New Religion," and secondly, the same eternal energy, paganism, which the Apostles faced from the first day when to the Gentile world they preached Christ crucified. And the Catholic Church to-day, holding firm and fast to the same principles and the same doctrine and the same law which Peter and James and John delivered to Jerusalem and

Rome and Athens, standing on the ground of the same eternal truths, never changing, yet always moving the whole moral world, remains in spite of new thought and new theories the only permanent strength in all the world, the only reliable moral force upon which all order and law and authority can depend, and therefore the only moral organization and institution which withstands alike the false pretensions of conceited novelties in religion and the turbulent restlessness of all revolutionists against civil order.

It is wonderful how men can deceive themselves with a little flattery, and it is pathetic to see what intellectual vanity can do to cover up the glaring fallacies of new systems. To accept what the experience of ages has proven has for some temperaments little attraction. Newness, originality, is the first requisite for them, and so under the guise of a new need for new conditions they invent for themselves new principles, a new doctrine, and call them a new church. And with a blindness which is beyond comprehension they fail to see the double fallacy of their position from the point of view of both history and philosophy. For the profound student of history knows that every so-called new condition of society has been repeated one hundred times before in the story of the race. The names of the people and places change, the conditions are identical. There is not a single condition existing to-day in the whole world, civilized or uncivilized, which the Church of Christ has not faced one hundred times before and settled with the same identical principle. And the student of philosophy knows that truth is always truth, and the only originality in the moral order is immorality; and yet we are expected seriously to listen to all this talk about the growth of truth and the new religion. If this growth consists, as we plainly recognize that it does, in a return to the paganism of twenty centuries ago, we fail to see what the twenty centuries of growth have accomplished. If this so-called "new thought" and new religion mean the blotting out of the whole morality of Christ, as in the end it certainly does, all meaningless phrases to the contrary notwithstanding, prating about progress and intellectual advance is the progress of the crab walking backwards.

Take away from the Christian religion all that makes it essentially Christian, the divinity of Christ, the reality of the supernatural world, the necessity of grace, the inherent moral weakness of human nature— take them away as the "new thought" and new religion have done, and we ask why speak of Christianity at all, except as a mockery and a snare. It is strange that with all their boasting they still fear to call themselves openly the pagans that they are. They pretend still to reverence Christ. Strange logic! for if Christ be the man they represent, He is the greatest imposter and criminal the world has ever known. For He has deceived the human race in the most vital matter that concerns humanity. Why then this mockery of their allegiance to Christ and the name of Christian? It would seem as if they had a superstitious dread of taking the last and most logical step of all—that of renouncing the entire Christian name, and openly joining hands with those who have opposed it from the beginning. And we repeat, driven as we are by the inexorable force of the true logic of their position, that they stand before this only alternative: either to go back to the shadow of the cross upon which the God-Man died for their salvation, back to the rock upon which Christ built His Church, that Church against which neither new religions nor new revolution can ever prevail; or, frankly disavowing His principles and His law, to throw off His yoke entirely and take the only other logical stand, the stand which all the world had taken before Christ came, that there is nothing but conjecture in the whole realm of spiritual life, no certainty of hope beyond the tomb, no philosophy of life but that which bids man to eat, drink and be merry, for to-morrow we die, and death ends all.

This is the true and logical terminus toward which modern life, rejecting the guidance of divine Faith, inevitably is tending. It is unquestionably the final conclusion of the premises which the so-called "new thought" has openly espoused. Are they prepared to accept the bitter logic of the situation, a logic which has begun to work itself out under our very eyes, and the fruit of which, however unwelcome, is now at their very doors? Why talk about the evils of divorce? Why bewail the diminution of the birthrate and the threatened extinction of family life? Why decry the rising discontent visible all around us? Why complain of the social disorders that are rending the civil fabric? Why exclaim in horror at the lawless uprisings of anarchy and riot against constituted authority? Why bemoan the growing divisions between the rich and the poor, and the clamor of class against class which fills the land? These are, after all, only the practical working out of the very principles which for a century and more the apostles of this new religion have been upholding. They are the scourge which infidelity and agnosticism have brought down upon the shoulders of those who have preached them.

The people are more logical than their leaders, these wise-acres with intellects too great to accept historic Christianity. Poor, dull people, with whom these modern philosophers so often have grown impatient because they learn so slowly! They are learning fast enough now; they have seized at last the full meaning of the new principles of

salvation which make each man both pope and king, which hand over
to the interpretation of each individual the mystery of life to solve according to his own judgment and his own taste. Yes, they are learning
fast now, so fast that their teachers are horrified at their aptness. And
when, at the lightning speed which they now have attained, the new
principles have arrived at their full application, when all Government
is threatened, except the government of each man by himself, when at
last the only sanction which human law has is force, as it must be when
the groundwork of the supernatural is abolished and moral obligations
have no more meaning, what will there be left to oppose to force but
force, and what is that but war? And the war, not of nation against
nation, but of man against man; and that is anarchy.

It is idle for them to imagine that philanthropy will have any power
to stem the tide which infidelity and irreligion have started. It is mere
folly to attempt to supplant faith by humanitarianism. This is the latest of all their fallacies and will be found as fruitless as its predeces-
sors. The evil is deeper than mere surface ills, and the momentary
relief of them can never change the radical wrong. There are certain
appetites that only grow by feeding, and if life is to be reduced to
the mere process of getting, no amount of material giving will ever
satisfy its insatiable hunger. That remedy has been tried before and
failed utterly; and that for the simple reason that moral content alone
produces real happiness, whether a man be as rich as Croesus or as
poor as Lazarus. And there can never be moral content without moral
life, and there can never be moral life without spiritual law, and there
is no spiritual law that has any lasting foundation, any substantial
hope, any universal and eternal motive, but the law of Christ living
in His Church.

If there is any form of government which needs for its permanence and prosperity the conserving force of right moral Christian
sentiment it is a republic. Under a monarchy, loyalty to the reigning
house and its traditions and glories, together with the aristocracy of
inheritance, can, as history has often proven, hold in abeyance the
forces of disunion and dismemberment. To-day the greatest power
which holds together the whole Japanese people is the veneration in
which the Japanese rightfully hold the Mikado and the Imperial family. In a republic there is no such conservative influence. The principle, at least in theory, of a democratic form of Government is that
the will of the majority of the people is the law. Popular sentiment
then is the very groundwork and foundation of its existence, and the
moral atmosphere which pervades the mass of the citizens is the only

safeguard of its permanence. It is for this reason that, while changes in a monarchy are slow, in a republic they sometimes come with the rapidity of lightning. The germ of disorder, which in an empire may take centuries to develop, in a republic may require but a single year. It is for this reason that no one who loves this thrice blessed land of ours can behold with indifference the smallest beginnings of those principles which, in these latter days more than ever before, have become evident among us—the principles, I repeat, of a new paganism imported from the schools of German agnostic philosophy, finding their way through the universities and the pulpit clown among the people. Wait but a little longer and the nation one day will awake startled to find the principles which it once applauded doing such mischief as these myopic teachers never contemplated.

For the people are merciless in their logic when once they have learned well their lesson. If the whole period of their early education is spent with no instruction in the divine truths which lead towards God, they can hardly be expected later, when passion and self-interest have grown stronger, to find their way to Him. If all their childhood passes in the effort of merely mental training and no thought is given to instilling into their childish hearts the moral curbs and restraints and influences which hold the appetites in check, or if the only basis of moral restraint is human respect, who is to blame if in later life self-will and self-seeking shall burst these weak bonds and sweep before them whatever stand in their way? The lack of religious influence in early years, in the home and in the school, has begun already to bear its fruit in every phase of our national life. And this unwelcome fact is so palpable that at last the once enthusiastic devotees of a purely secular education cannot close their eyes to the inherent weakness of the system and its vicious effects upon the whole life of the people.

We Catholics have pointed it out like many another danger for a century past, and our only thanks were to be rated as enemies, of popular instruction and belittlers of the great panacea of public school training. But we are well accustomed to this kind of gratitude, and, having sounded the warning for others, we have done our own duty to our own under circumstances which have proven our sincerity; for, while our people are among the poorest of this country in material goods, and the least able to bear new burdens, they have attested their fidelity to the welfare of the nation in a way that not even the richest have done. Out of their slender means they have erected, at the cost of millions and millions of dollars, schools and institutions wherein their children might be taught that there is a God to Whom all men must be responsible, that the moral law emanating from that God binds them during all their lives, that all authority is from God, that civil rulers are sacred in that authority, that the law of the land is to be obeyed under penalty of God's displeasure, that the rights of property are sacred, and all those other inviolable principles of right and duty which stand for order in the world and the peace of humanity.

What other organization in this whole country is doing at such tremendous sacrifice what we have done? And for all this we have received up to the present nothing but suspicion and distrust. Nay more, while doing for the children of the nation what even the nation itself cannot do, we have been burdened with a double taxation, which is, let us say it boldly and continue to repeat it until the burden is removed, nothing short of outrageous tyranny. For we have been forced, while expending enormous sums which we could little afford in the training of our youth in the sane principles of Christian morality which are the best safeguard of the nation, to pay more than our share of the taxes for the support of schools which, however good they may otherwise be, can never by their very constitution even so much as lay one stone in the moral foundation of civil life. For, I repeat, there is no morality without religion. There may be ethical speculation which the child is free to accept or reject, and surely that is a poor morality. And so this most recent effort to inject into secular education some appearance of moral training is almost worse than none at all, since by its doubtful attitude it must inevitably weaken the whole basis of moral law by making it appear to the child as a matter of choice and selection, or even of complete rejection, for its foundation is, not the eternal principles of the divine will, but the mere question of human agreement. And I call upon this Federation and upon every Christian in the land to oppose with all their influence this latest attempt of an infidel propaganda to thrust into the schools what appears on the surface to be an innocent system of ethical culture, but which in reality is only another clever ruse to substitute a pagan philosophy for Christianity. Better one hundred thousand times never to mention the name of religion, leaving it to the homes and the church to do what they can in supplementing the moral and religious training of the child, than this astute manoeuvre to root out of the child's life every idea or sentiment of supernatural law. And if this meeting of Federation will have accomplished only this one great achievement—namely, of arousing the whole American people to a knowledge of the awful dangers which the nation must eventually face if this system of irreligious or, unreligious training of the young continues, it will have done something to pin the eternal gratitude of all true patriots. Meanwhile we must ourselves stand fast to our own principles. Our growing numbers and influence impose upon us greater responsibilities. As the Christian faith in those around us is flickering out, our own must burn ever more brightly. And the louder the cry is raised of those whose only faith is in their own wisdom, Who made humanity out of dust and by Whose knowledge alone man may hope to learn. The world is clamoring for peace, and yet often they who are seeking it are but unconsciously sowing the seeds out of which discord alone can grow. It is our duty to turn their eyes out upon the hills where Christ still sits weeping over the world, blinded by its own folly, its heart still as hard as the people of His own Jerusalem, its mind still as proud as the proud teachers of His time. Let us love our dear land as He did His; and by the knowledge which His faith alone can bring and by the charity which His law alone can kindle, let us by word and example show forth, to all who are willing to see, those things which are for our country's peace.

2

Is Catholic Education a Waste of Time and Money?[1]

Bishop John G. Dunn

"And the disciples seeing it had indignation, saying to what purpose is this waste, for this might have been sold for much and given to the poor." —St. Matthew, xxvi, 8–9.

The question indignantly asked by the disciples in the house of Simon the leper is, I venture to say, hesitantly asked by many in New Orleans to-day—not in reference to a box of ointment poured on the head but in reference to this Ursuline monument erected for Christ's little ones. Does it not look like a waste? It is not a waste.

Could not the money have been better spent? Could a better investment not have been made? And the imagination at once invests it all, and pictures the improved mills and factories, and the cottages for the toilers, the homes of shelter for the homeless, the Magdalen retreats for the white and dark and red-skinned slaves of luxury and vice! Why all this waste? A waste running into the hundreds of thousands of dollars at the very start, and all for what—a school, another school, a Sister school, with no difference between it and thousands of other schools except the difference of a cross on the outside, a little catechism on the inside and the presence of a religious garb, sadly out of harmony with prevailing fashions.

The cry of waste—of economic waste—is heard to-day not only here, but all over the United States in regard to our education system,

1. Sermon preached by the Right Rev. John G. Dunn, D.D., Bishop of Natchez, Mississippi, at the dedication of the Ursuline Convent, New Orleans, Louisiana, September 24, 1912.

and truly it is hard to realize the enormity of this so-called economic waste.

We Catholics number one-fifth or one-sixth of the American population, which last year spent $403,000,000 on education, our contribution being about $80,000,000. In addition to this we provide schools and teach one and a half millions of Catholic children. On the public school basis of $35 per year for each child, this means an additional tax on Catholics of nearly $50,000,000 a year. We look upon this as a conscience tax, or we consider ourselves penalized to that extent because we happen to have Catholic consciences. We have 50,000 of the best-trained teachers in the world employed in our schools, men and women who are sacrificing the ambitions of business, the comforts of home, for unremitting, unremunerated labor in the schoolroom, and voluntary lives of public effacement, and all the private discomforts of poverty, chastity and obedience. Again why this waste, not of money, but of men and women, this waste of talent, this misdirection of a volume of exceptional energy and efficiency?

Pardon me if I attempt to give the cause of this effect, to justify this apparent waste, to assign a reason for the attitude of American Catholics to education.

Assuming that education is a preparation for life, or, as Herbert Spencer puts it, a preparation for complete living, there are to-day three systems of education before the public. Of these two are logical and reasonable, one is at most a makeshift and illogical; the first is atheistic, the second is Christian, the third is known as the American public school system.

The atheistic system is French, it asserts that there is no God, no soul, no future life, nothing but the present world. Admitting this assumption, the system is logical and reasonable, for if there be no God to know or worship, no soul to save, no future, it is logical and reasonable to eliminate all this out of education, which is a preparation for complete living. The atheistic concept of education dates from the French Revolution, and became a system in 1794, when religion was by law driven out of the schools in France. The system was revoked after Waterloo, and revived a few generations ago under the catchy names of the "neutral," "unsectarian," "un-denominational," "secular" school system.

This system suited admirably the atheistic temper of the French rulers. When the high-sounding words "neutral," etc., had fooled the people into accepting and following the system the mask was torn off, the truth was told that the titles were used not to define or describe the system, but to get atheism introduced under false colors, without unduly alarming parents or children.

Hear Viviani, the Cabinet Minister, as reported in the *Journal Officiel* of Nov. 14, 1906: "It is now time to say that school neutrality has never been more than a diplomatic lie. We appeal to it for the sake of closing the mouths of the timid and the scrupulous, but as that is not necessary now, we play an open game. We have never had any other design than to produce an anti-religious youth, and anti-religious in the active, militant, combative way."

The same Cabinet Minister, in his famous cabinet speech which was placarded all over France in 1906, told the world the real meaning of "secular," "neutral" and "un-denominational" education.

"All of us," said Viviani, "together, by our fathers, our elders, ourselves, have devoted ourselves in the past to a work of anti-clericalism, a work of irreligion. We have torn all religious belief from human conscience; we have extinguished in heaven the lights which it will never kindle again."

So much for the first or atheistic system, logical and reasonable for those who deny God, soul and immortality. We note the diplomatic lie of neutral, unsectarian, "to close the mouths of the timid and scrupulous," and we notice the results of "tearing all religious belief from human consciences and extinguishing the lights of heaven."

Opposed to this is the Christian school system, which is based on belief in God, in the existence of an immortal, undying soul, and a certainty of an eternal life for each and every member of the human family. Assuming this, education must be a preparation for this double life, the temporal here, the eternal hereafter. The intellect must be taught all truth, or at least the principles of all truth, whether of science or of faith, and the will must be gradually educated to all good, error of all kinds, scientific or religious, must be banished from the intellect, evil of all forms against natural or supernatural good must be banished from the will. The intellect and the will have an infancy, a development, a plastic, formative period, which true education must not overlook. To make a man smart, but not good, is not to educate, it is like giving tools to a burglar, a razor to a child, dynamite to an anarchist. To educate is to prepare a man to live well here and hereafter, for man's two great duties of citizenship and sainthood. The Christian system is based on Christ's discourse in the eighteenth chapter of St. Matthew, in which is given the Magna Charta of children. There he told those who aspired to His kingdom to become as little children, that angels guard them, that dire woes are in store for those who by word or example lead Christ's little ones from the narrow road of eternal life. That charter protects the unborn child, brings to the font the infant, and to the school the little one beginning life. "Suffer little children to come to Me," is a command given the three agencies of education, the home, the church and the school, and woe is pronounced against forbidding the child at any period of its existence development from coming to Christ or being Christian.

The Christian system is opposed directly to the atheistic system of France, at first called "neutral," "secular," "unsectarian," but now known as positively atheistic. Since there is a God, a soul, a future, the child has a right to know God, to save his soul, and to attend to the business of the future, as well as to the present life, and to be trained or educated accordingly. The Christian system adds to "secular" religious training, adds faith to reason, the supernatural to the natural. This is our "preparation for complete living."

The third system of education, known as the public school system, is neither atheistic nor Christian. It aims to be a kind of "via media," to avoid the extremes of both and to secure the advantages of both. It claims to be a creature of necessity, in view of the many conflicting forms of belief and unbelief in this country. It proclaims all that Christians want for public and private life; it does not deny anything Christians affirm; it abhors private or public irreligion; it is horrified at the excesses of atheistic education, and loudly proclaims through Church and State that this is a Christian country, and Americans a Christian and God-fearing people.

The public school system divides life into two phases, one part that is school life, the other that is not. It divides training into two spheres, one that is secular, the other that is religious. As a system it confines its energies to only school life and to that form of instruction which is known as secular. Its mission is to exclude all religious training and instruction from the life of the child during the school period, but not to hinder church or parent from supplying the deficiency. On account of this positive exclusion of religion from the school day the system is called "unsectarian," "undogmatic," "neutral" and "secular." It does not oppose religion, it does not include religion. The system is supported by the taxpayers, and as such it may be called national or American.

The three systems then are these: (1) Where religion is excluded from every department of life. (2) Where religion is included in every department of life. (3) Where religion is included in every department of life except school life.

What is our attitude to these three systems? Briefly, we reject the atheistic, we adopt the Christian, we fear the so-called American. With regard to the latter, we Catholics support it financially by paying one-fifth or one-sixth of four hundred and three millions yearly; we fear and dread it, by contributing almost as much to keep our children out of it; we fear it: (1) Because the very name brings back to our memory the story of the rise and growth and success of the French so-called "unsectarian" schools. We remember how names were used there as diplomatic lies, to introduce irreligion under false colors, to tear religious belief from human conscience, and to extinguish the light of heaven; if schools called "neutral," "unsectarian," "undenominational," dechristianize one land, why may they not do the same for another? (2) Because we cannot admit the principles on which the system seems to rest, viz.: That religion and education are inconsistent with or useless to the true life aim of the child; that there is any power which has the moral right to exclude religion from the school; that such exclusion is a good preparation for life.

These dogmas or principles seem to favor irreligion; they force religion into the background of the child's life and warp its moral consciousness.

We fear it because it is pronounced inefficient; those who know the system tell us so. As a sample, let me read you the comments of an experienced public school teacher, published during the summer, in which the system is called "the most momentous failure in our American life"; in the exact words of this teacher the present "idiotic system, which costs over $403,000,000 a year, is either wrongly educating, maleducating, or absolutely harming nearly 18,000,000 children every year." It is called a system not only "ineffective in results," but also actually "harmful in that it throws every year ninety-three out of every one hundred children into the world of action absolutely unfitted for even the simplest tasks in life." If we can believe such statements, supported as they are with figures supplied by the United States Commissioner of Education, the system is a failure as a preparation for the present world, for American life of to-day; or it is, as the same writer bluntly puts it, "a system that is to-day a shame to America, a system that is antiquated and absolutely out of touch with the times, and therefore stupid and wholly ineffective."

We fear it because it is un-American. It is un-American because it is not Christian; it does not suffer little children to go to Christ during the school hours, it even forbids them, and here we ask why use a system for American children which has successfully dechristianized other children? What right has any system to exclude religion from school life, to sterilize American education of everything Christian and religious? How is religion recognized by Americans as a necessary element in the reformation of the criminal, but not in the formation of American children? Belated reformation seems better than early formation. What about an ounce of prevention? Again, where did God authorize anyone or any system, power or party to insult Him by implying that He was unwelcome, undesirable, something to be avoided in the American schoolroom? And, finally, we ask with something like fear and trembling, that if there is a power in this Christian land to banish God and Christ from school life, what guarantee is there that the same power may not banish everything religious from the life of the individual, the family and the nation?

It is un-American because it is unfair. It is unfair to impose a conscience tax on a large number of American citizens; it is unfair to dogmatize to the advantage of the unbeliever by supporting a system that discounts religion, that implies that religion has no rightful place in education, that religion and science should be divorced and that American Christians must accept a system sterilized of all religion. Is it not unfair to thus favor religious indifference or irreligion while taxing Christians for the ways and means of bringing abut their own destruction?

It is un-American because it seems to undermine the very foundation of our national existence; that is to say, our national morality. In his farewell address, George Washington has warned us "that reason and experience both forbid us to expect that national morality can prevail in exclusion of religious principles"; but from our public schools, from those vast incubators, come forth yearly 20,000,000 American fledglings whose education has been as completely sterilized of religious principles as the $400,000,000 a year system can make them. What is the system doing to secure a national morality, without which there is national ruin? If it does nothing , it is un-American and unpatriotic.

Look a little closer and follow the system in its results. To-day forty per cent of our population do not go to church; twenty-five per cent do not even acknowledge God. It is said that two-thirds of our population are today religious illiterates. Our children learn nothing of God in school, and little about Him in the church, because they don't go there. We have, I fear it is a consequence, the unenviable distinction of heading the crime list, the murder list, the divorce list of the world. That national nightmare of ours, divorce, is breaking up one home in every twelve; we have unrest and discontent among the masses, increasing greed among the moneyed classes; we are cultivating the atheist in this generation, forgetting that the atheist of one generation begets the anarchist of the next. We are witnessing a baby famine among those who are loudest in proclaiming Anglo-Saxon supremacy; we see a nation shutting its eyes when the barbarians are swarming at its gates. We are assisting at the funeral of that old stock that was splendidly represented at Bunker Hill, Yorktown and New Orleans, and watching with national unconcern other races who are supplanting us and winning our heritage, not by their learning or intelligence, but by their cradles. Is this American? Is this patriotic?

To say the least, these are symptoms of a national disease; they are storm signals, warning us that there is something wrong in our national life. Seeing this, as we must, we American Catholics come out publicly and boldly and proclaim that as a nation we are strangling the Christianity of the future, we are undermining the religious principles, the morality, the very foundations and props of our national life, by excluding religion from the schools of the nation.

Not satisfied with raising our voices in alarm and in protest, we go further and build schools where Christ may enter; where His principles, His teachings, His morality are taught, learned and followed. Fifty thousand of our Catholic Sisters hold out their arms exclaiming with Christ: "Suffer little children to come to Me and forbid them not," and behind the teachers and children stand 15,000,000 of our Catholic citizens building schools, paying teachers, giving their children as pupils, and as Sisters encouraging every effort made to save the faith of the American child, and the morality and the Christianity of the American nation.

Foremost and first in this great educational work of religion and patriotism has ever stood the great Ursuline community of New Orleans. While politicians wrangled and governments fought about trusts and tariffs these truly great ladies bent all their energies in looking after the girls of the Southland, the welfare of its women and the future mothers of the race. The Ursulines, the first in the educational field, have a glorious history of achievement, the most fearless, devoted, enterprising and successful contributors to what Archbishop Spalding calls "the greatest religious fact in the history of humanity—the American Catholic school system." Without wealth of their own, without endowments from others, without the aid of State, national or Federal, these heroic Sisters, like the sisterhood all over the country, have beaten out highways along the trails of the missionaries and everywhere broadened the paths to knowledge.

What is the program—the purpose—of this new Ursuline Home of Education? It is to give a thorough Catholic education, and that says everything. It means the whole field of human knowledge will be cultivated; it means especially all that is included in the higher education of American womanhood. Here the arts and sciences will flourish; here the exact sciences will be taught; here that Christian philosophy which has stood the test of centuries and continues still, to mold and fashion correct thought and thinking, forming not only those who are guided by it, but indirectly every form of society and the very life of the nation. Here will be epitomized in one magnificent teaching academy the highest and the best teaching effort of the American sisterhood.

There are things which will not be taught here; women will never be taught to be suffragettes nor suffragists; they will never be taught to claim the privileges of both sexes, with the result of getting neither; they will be banded in sodalities, and not in Greek letter societies; they will be taught more about saving their souls than photographing them; they will be taught faith in God, His Bible and His Church, and not that little knowledge which turns out a doubter, a skeptic or a scoffer.

In addition to the entire field of arts and sciences, and to everything that an American girl should know, something more will be taught—the intellect will be taught, the will be trained; the intellect is the lamp of the soul; its light must be steady; its course must be true; it needs certainty, stability, firmness; it needs faith; it needs a creed; it needs authority; its strength does not depend on the extent or variety of its knowledge, but in the depths of its roots. Our teachers here have to make the intellect animated by faith, a lamp on the road to heaven, to light up the way with religion and science, with truth, human and divine.

The will also has to be educated; it has to be taught that its strength does not lie in independence of authority, human or divine, but in conformity with both, in obedience to law, in respect, reverence, rectitude and purity. Now, this is no easy lesson, to learn that the strength and perfection of will is obedience to God's authority, and to all authority emanating from Him. Will culture is pre-eminently the work of education; bright intellects have gone to hell, but heaven itself has announced peace to men of good will.

I asked why this economic waste represented in this costly building, represented in Catholic educational expenditure of men and money all over the country, and I answer:

First—That it is not a waste, but an investment. We find here a public school system of education which is at least ineffective, where religious principles are not taught during the springtime of life, during the plastic, formative period, during the planting and sowing season. Our so-called waste is to complete this deficiency, and we think it both Christian and patriotic.

Second—Another reason for our waste is that we deplore the exclusion of religion from the public schools; we protest against such religious quarantining; we deplore subjecting the youth of the nation to the opposite influences of religion at home and no religion in the school. We regret, with shame and pity, the fact that in any part of our fair, free American land Christ is considered an unwelcome visitor; our waste is a protest against sterilizing educational Christianity.

Third—This waste is to contribute our part to those religious principles without which there is national ruin. The father of our country calls for national morality; our so-called waste is our contribution; we believe that without religious principles taught in our schools national morality is an impossibility. True, we are still a Christian nation, but may we not say with the poet, while remembering the rugged faith of our pioneers and the founders of all the big denominational universities in the country, may we not say:

"You may break, you may shatter, the vase if you will,
But the scent of the roses will hang round it still."

Why this ointment waste, complained the disciple in the house of Simon the leper; why this school waste, complain the thoughtless in the land of Columbus. To both the same answer may be given: "She hath wrought a good work upon me." . . . "Wherever the Gospel shall be preached in the whole world, that also which she has done will be told for a memory of her." The historian of future ages will record the fact that Catholics, that the Catholic sisterhood, have done a good work in keeping religion in the schools, in permitting little children to come to Christ in the school time of their lives. Future generations will bless the Sisters of to-day as we do for an investment both religious and patriotic of the highest, safest and most enduring character, bearing interest and paying dividends in America's most valued assets—an educated, Christianly educated, American womanhood.

3

Catholicism and Americanism[1]

Bishop John Ireland

My religious faith is that of the Catholic Church—Catholicism, integral and unalloyed—Catholicism, unswerving and soul swaying—the Catholicism, if I am to put it into more positive and concrete form, taught by the supreme chieftain of the Catholic Church, the Bishop, the Pope of Rome.

My civil and political faith is that of the republic of the United States of America—Americanism, purest and brightest, yielding in strength and loyalty to the Americanism of none other American surpassed in spirit of obedience and sacrifice by that of none other citizen, none other soldier, sworn to uphold in peace and in war America's Star Spangled Banner.

Between my religious faith and my civil and political faith, between my creed and my country, it has been said, there is discord and contradiction, so that I must smother something of the one when I bid the other burst forth into ardent burning, that I must subtract something from my allegiance to the one when I bend my full energy to service to the other. Those who so speak misunderstand either my creed or my country; they belie either the one or the other. The accord of one with the other is the theme of the address I am privileged this evening to make.

1. Address delivered at Milwaukee, Wisconsin, on August 11, 1913, at the mass meeting incidental to the Twelfth Annual National Convention of the Federation of American Catholic Societies.

No room is there for discord or contradiction. Church and State cover separate and distinct zones of thought and action: The Church busies itself with the spiritual, the State with the temporal. The Church and the State are built for different purposes, the Church for heaven, the State for earth. The line of demarcation between the two jurisdictions was traced by the unerring finger of Him who is the master of both: the law of God is—"Render to Caesar the things that are Caesar's; and to God the things that are God's."

I rehearse a vital dogma of Catholic faith with regard to the mutual relations of Church and State—the solemn teaching of a sovereign pontiff, Leo XIII. The pontiff writes: "God has divided the government of the human race between two principalities, the ecclesiastical and the civil; the one being set over the divine, the other over human things. Each is supreme in its own sphere; each has fixed limits, within which it moves. Each is circumscribed to its own orbit, within which it lives and works in its own native right. . . . Things civil and political are subject, as reason and equity demand, to the civil authority, Jesus Christ Himself having commanded that the things of Caesar be given to Caesar, as the things of God are given to God." Language could not be plainer, more emphatic, more authoritative with regard to the rights of the civil power, its independence within its proper zone of action. The position of the Catholic Church, consequently of Catholics, toward the nation or State, is defined in clearest terms by the highest authority of the Church.

What is to be feared from the Catholic Church? To priest, to bishop or to Pope, who—I am willing to consider the hypothesis—should attempt to rule in matters civil and political, to influence the citizen beyond the range of their own orbit of jurisdiction—that of the things of God. The answer is quickly made: Back to your own sphere of rights and duties—back to the things of God! Or, in like manner, should the State, or its officials, in law or in act, step beyond the frontier of temporal jurisdiction and dare lay hands upon the things spiritual and divine, the answer is: Beware, touch not the things which God has reserved to his duly appointed representatives in the spiritual order.

A recent proclamation from an anti-Catholic association in America reads: "We hold that no citizen is a true patriot who owes superior temporal allegiance to any power above that of his obedience to the principles of the Constitution of the United States." The shaft is loomed against a supposed tenet of the Catholic Church; it pierces the vacant air; it is a missive of pitiable ignorance.

Is the issue that of the temporal sovereignty exercised for ages in a part of Italy by the Roman pontiffs, still claimed by their successor as an international right? But in the States of the Church the Pontiff was king as well as pontiff. To his own kingdom his temporal rule was strictly limited. Beyond the frontier of his own States he claimed no civil or political power; none was allowed him by the most Catholic of nations, by the most loyal of Catholic believers.

Is the issue that of happenings in ages when bishops and popes, the sole visible tenants of authority able to wrest tribes and peoples from chaos and anarchy, were compelled by social needs and popular appeals to sit as civil lawmakers and judges—when the crozier and the tiara were the sole arms to stem the onslaught of imperial and regal despotism, and peoples in despair cried to them for mercy and help—or in ages when Christendom was of one creed in faith and morals, and special gifts of power were made to the papacy, willed by all as an international arbitrator and pacemaker—when special opportunities for beneficent intermingling of the spiritual and the temporal in the life of nations were created for the papacy, to which it was bound to give heed, under penalty of betraying the behests of charity and of justice, and turning back from the face of the earth the upwelling stream of culture and civilization?

Into past ages I do not now hold the field glass of scrutiny, although, were I to do so, I were readily able to descry glorious work done by the papacy, and to the wondering eye of a modern world show it to have been ever the guardian of personal and social rights, ever the foster mother of popular liberty and popular justice, ever the resplendent mirror of Him of whom it was written: "He passed by, doing good." My contention is—the papacy and the Church when and where, as in America, a new social order has arisen, within which the State or the nation wills to live of its native life and rights, and the Church, freed from burdens imposed upon it by social phases of other times and other places, willingly betakes itself to the folds of its own mantle, to the circle of its own spiritual orbit, saying with its founder and master: "To Caesar the things that are Caesar's, to God the things that are God's."

And now, in America, some do say, that the Pope of Rome is ambitious of temporal rule over America, of planting here the "Yellow and White" instead of the Star Spangled Banner; that priests and bishops are active agents of his yearnings; that Catholics dream of the day when his command in civil and political matters will sway the White House and Capital; that to do this intent associations are nightly befitting themselves by sanguinary oath and secret drillings, to murder their fellow-citizens and in the name of a foreign potentate take forcible possession of the land of the brave and the home of the free! I allude to such wild elucubrations of diseased brains only to ask, in unanswered wonderment, how such follies can be thought out and acted upon, even by a handful of them, in the twentieth century, in America? But, of course, the insane are ever with us, and all the insane are not put into safe keeping.

The partition of jurisdiction into the spiritual and the temporal is a principle of Catholicism; no less is it a principle of Americanism. Catholicism and Americanism are in complete agreement.

The Constitution of the United States reads: "Congress shall make no law respecting an establishment of religion, or prohibiting the free exercise thereof." It was a great forward leap on the part of the new nation towards personal liberty and the consecration of the rights of conscience. Not so had it heretofore been on the soil of America. Save in Maryland while reigned there the spirit of the Catholic Lord Baltimore, and in Pennsylvania under the sweet-tempered rule of William Penn, religious freedom was barred by law in the colonies—Protestant creeds warring one with the other, all warring with the Catholic. But it was decreed—the new flag must be unsullied by religious persecution, the new nation must be, on every score, the daughter of freedom, the guardian angel of personal rights in each and every American.

The proclamation of the Constitution was as the Milanese edict of the Emperor Constantine. Before the time of Constantine all things, even the things of God, were Caesar's. The State made and unmade divinities; it was itself a divinity; its highest representative, the Emperor, claimed place among the Olympians, and incense was burned before his statue as before that of a god. The personal conscience was allowed no recognition. The subject must worship as Caesar ordered. It was servitude most absolute. But at last the conqueror of the Milvian bridge spoke; liberty triumphed in the triumph of the Labarum. "We have determined, with sound and upright purpose," said Constantine, "that liberty is to be denied to no one . . . that to each one freedom is to be given to devote his mind to that religion which he may think adapted to himself." Conscience was made free in the Roman Empire by the Milanese edict; it was made free in America by the Federal Constitution. In the one and in the other, it is the injunction of the master: "To Caesar the things that are Caesar's; to God the things that are God's."

By the terms of the Federal Constitution as by the teaching of the Catholic Church, no room is given in America for discord between

Catholicism and Americanism, between my Catholic faith and my civic and political allegiance.

America is a republic; the spirit, the form of government is democracy—the government of the people, by the people, for the people. Is there not here, it is asked, at least a touch of conflict between my religious faith and my civic and political faith? I tread upon easy ground, so plain are the teachings of the Catholic Church in favor of the rights of the people in matters of civic and political government. I again quote from the encyclical letters of Leo XIII. The pontiff writes: "There is no power but from God. The right of command, however, is not in itself linked to any one form of government. One or the other form the commonwealth may rightfully give to itself, provided such be really promotive of the common welfare. . . . No reason is there why the Church should prefer one form of government to another, provided the form that is chosen be just in itself and favorable to the common good. Therefore, the rules of justice being duly observed, the people are free to adopt that form of government which befits their temper, or best accords with their traditions and customs." America declared itself a republic; its government is organized democracy. In America, according to the teachings of the Catholic Church, the republic is the sole legitimate government; to the republic Catholics are in conscience obliged to yield sincere and unswerving obedience.

God is the source and the giver of all power; of themselves men have no authority over other men. The authority of the parent over the child is from God, who created nature and so created the family; the authority of the State is from God, who willed that men should live within the fostering embrace of a social organism. In this sense, but in none other, a government, whatever the form, rules by divine right. God gives the power, but the people choose those that hold it, and mark out the conditions under which they do hold it. This is supreme democracy; it is the dogma of Catholicism.

In America the government is the republic—the government of the people, by the people, for the people. With you, fellow Catholics, with you, fellow Americans, I salute the Republic. I thank God that the people of America are capable of possessing a government of this form. The Republic—it is the fullest recognition of human dignity and human rights, the fullest grant of personal freedom, that due respect for the rights of others and the welfare of the social organism may allow. Permit the barbarous onslaughts of lawlessness and anarchy to undermine its foundations or loosen the cement binding together its walls! Never, so long as life still throbs within our bosoms! Alter it to empire or monarchy! Never, so long as our lips may praise it, or our hands wield arms in its defence.

Would we alter, if we could, the Constitution in regard to its treatment of religion, the principles of Americanism in regard to religious freedom? I answer with an emphatic no. Common sense is ours. Common justice is ours; a regard to our own welfare and safety is also ours. The broad fact is that the American people are divided in matters of religious belief: to the American people, to the whole people, does the country belong. What else, then, could the framers of the Constitution have done, what else since their time could the legislators of the land have done, in equity towards all, in equity to the country as one nation, to its people as one people, but solemnly decree, as they did, as they running through all its walls and battlements, the safeguard of its peace and prosperity. Violate religious freedom against Catholics: our swords are at once unsheathed. Violate it in favor of Catholics, against non-Catholics: no less readily do they leap from the scabbard.

Does Catholicism in America suffer from religious freedom, allowing equally to Catholics and to non-Catholics? Compare the lot of Catholicism in America to that of Catholicism in so many trans-Atlantic lands, where the tenets of pagan Caesarism, as to the supremacy of the State over the conscience of its subjects, do still prevail. There manacles bind hand and limb the bride of Christ: here she walks, in queenly mien, free and unfettered, putting forth, without let or hindrance, the full exuberance of her native force and beauty, proving at every stepping that her life is all her own, since she lives it without outward help or prop: that her blossom and fruit are all her own, since they spring exclusively from her bosom, and of their own vigor defy triumphantly darkening clouds and battling tempests.

Had the Catholic Church not lived and thriven in freedom, truth were not its armor, grace from heaven were not the comeliness of its countenance.

They know us little who accuse us of coveting civil and political power, that we may dim the splendor of the fairest flower in the garden of Americanism. Our combats, if combats there be, are never against the liberties of America, but in defense of them; never against Americanism, but against such of its sons whose souls never yet have thrilled in full response to its teachings and inspirations.

The charge is made, if not anti-American, the Catholic Church is un-American—it is in America an alien institution. More definitely the charge is this: The Catholic Church does not bear the stamp, "Made in America." It is un-American to go across the Atlantic or the Pacific for aught that American uses or needs—even for its religion. Now the head of the Catholic Church is the Bishop of Rome, a foreigner; its general councils, composed of men of all nations—foreigners in the majority, Europeans, Asiatics, Africans—legislate in faith and morals for America. Why not a Pope strictly American? Why not councils, as those of other religious bodies, exclusively made up of Americans—capable, as only Americans may be supposed to be, of interpreting the American mind and guiding the American aspiration?

The late Bishop Doane of Albany once wrote: "It is hard to find any other word (than that of 'alien') which describes the whole communion of a Church which owes its highest allegiance to a single head, who is a foreigner across the sea." A few weeks ago, in the *Yale Review,* the secretary-general of the university, while treating of, what he is willing to call the helpful influence of the Catholic Church over recently arrived immigrants, complains: "But it (the Catholic Church) links them (the immigrants) with their past rather than with that of United States. It has been outside the main current the Anglo-Saxon progress. Its emphasis is neither on freedom nor on democracy; so unless it proves untrue to its own ideal it will not satisfy the American people." To Bishop Doane, Catholicism is "an alien" in America objectionable to Americans, because its sovereign pontiff is not an American, living in America. Anson Phelps is sure that Catholicism, to satisfy Americans, should have been woven in a loom-room even of Anglo-Americanism. In the late June number of the *Atlantic Monthly* a writer heads his article with this caption: "Reasonable Hopes of American Religion," and actually delineates a creed suitable in his judgment to the people of America.

Faith and morals made in America on a design strictly American! Great and good as is America, it must not arrogate to itself the realm of the Almighty God, that of faith and morals. Shall we call the Almighty God a foreigner? Yet he is not exclusively the God of America. Shall we call the Saviour of Calvary a foreigner? Yet He was neither a native nor a naturalized American; and His message was—"Teach all nations"—instead of teach only America. And now shall we call the Bishop of Rome a foreigner, "an alien," because he stands before the world the universal teacher, the Vicar of Jesus Christ, teacher of all nations, teacher of the whole human family?

Argue that the Almighty God is not the supreme author and norma of an eternal righteousness, that Jesus Christ is not the proven revealer of the thoughts and the love of the Almighty God, that the Bishop of Rome is not the historic successor, of Christ's apostolate—

then, counsel, perhaps, you may an American-made Church for
Americans an American-made code of faith and morals. But religion
is not a product of the mind of the individual man, or of the environment within which he lives: it is not a sheer human growth, change-
able as the seasons of the year, fitful and capricious as the likes and
dislikes of man and of peoples.

Religion is the mind and the will of God, existing as God exists,
objectively outside of men and of peoples, superior to all in men, ex-
acting from man the obedience due by the creature to the creator. The
question is never—what is it that suits a man, or a people, but what is
it that God has imposed upon men by the eternal laws of his supreme
righteousness, or by the teachings of his historic revelations? What
Americans require is, not an American made, but a God made religion. And so, at the bar of American common sense itself, the proposals of the writer of the *Atlantic Monthly* must only be—as he himself
despairingly inclines to term them, "dreams that are the shadows of
hopes, hopes that are the shadows of dreams."

The Catholic Church is extra-American, supra-national, begotten for
all nations, not for America alone; its supreme pontiff is extra-American, supra-national—a foreigner on no spot of earth's surface, everywhere at home, as the spiritual father of all tribes and of all peoples
who seek divine truth from a universal God and a universal Saviour.

And this, the beauty; this, the grandeur of the Catholic Church,
that it is Catholic, as the eternal God is Catholic, as the salvation given
by Jesus Christ is Catholic. Narrowness, provincialism in religion, in
faith and morals, in the first face of things, is a perversion of God's
eternal law, and of the revelation given to men 1,900 years ago. The
days of tribal religions are past; they must not be revived in America.

Another charge of un-Americanism—the attitude of the Catholics
toward State schools. My answer is quickly at hand. The State takes
to itself the task of instructing the children of its people in branches of
secular knowledge; in order that this be done the more efficiently and
the more generally, the State pays from the public treasury the financial cost of the schools opened under its patronage. Do Catholics
make objection to the task or to the financial expenditures it entails?

Convinced they are, as the most zealous supporters of State
schools, that no child, whether for its own, or for the sake of the State,
should grow up without an adequate share of secular knowledge;
and convinced no less are they that it is right and proper on the part
of the State to disburse its funds in favor of universal secular instruction. What then our claim? One that we most licitly put forth on be-

half of America itself—that this secular instruction be given so that the religious creed of the least of the little ones be not made to suffer; that it be given so that the influences of religion—influences, however much outside the direct grant of the civil power, still vitally necessary to the social life and security of the State itself, as they are to the spiritual life of the souls of its citizens—be not contaminated or nullified. Not against State schools, as such, do I raise objection, but as to the methods in which they work—methods that, whatever the theory, do in fact consecrate secularism as the religion of America, and daily are thither driving America with the floodtide of a Niagara. Somehow, secular knowledge should be imparted to the child so as not to imperil its faith in God and in Christ. Prove to me, I say, that this contention does not fully fit into the Constitution of the United States, that in making it I have not in mind the welfare, the salvation of America—prove this before you denote me as un-American.

A pernicious mistake is made regarding our complaint of the methods in which State schools are conducted. It is that Catholics are looking exclusively to themselves and to their financial interests. Not so at all: we look to ourselves; but even more so, we look to the people of America, to the Republic of America. We need not be much concerned for ourselves. We have our Catholic schools; to-morrow we shall have them in greater numbers, where our children receive secular knowledge without peril to faith and morals. Nor do we count the cost of maintaining those schools, in view of the priceless protection they give to faith and morals. But the vast population around us are limited to schools of secularism—and in this way secularism is fast becoming the religion of America. Say what you will, to-day, in America, the evil is the decay of religion, and, in logical sequence, the decay of morals. In both instances the cause of the decay is the enforced secularism of the State schools. Others than Catholics, heedful observers and intelligent thinkers, admit the evil, admit the cause and give the alarm. I trust to the awakening common sense and patriotism of the American people to discover the remedy. Meanwhile in telling of the evil and of the cause, my right hand on my conscience, I rank myself among truest and most loyal Americans.

An axiom of Americanism is equal rights for all, fair play, "the square deal," as it has been termed. That, and naught else, is the demand of Catholics in America. Catholics demand their rights—all the rights guaranteed to American citizenship by the letter and the spirit of the Constitution; and for the acquisition and the preservation of those rights they shrink from no means or method allowed by the

Constitution and the laws of the land. Were they to act otherwise, they were the unworthy sons of America. The rights of Catholics are the rights of the personal conscience of the Catholic citizen. It is not the Catholic Church in its official name that comes into issue; it is the American citizen, whose religious faith is the faith of the Catholic Church. Not to know one's rights is low mindedness, not to defend them is cowardice. The true American, differing from us in religion would despise us if we laid down our arms before bigot, and injustice, and by so doing disgraced the shield of Americanism, ever vowed to justice and to valor.

Do we, however, demand special privileges not accorded to other citizens of America? No—never—no more than we would allow others special privileges not accorded to ourselves—less even than we would allow such privileges to others. If the members of a church or a religious or a semi-religious organization of any kind, arises in America calling for special privileges, be the shame of un-Americanism their portion. Such a contention never will be the disgrace of Catholicism. The common law of the land Catholics propose for themselves; it is what they propose for others.

Catholic fellow-citizens, claim your rights—the rights given by the Constitution of the land, the American spirit of fair play, the laws of American citizenship. But in doing this be on your guard, lest even in slightest semblance you give offence to men too ready to take offence. Be sure before you act that reason and justice are with you. Act always in calmness, certain always that, upon proper presentation of your case, sooner or later America will deal rightly with you. Remember that your complaint is not with the American people, but with individuals, or small classes of men, who, whatever their nominal Americanism, are beyond its sweetest whisperings, below its rapturous elevation of thought and sentiment.

Of the American people this must be said—I say it from my heart, in full knowledge—a people more deeply penetrated with the sense of civic and political justice, more generous in concession of rights, where rights belong, more respectful of their every brother, their every fellow-citizen, is not in existence on the broad surface of the globe. This my tribute to the American people, the verdict, my fifty years of private and public commingling compel me to pronounce.

Good citizenship is the need of America, the basis of its safety, the spring of its hopes. It is the imperious law of Catholicism. I say the law of Catholicism—the law, consequently, of all who live its spirit, who obey its mandates. Those who bear the name of Catholic, but are faithless to the injunctions of their religion I disown. They are bad citizens despite their creed, which with all the forces innate in it makes for good citizenship. To the Catholic obedience to law is a religious obligation, binding in God's name, the conscience of the citizen. Let every soul be subject to higher powers; for there is no power but from God; and those that are, are ordained of God. Therefore, he that resisteth the power resisteth the ordinance of God. And they that resist purchase to themselves damnation.

I do not discuss the hypothesis of laws wrong in morals, clearly beyond the province of the civil power, violations of the rights of the personal conscience. Such laws were not ratified by the supreme master of righteousness. Personal conscience is the ultimate asylum of the soul, in presence of civil or of ecclesiastical authority. Both Americanism and Catholicism bow to the sway of personal conscience.

It is Americanism that the ballot box is the sanctuary of good citizenship—opening its doors only to the weal and honor of the country. A sacrilege it is to step towards it with bride in hand, fraud in mind, to reach towards it the offering of selfishness, or of injustice. None more careful of the unstained ballot box than the good Catholic, loyal to the Catholic faith; America is the sole issue before him—its weal for honor. Aught else mind or in heart, he is a traitor to his creed, as he is traitor to his country.

The best men for the office, whatever the religious creed of the man. To put a Catholic into office, merely because he is a Catholic, though otherwise unworthy and incapable, is a crime against America, a sin against the Almighty God.

In choosing his candidate the Catholic voter is the freest of the free. It is a calumny that we deeply resent, to say that in civic and political matters Catholic voters are under the influence of the Church. Priests and bishops do not dictate the politics of Catholics; if they strove to do so their interference would be promptly repulsed. It is of public knowledge that the Catholic vote is distributed among the several political parties of the country. To speak of myself, privately and publicly as a citizen, I give my allegiance to a particular political party. Do I dare preach from my pulpit the tenets of that party to the discredit of another? Do I dare allow that, if heeded at all by others, my choice of a ballot should or could receive other attention than that due to its civic and political merit? As a matter of fact legions of Catholic voters in America believe me hopelessly wrong in politics. As a citizen I may regret that my political influence is not wider; as a Catholic I am glad of the independence of the citizenship of America.

There is in America no Catholic political party, nor should there be. As a matter of course, were a special issue raised in which rights of Catholics were menaced the conscience of Catholics were impelled to defend those rights on the ground of American fair play itself. That—and nothing more.

Now and then I myself made the complaint that in America Catholics are not represented in the higher offices of the land proportionately to their numbers. My words were interpreted as if I had urged Catholics to take political control of State and nation in the interest of the Catholic Church. Nothing is further from my mind. My sole contention is that seemingly Catholics are lacking in legitimate civic ambition, or in high civic qualifications, else their fellow-Americans would have been more willing to honor them. Is this position not squarely American—equal rights to all, provided the merits be equal? I repeat the lesson to Catholics who now hear or may later read my words. For your own sake, for the sake of America, upward be your march in social and political ambition, in ability to render service to the country, in moral worthiness, in intellectual culture: then trust yourselves to the social and political justice of your fellow-Americans. Some Catholics there are who complain that hostility to their religion keeps them in the dark vale, while too often the fact is that their own short-comings forbid them to ascend to the sunlit hills.

Either they have not fitted themselves for high positions, or they have been without the legitimate ambition to honor themselves by giving to the country highest and best service. I have said: trust to the justice and fair play of your fellow-citizens. Should, however, the particular case arise where it is plain you are set aside because you are Catholics, then, in the name of Americanism, protest so loudly that never again will similar insult be offered to your American citizenship.

I have told of the American Catholic in time of peace. Shall I tell of him in time of war? Here I proffer no argument; I relate a historic occurrence. It was at Gettysburg, fifty years ago the second day of July, 1863. The command is hurried to the Irish Brigade to check the onrush of Gen. Anderson's Confederates. The chaplain, the Rev. William Corby, leaps to the top of a large, boulder stone: "The Catholic Church," he shouts, "refuses Christian burial to the soldier who turns his back to the foe or deserts his flag," adding that he is ready to impart sacramental absolution to those who in their hearts make a sincere act of sorrow for sin. All are on their knees; Gen. Hancock in his saddle, removes his hat; the absolution is given; the charge is made; the Confederates flee backwards.

Gettysburg is but one of a hundred instances my tongue could easily name. Somehow, Catholicism and Americanism commingle graciously their intertwinings when the honor of the Star-Spangled Banner is in peril.

As a religion Catholicism is in the arena, with the spiritual arms forged by its founder—faith, hope and charity. It is avowedly expansive and propagandist. What else, so long as the divine commission read: "Going, therefore, teach ye all nations."

Is America to be Catholic in religion? Fain would I have it so. I am not, however, so ignorant of history and of present conditions as to imagine that the goal is within near reach. But Catholicism in America, all consideration given to ebb and flow, is growing apace. I will not deem myself in error when I estimate the Catholic population of the United States to be 18,000,000, to which figure are to be added nearly ten other millions, if we number all whom to-day the flag owns or protects.

Need America fear the spread of the religious creed of Catholicism? In reality the question is none other than this: Need America fear the spread of the Gospel of Christ? If the Catholic Church wins in the battle with unbelief, or with the present varied forms of Christianity, it will only be because it demonstrates in itself the perpetuity of the Kingdom of Christ, to which solely it makes its appeal. Its doctrines, its life and action, must be those of Christ; else, as it should do, it vanishes from the scene. Argument in opposition to its claim as the religion of Christ, it calmly awaits. Of arguments it does not complain. It only asks that passion be absent from the contest, that calumny and misrepresentation be not made use of—promising on its part that whatever on this score the tactics of offence other than those of truth and charity—the methods of the Lord Himself. The work of expansion, as done by the Catholic Church, will be the work of peace and of love. No social discord can come from it—no break in the harmony that should sweeten the ties binding together fellow-citizens and neighbors in the common service of a common country.

To the civil and political institutions of America no harm can come from the spread of Catholicism. Yea—to those institutions Catholicism brings elements most vital to their life and growth—those of a positive, authoritative religion. Never does materialism beget or sustain a well-ordered social organism; never does a vague uncertain Christian sentiment give to it strength and cohesiveness. The Catholic Church puts forth a clear and definite message; it speaks with authority. In its dogmas and enactments it is thoroughly social, laying supreme stress on the principles of law and order, so necessary to society, especially in a free democracy. It teaches that disobedience to law is a sin against God; that society is from God; that to undermine the foundations of society, make null its purposes and mission, is to resist the ordinance of God. It teaches the sanctity and the indissolubility of marriage, setting its whole power in restraint of that terrible plague of divorce, so ruinous to-day of family hearthstone, the fundamental unit of the whole social organism.

And it teaches, most firmly and most imperiously, the principles of moral righteousness, that repress passion and self-interest, the fatal foes of the social organism; and it teaches, also, as the final outcome of earth's strugglings, the inspiring doctrine of hope in another life which alone dispels the pessimism of despair, the ferocious thoughts and acts to which this pessimism must needs give birth. To-day society—blind they are who do not see the awful peril—is close to precipice and abyss. The cause is the decay of religion. Salvation for the social organism is in the name and the power of the ever living God: the potent agency to preach God and uphold His authority is the Catholic Church.

I repeat my profession of faith—my religious faith, Catholicism; my civil and political faith, Americanism.

Some twenty years ago, on a memorable occasion, an illustrious prelate, at that time the official representative of Pope Leo XIII, said to the Catholics of America, "The Gospel of Christ in one hand, the Constitution of the United States in the other, go forth to work and to victory." Our signal of combat! It is the word of Francis Satolli: It is Catholicism and Americanism.

4

THE NEEDY FAMILY AND INSTITUTIONS[1]

Richard H. Tierney, S.J.

The family is one of God's gifts to men. It has its origin in His law ordaining all things unto the best. It began in Eden by a direct act of God, giving Eve to Adam, that each might be to the other a support and consolation in life. God did more than this: not only did He institute the family, but in fashioning hearts He put into them a law that naturally attracts men and women to wedlock, and bids them be true to each other to the end.

Apart from supernatural considerations which we shall see later, this is our idea of marriage. True, much to the detriment of public morals, this concept is not in universal favor. The wretched hypothesis of certain anthropologists, advanced by Buchofen in his "Das Mutter-reclit," is more partial to the flesh, and hence more congenial to a set of men who were better unborn. The same is true of polyandry and polygamy, successive or simultaneous. In a greater or lesser degree all these are repugnant to the natural law, and they are besides forbidden by the divine law. Nor, despite isolated exceptions arising from abuse, does history support any of them. Westermack, perhaps the greatest authority on this subject, insists that monogamy was by all odds the most common form of marriage "amongst the ancient people of whom we have any direct knowledge." When Christ came and promulgated His saving doctrine He insisted on the original and only true form of matrimony, and added to it besides a sacramental element. He made

---

1. Paper read at a meeting of the Illinois State Charity Organization, La Salle, Illinois, October 27, 1914.

matrimony, therefore, a lifelong union between one man and one woman joined together by an inviolable pact that is at once a natural contract and a Sacrament instituted by Him, and sanctified in His Precious Blood. This union, which St. Paul likened to the union between Christ and His Mystic Spouse the Church, has as its chiefest justification a home into which children are to be born for the good of the State and the glory of God. Thus, the Christian family is instituted and perfected. Now the family has a double set of relations, one internal, the other external. The former do not concern us; the latter, the relations to the State, do concern us.

The family is the social unit, the basis of civil society, in the sense that the State is formally concerned with it. This relation obliges the State to perform certain services and to abstain from certain other acts. Thus, for instance, civil society can interfere with the control and education of children only so far as may be necessary to prevent neglect of parental duty in these matters. The control and education of offsprings pertain to parents by a natural right emphasized, at least indirectly, by a positive divine command.

It is a woeful thing to tamper with a family; it is a crime to break it up, except in abnormal cases. Mark it well. Nothing can take the place of the sanctuary of the home; not even a most perfect institution. The family is the child's natural place; within its circle all the ideas and emotions that are ultimately based on the natural law find easy expression, thereby exercising an influence that were otherwise lost. The child outside the family circle is in an unnatural place; a place where many promptings of the heart are not called into action. Be an institute ever so perfect, yet the mother of the child is not there, nor its father, nor its brothers and sisters. The chastening, uplifting influence of such factors is lost on the orphaned soul which goes forth to the world abnormal in some ways, for that it had not been touched into the full and complete life ordained for it by God. It knew not a mother's smiles and tears, a father's tender solicitude, a sister's caresses. There is a lack in the heart. The family, then, should be preserved even at great hazards. But often, alas! the home must be broken up. Excess in liquor, or unchastity, twin agents of the demon, or some other cause, leaves children without shelter and care. No other family will take the waifs. They must be sent to an institution. The institution selected is private. What should it be like? What care should its inmates get? The answer comes as a deduction from what I have already said. The institution should be as homelike as possible; those in charge of it should do as much as possible to prepare the child for the battle of life. Herein should be found discipline founded on the religion of the child, and love and some adequate process of equipping the children to earn an honorable livelihood. In other words, the institution should be as "uninstituted" as brain and goodwill can make it.

Children are ruled by love not by the rod; children are subdued by firm, kind words, not by angry commands; children are taught respect for authority by learning first to love the person clothed with authority; children are trained not in herds, but as individuals, each with its own immortal soul needing a personal, unceasing care to meet exigencies that arise.

Do not think that sounding gongs and ranks and the measured rise and fall of many feet and tense baby faces and stern frowns of masters and mistresses are the sum and substance of discipline. They may connote supreme disorder: to wit, interior rebellion against authority. Better far to have a scampering boy or two, and a giggling girl or more, who realize that they are disorderly than one thousand, yes, ten thousand little souls dragooned into external decorum without any interior response. In the end the latter method if indeed it does not kill all initiative causes a rebound of soul, and great is the ruin. All good discipline is self-discipline. It is not imposed from without; it is a growth from within. It is not suppression; it is expansion under guidance. It is not a process of suffocating faults; it is an implanting of virtue. Such is discipline. It begins in the intellect and proceeds to the will. The child must first realize the difference between right and wrong; must then determine to adopt righteousness, and finally must live up to the determination. Ladies and gentlemen, you and I can bring this about only when we have won the love of the child and hold its little soul in the hollow of our hands, to train it in God's ways. That is home discipline, and such is the ideal for the institution. The child, I repeat, is to be trained in God's ways. Without Him there is neither lasting joy in life nor hope in death. Here sociology is not sufficient. It may do something, but that which it does is ultimately useless unless supported by a divine sanction. Let us not be either afraid or ashamed to confess it, the human soul needs God, both for peace and safety. There are depths therein that can be sounded by the plummet of God's love alone; crevices that can be illuminated by the light from His face only; rough places that He alone can make smooth. The last, strongest, sweetest appeal to man is God's; religion must permeate the atmosphere in which the child lives, the religion demanded by the child's parents or legitimate guardians. For it is an infamous crime, a monstrous violation of the natural and divine law to rob a needy child of its faith.

Moreover, he who does so has made his victim false to God, the norm of morality; infidelity to the norm eventuates in disregard of morality itself, a sorry result of misguided zeal.

From all this it is quite apparent that love must always be supreme in the institutions under discussion. All employed therein must love their work, otherwise they are hirelings, task masters who are better employed elsewhere. Many people adopt a peculiar attitude toward unfortunate children. They seem to consider them criminals undergoing a term of punishment. They are harsh with them and overbearing and dictatorial, and formally authoritative in everything; in short, they are unlovely and unlovable, never fatherly or motherly. They create an atmosphere which even frogs—to say nothing of children—would find chilly and uncongenial. The result is a frightened, deceitful child, which looks at you out of the corner of its eye, and grows up an Ismael, hand raised against his fellows, suspecting all of brutality. Unaffected love, then, must enter into the training of the children. Our exemplar is Christ, Who preached and practiced corporal and spiritual works of mercy, and promised reward even to so mean a gift as a cup of cold water given in His name.

This love will prompt officials of private institutions to look to every need of their charges. There will be plenty of wholesome food. There will be sufficient provision for play—an item sometimes neglected. Yet play is both a physical and psychological necessity. A primal instinct fairly drives the normal child to play in order that its limbs and muscles and sinews may be made fit for future stress. So much for the physical aspect of this question. The psychological aspect is just as simple. For reasons known to you, unnatural violence against an instinct of nature is harmful. Play is an instinct of nature. The conclusion is too obvious and clear in substance to call for deduction or labor.

Over and above all this, sense of duty, if not of spontaneous love, will prevent the masters of these institutions from sending any child away unprepared to work its way to an honorable place in society. The children should be given an elementary education. It is shameful to allow a boy or girl to grow up in ignorance, unable to read, write, compute and talk grammatically. Moreover, the children should be equipped to earn a living wage, in the shortest possible time after leaving the institution. Mops and washtubs and ironing-boards are poor enough instruments for that. The boys should be taught a trade, or farming or some other useful means of livelihood. The girls should be drilled in dressmaking, or millinery, or typing, or accounting and so on. And every girl should be exercised in systematic housekeeping, learning the art of a competent housewife. Remember that under normal conditions these boys and girls of to-day are destined to become the fathers and mothers of to-morrow, not mere floaters on the stream of life, much less outcasts from society.

Let us not deceive ourselves in this. Any institution that fails to turn its inmates into useful citizens falls short of its primary purpose. It is a sham, a lie in stone; it were better out of existence; it is ruining souls that otherwise would be fashioned into good men and women. A study of the lives of those brought up in institutions which neglect the elements insisted upon, oftentimes reveals a mass of wreckage tossing on the sea of life.

No institution completes its work for children which does not employ a "follow-up" system. It is of little avail to watch over a girl for eight or ten years and then place her among strangers, innocent and ignorant of the ways of modern folk. Unless she be a tower of strength, the psalm of her life is apt to end abruptly on a broken chord, like the "wail of the dead in the night." And if accidental conditions make the life of a boy similarly situated less disastrous in the eyes of men, they do not make that life less sad before the face of God, Who loathes with infinite loathing that base hypocritical thing called in polite society the "double standard," a relic of savagery when man's lust was his god, and woman his victim, not his heaven-sent helpmate, a mother, mine and yours! There should be an effective "follow up" system in charge of up-standing, godly men and women who know their duty and dare do it. Happily no words are needed to explain or illustrate this system. You know it better than I.

Ladies and Gentlemen, your work is sublime; I envy you it. It is a privilege to be allowed to care for the little ones whose Angels see the face of the Father Who is in heaven. May you accomplish your task in the spirit of the Master, Who bade His followers suffer the little ones to come unto Him, and threatened dire punishment to all who should scandalize them. He is the Way, the Truth, and the Life, the great Hope of individual and State. Children trained in His spirit will be self-respecting, honorable citizens, a consolation to you who have given your lives to their upbringing.

5

THE EIGHT-HOUR DAY

Joseph Husslein, s.j.

It is clear that labor, as a body, cannot gain by the undue shortening of the working day. The increase of wages per hour that might accompany this would be nominal and not real. The purchasing power of money would necessarily shrink in proportion to the overpay that was exacted. It is imperative, therefore, that a fair day's wage be the outcome of a fair day's work. Are eight hours of honest labor sufficient for this? Or, on the other hand, are they more than is required.

We are familiar with the contention of Lord Leverhulme, in England, that the six-hour day should be adopted. Such views are based on the supposition that six hours of scientifically efficient and intensified labor can attain the height of human productiveness. But men will not scientifically conserve their strength for just six hours of concentrated work, nor can every form of labor be thus intensified. Many occupations are of their very nature more leisurely and protracted.

Certainly, the six-hour day will find little support from public sentiment. It would not, as a rule, suffice for industry. Particular reasons can justify it in particular cases. The six-hour day demanded by the miners in the after-war period was not intended to lessen the hours of work, but merely to divide the work in such a way as to make it continuous, where enough employment had not been given the miners to average even six hours for five days in a week.

Unemployment, too, is given as a reason for the six-hour day. As I turn to a trade journal I find the argument thus expressed by a trade-union writer: "There are constantly hundreds of thousands of workmen out of work in this country," he says, referring to the United

States. "It is certain that under the present way of doing things there is not enough steady work for all hands. What can be more obvious then than, that if the hours of labor are made fewer, more men can be employed?" He therefore concludes that the six-hour movement "is not selfish at all, but is designed to give a fair share of employment to all."

Unemployment may, in a certain measure, be chronic, but not to such an extent as to warrant a six-hour day. The universal application of this would lessen production and force up prices to an appalling degree, so that labor would be the great and ultimate sufferer. Unemployment must be met in other and saner ways. If men are everywhere assured a family wage, mothers are freed from industry to apply themselves to the care of their homes, and children are not exploited for gain, there will be no need of a six-hour day, except to meet a local and temporary crisis. Under this last condition there can be no objection made to it. Considerate employers have at all times had resort to this solution of the unemployment problem when they were concerned to provide for all their men, so far as this was possible in days when industry was slack.

Labor in general is satisfied with the eight-hour day. Towards this the labor movement in the United States had been tending for many years before its consummation was practically achieved. As far back apparently as the seventies of the last century we come across a song by J. G. Blanchard, from which I quote the following snatch:

> Oh! bands and hearts are weary, and homes are heavy with dole;
> If life's to be filled with drudgery, what need of a human soul!
> Shout, shout, the lusty rally, from shipyard, shop and mill,
> The very stones would cry it out if labor's tongue were still:
> Eight hours for work, eight hours for rest, eight hours for what we will.

On its economic side it is quite probable that the eight-hour day, with one or more proper rest periods, will yield the utmost efficiency in modern industry, if men will indeed apply themselves reasonably to the best accomplishment of their tasks. Here, for instance, is a passage from the interesting statement that was issued years ago by the Ford Motor Company, under the title of "The Advantages of the Eight-hour Workday over the Nine and Ten." The company offers these telling figures:

> A certain group of men, working nine hours under the old system, assembled 750 radiators. The same group, working eight hours under the new plan, assembled 1,300 radiators.

A group of men, working nine hours under the old plan, turned out 38 fenders. Under the new, working eight hours, the same men turned out 50 fenders.

A group of 65 men, working nine hours under the old system, turned out 800 gas tanks. Under the new, working eight hours, the 60 men turned out 1,200.

Hours were reduced, wages increased, and cost went down.

These results, of course, implied resources for the promotion of efficiency which all employers cannot command. It is but fair to say that at the present moment there are complaints from social experts in France and Germany, where the eight-hour day has been newly applied, that in many trades, the production under this system is inadequate to meet the needs of these countries. This may largely be due to a want of serious application on the part of the workers. There can be no doubt that particularly earnest and effective labor is required in unskilled occupations, that an industry may be able to pay a full family wage to the eight-hour workers. One of our leading social experts even doubts whether this can be done, since he holds that the most unskilled labor is the most costly, though he believes that a maximum of ten hours should be sufficiently productive for industry to warrant such a wage in these employments. Scientific efficiency, however, should warrant an eight-hour day in continuous and strenuous labor.

We must further draw a clear line between occupations in which labor can be intensified and those in which shorter hours mean merely a falling off in production. Some employments are such of their very nature that they afford leisure and interruption for the worker. In other occupations, too, the eight-hour day is simply impossible. Thus the conductor and engineer upon a railway train cannot abandon their positions when the clock strikes. They must bring their passengers safely into the appointed station. The famous eight-hour railway law was in such cases basic for wages and not for work. It meant extra pay for overtime. With this the men were satisfied, though Mr. Woodrow Wilson, then President, expressly made this general announcement regarding the eight-hour day:

> We believe in the eight-hour day because a man does better work within eight hours than he does within a more extended day; and the whole theory of it, a theory which is sustained now by abundant experience, is that his efficiency is increased, his spirit in his work is improved, and the whole moral and physical vigor of the man is added to. This is no longer conjectural.

There is much to be said in favor of a general eight-hour day in industry, provided we admit the reasonable exceptions that must be made and provided also that efficient service is rendered. At all events, it secures the necessary leisure for those who else would never be granted it. There is a simplicity in the conception that makes its enforcement possible. It is absolutely necessary, both for efficiency and human comfort in the extremely fatiguing processes that are sufficiently common in modern industry. Its logic, as expressed in the poem we have quoted, appeals to the heart and mind: "Eight hours for work, eight hours for rest, eight hours for what we will." Hence the wide favor with which the eight-hour day has met.

Yet it does not follow from this that it is the ideal time-measure for the labor-day in every gainful occupation. Of particular interest in this regard is the resolution drawn up by the Congress of Canadian Catholic Trade Unions in the convention held at Three Rivers in 1919. It strongly opposed a universal eight-hour law, thus expressing its conviction:

> The convention voices the opinion that all measures tending to prescribe a determined number of hours for the legal working-day in all industries is arbitrary, unwise and inopportune. It believes and maintains that the length of the working-day should be such as to assure the worker a reasonable allowance of time to repair his physical strength, to fulfill his duties as husband, head of the family, citizen, and a member of the Church; and finally to satisfy the obvious demands made upon him by commerce, industry and financial considerations.

The main point in the contention of these labor unionists was that some trades admitted of more than eight hours while others demanded a shorter working-day. This is undoubtedly true. Their proposed solution was that different trades should themselves determine their own specific needs in this matter. Here surely would be the ideal method, if employers and employees could agree within each trade upon a length of hours that would be equally fair to themselves and to the public. The difficulty lies of course in the frequent selfishness of both capital and labor, and in the disregard of the common good too often shown by both alike.

Turning to the traditions of Christian times, we find that the eight-hour day was by no means unknown in the Middle Ages. Yet the more ordinary rule appears to have been to utilize the full day, with proper intermission, from sunrise to sunset. There was no night work permitted, and the long summer days were offset by the shorter winter hours.

Besides, there were the many holidays of the Church on which all labor was suspended, while work often terminated at an earlier hour on the vigils of certain great feasts, even as on all the Saturdays of the year. The complete Saturday half-holiday indeed was not uncommon. In his volume on labor M. d'Avenil holds that from the twelfth to the sixteenth century the number of working-days in France were not more than 250 for the entire year, leaving 115 days free from labor. M. Levasseur even states that for certain trades the annual rest days were no fewer than 141. Not nearly so many holidays appear to have been given in England. But certain it is that nowhere is there a complaint of excessive working-hours; for labor then was not without its joy, and men took pride in their trade, while religion sanctified the humblest duties by the sublimest motives. The toiler knew that in his daily task he was but following in the footprints of the Carpenter of Nazareth.

6

A LIVING WAGE[1]

John A. Ryan, D.D.

"A Living Wage" forms the title of a chapter in Professor William Smart's *Studies in Economics.* This chapter was written in Scotland, November, 1893. In its opening sentences we are told: "The last few weeks have seen the birth of a new and attractive catchword. Before it has even been defined, it is already put forward as arguing a claim. . . . The expression 'living wage' seems to give a reason and a basis for a certain amount of wages. It has, accordingly, found its way into everyday language, and we may expect soon to find that the conception which it expresses has taken its place among the convictions of many."

In all probability, these sentences describe the origin of the phrase, "living wage." But the idea that it expresses goes back much farther than the summer of 1893. Because the idea is so much older than the expression, it has "taken its place among the convictions of many" to a far greater extent and with much more rapidity than Professor Smart expected when he wrote the words just quoted. Because the expression neatly and concretely sets forth the idea, it likewise has obtained a currency that the professor never anticipated. Both the idea and the expression owe their vogue and their popularity to the fact that they represent a fundamental principle of justice.

Although the idea of a living wage goes back at least to the early Middle Ages, it received its first systematic and authoritative expression in the Encyclical of Pope Leo XIII, "On the Condition of Labor."

---

1. From John A. Ryan, *The Church and Socialism and Other Essays* (Washington, D.C.: The University Press, 1919).

This was published in May, 1891, something more than a year before the "catchword" was first heard in Great Britain. In that document the great pontiff flatly rejected the prevailing doctrine that wages fixed by free consent were always fair and just. This theory, he said, leaves out of account certain important considerations. It ignores the fundamental fact that the laborer is morally bound to preserve his life, and that his only means of fulfilling this duty is to be found in his wages. Therefore, concluded Pope Leo, "a workman's wages ought to be sufficient to maintain him in reasonable and frugal comfort." This proposition, he declared, is a "dictate of natural justice."

What is "reasonable comfort"? Evidently, it is something more than the conditions and essentials of mere existence. To have merely the means of continuing to live and to work is not to be in comfort. What degree of comfort is reasonable? To this question we could get a hundred different answers from as many different persons. Each of the one hundred might conceive reasonable comfort as that to which he had become accustomed, or that to which he aspired because it seemed to bring happiness to others. The reasonable comfort that the Pope had in mind is merely the reasonable minimum. It is that smallest amount which will satisfy right reason. One way of finding out how much is required by this standard is to consult the judgment of competent and fair-minded men. Another and more fundamental method is to interpret reasonable comfort in the light of man's nature and essential needs. These are the ends to which any degree of welfare is but a means. Man's nature and needs, therefore, should indicate the amount of goods that constitute the minimum measure of reasonable comfort.

Like every other human being, the wage-earner is a person, not a thing, nor a mere animal. Because he is a person, he has certain needs that are not felt by animals, and his needs and his welfare have a certain sacredness that does not belong to any other species of creatures. A dog or a horse may be used as mere instruments to the welfare of man. They may rightfully be killed when man no longer wants them. Not so with the human person. He has intrinsic worth and dignity. He is made in the image and likeness of God. He is an end in himself. He was not created for the pleasure, or utility, or aggrandizement of any other human being or group of human beings. His worth and his place in the universe are to be measured with reference to himself, not with reference to other men, or to institutions, or to states. He is worth while for his own sake.

When, then, are the needs to which are attached this prerogative of intrinsic worth and sacredness? How much of the good things of life must a man have in order that he may live in a manner worthy of a person? In general, he must have sufficient goods and opportunities for the exercise of all his faculties and the development of his personality. On the physical side, this means food, clothing and housing adequate to maintain him in health and working efficiency. If he is underfed, or insufficiently clothed, or improperly housed, he is treated with even less consideration than wise and humane men extend to their beasts of burden. Since the worker is not merely an animal and an instrument of production, but an intellectual and moral person, he requires the means of exercising and developing the faculties of his soul. Therefore he needs some education, some facilities for reading and study, the means of practicing religion, an environment that will not make unreasonably difficult the leading of a moral life, and sufficient opportunities of social intercourse and recreation to maintain him in efficiency and to give him that degree of contentment that is essential to a healthy outlook on life. As regards the future, the worker requires a certain minimum amount of security against sickness, accident, and old age. Finally, all these goods should be available to the worker, not as a single man, but as the head of a family; for marriage is among the essential needs of the great majority.

All the foregoing goods and opportunities are included in the concept of reasonable comfort. Within the last few years, many groups of persons have attempted to translate these requisites into more concrete symbols. They have tried to describe reasonable comfort or a decent livelihood in terms of food, housing, insurance, etc. Their statements and estimates have shown a remarkable measure of agreement. This substantial uniformity proves that "reasonable comfort," is not only a practical and tangible conception, but one that springs from the deepest intuitions of reason and morality.

We pass over their specific statements concerning the amount and kinds of food required, as these are too technical for our present purpose. It is sufficient to say that these specifications cover an allowance of food adequate to the preservation of health and working efficiency. As regards clothing, the estimates include not merely what is needed for health and efficiency, but those additional articles and changes of raiment which are essential in order that the worker and his family may, without loss of self-respect, attend church, school, and participate in public gatherings, and various forms of social intercourse. The provision of apparel for these latter purposes may not be directly necessary on the ground of health, but it meets one of the fundamental needs of a human being. It is among the requirements of the mind and the emotions. To deny it to a man is to treat him as somewhat less than a man.

In the matter of housing, the authorities agree that the wage-earner and his family require at least four or five rooms, with adequate sunlight, ventilation, and all the elementary requisites of sanitation, and in moral and healthful surroundings.

The majority of social students believe that the workingman's wife should not be compelled to become a wage-earner, and that his children should not regularly engage in gainful occupations before the age of sixteen. If these conditions are not realized, the family is not living in reasonable comfort, and its younger members are deprived of reasonable opportunities of education and development.

All the members of the family should have some provision for recreation, such as an occasional trip to the country and visits to moving pictures or concerts, some access to books and periodical literature, in addition to schooling for the children up to the age of sixteen; and of course the means of belonging to a church.

The worker should have sufficient insurance against unemployment, accidents, sickness and old age to provide himself and those normally dependent upon him with all the above mentioned goods during those periods when he is unable to make such provision by his labor and wages.

Such are the requisites of reasonable comfort as determined by man's nature and needs, and as interpreted by all competent authorities on the subject. That the wage-earner, as all other persons, ought to have this much of the good things of life will not be denied by anyone who appreciates the dignity and intrinsic worth of personality. The man who would assert that the worker and his family may reasonably be deprived of these things must logically contend that the worker may be killed or deprived of his liberty for the benefit of others. For the rights of life, liberty, marriage and all the other fundamental goods rest on precisely the same basis as the claim to reasonable comfort. That basis is the inherent sacredness of personality. This sacredness is outraged, not only when the person is killed, crippled, or imprisoned, but also when he is prevented from exercising and developing his faculties to a reasonable degree.

Pope Leo XIII declared that the workman's claim to a wage that provides reasonable comfort is a "dictate of natural justice." That is to say, a living wage and reasonable comfort are not merely desirable advantages, goods which we should all like to see possessed by the working man and his family, things necessary for reasonable life, but they are required by the principle of justice; they belong to him as a right. To a large proportion of employers, and to many other persons, this is still "a hard saying." How can it be justified?

Pope Leo could not present an extended justification in a document that dealt with the whole field of industrial relations; hence he contented himself with laying down the general principle that a living wage and a condition of reasonable comfort are required in order that the wage earner may fulfill his duties of life and self-development. Obligations cannot be discharged without the necessary means; for the laborer, wages are the only means.

The latest ethical defence of the right to a living wage is that presented by the Rev. Dr. Cronin, in the second volume of his *Science of Ethics.* It is, in brief, that a wage which is not sufficient to provide reasonable comfort is not the just equivalent of the wage-earner's labor. Why? Because the worker's energy or labor is the one means that God has given him to provide the essentials of reasonable life and comfort. When the employer appropriates to his own uses this energy, he is bound in strict justice to give in exchange for it the amount of welfare which the laborer's energy is the divinely given means of obtaining. Other writers give other arguments and justifications. Among the Catholic authorities the differences in this matter are differences of view-point rather than of principle. The following argument seems to be more fundamental and thorough than some of the others.

When we consider man's position in relation to the bounty of nature, we are led to accept three fundamental principles. The first may be thus stated. Since the earth was intended by God for the support of all persons, all have essentially equal claims upon it, and essentially equal rights of access to its benefits. On the one hand, God has not declared that any of His children have superior or exceptional claims to the earth. On the other hand, all persons are made in the image and likeness of God, composed of the same kind of body and soul, affected by the same needs, and destined for the same end. Therefore they are all equally important in His sight. They are all equally persons, endowed with intrinsic worth and dignity, ends in themselves, not instruments to the welfare of others. Hence they stand upon an essentially equal footing with regard to the animal, plant, and mineral bounty of the earth. This bounty is a common gift, possession, heritage. The moral claims upon it held by these equal human persons are essentially equal. No man can vindicate for himself a superior claim on the basis of anything that he finds in himself, in nature or in the designs of nature's God.

Nevertheless, this equal right of access to the earth is not absolute. It is conditioned upon labor, upon the expenditure of useful and fruitful energy. As a rule, the good things of the earth are obtained in adequate form and quantity only at the cost of considerable exertion. And this exertion is for the most part irksome, of such a nature that men will not perform it except under the compulsion of some less agreeable alternative. The labor to which the earth yields up her treasures is not put forth spontaneously and automatically. Therefore the equal and inherent right of men to possess the earth and utilize its benefits becomes actually valid only when they are willing to expend productive energy and labor. This is the second fundamental principle.

Obviously we are speaking here of the original rights of men to the earth, not of those rights which they have acquired through the possession of private property. The rights in question are those which inhere in all men, whether or not they are private owners.

From the two principles of equal right of access to the earth, and universal obligation to perform a reasonable amount of useful labor, follows a third fundamental principle. It is that men who at any time or in any way control the resources of the earth are morally bound to permit others to have access thereto on reasonable terms. Men who are willing to work must be enabled to make real and actual their original and equal right of access to the common bounty of nature. For the right to subsist from the earth implies the right actually to participate in its benefits on reasonable conditions and through reasonable arrangements. Otherwise the former right is a delusion. To refuse any man reasonable facilities to exercise his basic right of living from the common bounty by his labor is to treat this right as nonexistent. Such conduct by the men who are in possession implies a belief that their rights to the gifts of God are inherently superior to the right of the person whom they exclude. This position is utterly untenable. It is on exactly the same basis as would be the claim of a strong man to deprive a weak one of liberty. The right to freedom of movement is not more certain nor more indestructible than the right of access on reasonable terms to the bounty of the earth. Were a community to imprison an innocent man it would not violate his rights more vitally than does the proprietor or the corporation that deprives him of reasonable access to the resources of nature. In both cases the good that he seeks is a common gift of God.

This, then, is the moral basis underlying the laborer's right to a living wage. Like all other men, he has an indestructible right of access to the goods of the earth on reasonable terms. Obviously, the conditional clause, "on reasonable terms," is of very great importance. Neither the laborer nor anyone else has a right of direct and unconditional access to those portions of the earth that have rightly become the property of others. Such a claim would be the height of unreason. The laborer's right to participate in the common heritage must be actualized in such a way as not to interfere with the equally valid rights of others. The laborer's right must be satisfied with due regard to existing acquired rights and the existing form of industrial organization.

From this principle to the principle that the laborer has a right to a living wage, the transition is logical and certain. Pope Leo XIII declared that the laborer's right to a living wage arises from the fact that his wage is his only means of livelihood. Owing to the manner in which the goods of the earth have been divided and appropriated in the present organization of industrial society, the wage-earner has no way of exercising his original and equal right of access to the earth except through the sale of his labor in return for wages. An occasional worker might get a livelihood by cultivating a piece of land, but the cost is so great that only those can defray it who are already receiving more than living wages. If such an opportunity and alternative were general, the living wage would not be a practical question. Men would not hire themselves out for less than that amount when they could obtain a decent livelihood by employing themselves on a piece of land. To assure a laborer that if he does not like to work for less than living wages, he can fall back upon his right of access to the earth by taking up a piece of land, is but to mock him. Such access as he has is evidently not access on reasonable terms.

For the wage-earner of to-day, therefore, access to the resources of nature can be had only through wages. The men who have appropriated the goods and opportunities of the earth have shut him out from any other way of entering upon his natural heritage. Therefore they are morally bound to use and administer these goods in such a way that his right shall not be violated and his access to the resources of nature not rendered unreasonably difficult. This means that the industrial community in which he lives, and for which he labors, shall provide him with the requisites of a decent livelihood in the form of living wages. On the one hand, the worker has performed a reasonable amount of labor; on the other hand, the industrial community is the beneficiary of his services. In the product which he has created the community has the wherewith to pay him living wages. To refuse him this amount of remuneration is surely to deprive him of access to the earth and to a livelihood on reasonable terms.

It is assumed here that the laborer's product is sufficiently large to provide this much remuneration, and that the employer would rather pay it than go without the laborer's services. The case in which the product falls short of this sufficiency will be considered presently. If the employer does not think the laborer worth a living wage, he has a right to discharge him. Otherwise the employer would be treated unreasonably. But when the employer regards the employee as worth a living wage, but refuses to pay it merely because the laborer is economically constrained to work for less, he is surely treating the latter unreasonably. He is depriving the laborer of access to the goods of the earth on reasonable terms. In the striking words of Pope Leo XIII, he is making the laborer "the victim of force and injustice."

The reader will have noticed that in the last paragraph the word "employer" is substituted for the word "community," which was used in the paragraph preceding. If the community in its corporate civil form—that is, the State—were the direct beneficiary of the laborer's services, if it came into direct possession of the laborer's product, it would obviously be charged with the duty of paying him a living wage. In our present industrial organization, however, the State permits the employer to obtain the product and imposes upon him the duty of wage paying. Therefore he is the person who is obliged to perform this duty adequately, that is, in the form of living wages. If he fails to do so, he abuses his social and industrial functions; he uses his control over the goods of the earth in such a way as to deprive the laborer of access thereto on reasonable terms.

What if the employer cannot pay living wages? Space limitations will not permit us to discuss the very interesting ethical question whether such an employer is morally obliged to go out of business. The employer has a right to take from the product the equivalent of a decent livelihood for himself and his family, even though the remainder will not provide full living wages for all his employees. For his claim to a decent livelihood is as good as theirs, and in a conflict of equal claims a man is justified in preferring himself to his neighbors. When, however, the employer has already obtained a decent livelihood, he has no right to take from the product one cent more until he has given all his employees the full measure of living wages. In the first place, the right to take interest in any circumstances on invested capital is only presumptive and probable, not certain. In the second place, the right of the laborers to get from the joint product the means of satisfying their essential and fundamental needs is morally superior to the right of the employer to the means of indulging in luxurious living or of making new investments. To deny this proposition is to assert that the claims of the laborers upon the common bounty of nature are morally inferior to those of the employer, and that they are but instruments to his welfare, not morally equal and independent persons.

One can easily imagine some employer exclaiming that a right of access to the resources of nature does not mean the right to take as much as the equivalent of a living wage. The objection ignores the truth that the access should be "on reasonable terms." Surely this phrase implies that the access and the wage should provide at least a decent livelihood. The employer who thinks that he may rightfully pay the lowest wage that the laborer can be forced to accept forgets that he himself is only a steward of the gifts of God. What he calls his product is his, not to use as he pleases, but to administer with due regard to the natural rights of his employees.

We have made no formal defense of the proposition that the just living wage for an adult male is one that will support decently his wife and children as well as himself. We have assumed that anyone who recognizes the claim of the laborer to develop his personality to a reasonable degree will take for granted that those advantages are possible only when the father's wage is adequate to decent family maintenance.

Up to the present we have given no more specific definition of a living wage than it is the equivalent of a decent livelihood, or a sum sufficient to maintain the worker and his family in conditions of reasonable comfort. The attempt to define it in terms of money is beset with many difficulties. Some housekeepers are much better managers than others in making purchases and in utilizing them; the number and quantity of concrete goods that suffice for decent living conditions, for example, in the matters of recreation and non-material things, do not easily submit to exact measurement; the variation in the cost of commodities from city to city and from section to section renders any single estimate inadequate; and, finally, the recent extraordinary rise in prices, culminating in the present abnormal cost of living, has made almost all previous estimates antiquated.

Nevertheless, the difficulties are not insurmountable. They can be overcome sufficiently to yield approximate estimates that will be of great practical value. That is all that we require in a matter of this kind. We are dealing with the realm of moral approximations, not with the province of exact science. While the cost of living of a workingman's family varies indefinitely on account of the varying proficiency of the housewife, we have to consider only the average level of domestic economy and efficiency. This average is ascertainable quite as definitely as a hundred other important social facts. The goods that are required to provide a minimum decent level of existence can be estimated with sufficient accuracy to safeguard the welfare of the laborer and his family. The variation of prices over space and time can be dealt with by making the estimates of a living wage apply only to specific places and specific dates.

Within recent years we have been provided with many such estimates. For example, the New York Bureau of Standards concluded in 1915 that the minimum cost of living for a family of five was a little less than $850 annually. In the same year a commission of members of the legislature gave an estimate of about $875 for the same city and about $100 less for Buffalo. In the summer of 1918 the experts of the National War Labor Board found that the lowest annual amount upon which a man and wife and three children could be maintained decently was $1,386.

Four methods are conceivable by which a living wage might become universal. The first is the automatic operation of economic forces. Some twenty or twenty-five years ago this theory enjoyed considerable favor among economists. It took substantially this form: Capital is increasing much faster than labor; therefore, its demand for labor is increasing relatively to the supply; therefore, the remuneration of labor will necessarily increase. The fatal flaw in this argument is its neglect of the fact that a large proportion of the new capital takes the place of labor, thereby reducing instead of enhancing the demand for laborers. Machines are constantly made to do the work of men, and so far as we can see, the process will go on indefinitely. The remuneration of underpaid labor measured by its purchasing capacity has decreased rather than increased during the last quarter of a century. No economic forces are discernible that are likely to cause a contrary movement within the next twenty-five years.

The second agency that might theoretically be expected to raise the wages of the underpaid is the benevolence of employers. Only visionaries put any faith in this method. In so far as experience is a guide, it warns us that only an insignificant minority of employers will ever voluntarily increase the remuneration of employees who are getting less than living wages. Were the number of those disposed to do so multiplied indefinitely, they would not be able to carry out their lofty design. Owing to the force and keenness of competition, the great majority of employers must conform to the wage standards fixed by their most selfish competitors. A benevolent majority might, indeed, raise wage rates to the level of decency by combining for that purpose. Our readers would not thank us for inviting them to consider seriously such a fantastic hypothesis.

The third conceivable method is that of organization by the laborers themselves. While labor unions have done much, very much, to increase wages within the last forty years, their influence in this field has been mainly restricted to the skilled trades. The proportion of unskilled and underpaid labor enrolled in the unions has always been very small, and it shows very little tendency to increase. Effective organization requires time, patience and considerable financial resources, the very things which underpaid labor lacks. Not within a generation would organization be able to obtain living wages for more than a minority of those who are below that level.

The one device that gives promise of making the living wage universal is a minimum fixed by law. This means that the public authorities, state or federal, or both, should enact legislation forbidding any employer to pay less than the equivalent of a decent livelihood.

7

What Is Social Justice?[1]

George G. Higgins

The virtue of social justice is easy to talk about but difficult to define, and even more difficult to put into practice.

What is social justice? Pope Pius XI refers to it as that virtue which demands "from each individual all that is necessary for the common good." A big order, to be sure, and one that even the best of Catholics, without any noticeable twinge of conscience, can rather habitually fail to carry out.

The Rev. William Ferree, who has written by far the best and most original American study on the nature and practice of social justice, examines our Catholic conscience on this most important virtue. (*The Act of Social Justice*. Catholic University of America Press.)

"Now leaving out the men of ill will, including the indifferent and the lazy," he asks, to our embarrassment, "what men of good will are rather habitual offenders against social justice despite their 'good intentions'?"

Abdications of Leadership

First of all, he replies, there are those who are so "impressed by the great mass of social disorder and the difficulty of reform," that "they consider that responsibility can apply to personal life only." Far from being a virtue, he says, this attitude (which, often enough, is

1. This text constitutes Higgins's column "The Yardstick, Catholic Tests of a Social Order" for release the week of May 5, 1947.

only a cover-up for cynicism) is "a sin against social justice because it abdicates leadership in the very institutions which it itself perpetuates by its participation."

Different illustrations of this all too often failing will naturally suggest themselves to different readers. The following are offered only as typical examples: Refusal to participate in union affairs because the union happens to be temporarily under the control of undesirable leadership—and besides, the argument continues, if people would only be decent, we wouldn't need to have unions. Refusal to vote in political elections on the ground that political life is hopelessly corrupt. Opposition to the United States on the theory that, unless and until all men return to God and to the moral law, there can be no hope of peace. An attitude of apathy and indifference about social and economic legislation based on the excuse that you can't change the attitudes of men by means of legislation.

"LET GEORGE DO IT"

Secondly, Father Ferree continues, there are those who "add to the lack of solidarity (social charity) of the former class (the abdicators), a lack of appreciation also for the very complexity of life which so impresses these former. While thus tragically simplifying the problem of responsibility to individual means only, they throw the whole crushing weight of social disorder upon unsupported and isolated individual consciences and upon personal 'heroism' in resisting evil."

And finally there are those who disdain the tedious and thankless work of organization itself, not necessarily because they are lazy, but because they look upon organization "as somehow below their dignity or wasteful of their time." Among the worst offenders in this regard, according to Father Ferree, are some who have been blessed with the advantages of a better-than-average education and who, for that very reason, might reasonably be expected to make a better-than-average contribution to the cause of social justice. Too often, instead, they let George do it, while they indulge in the comforting luxury of telling George by hindsight that he should have done it differently.

CERTAIN TIMID SOULS

If Father Ferree be unimpressed by our "good intentions" in the face of our frequent failure to do "all that is necessary for the common good" (which means our failure to correct the bad economic and social institutions to which we belong, or to organize good institutions where needed), he is in the best of company. He is merely re-echoing the authoritative opinion of the saintly Pope Pius X who told us more than a generation ago:

> "Catholic Action will not please certain timid souls who, though good living, are so attached to their habitual quiet and so afraid of every innovation that they believe that it is quite sufficient to pray, because God knows best how to defend the Faith and humiliate His enemies and make the Church triumphant. But these good people . . . will wait in vain for society to re-Christianize itself simply by the prayers of the good . . . It is necessary to join prayers with action . . . There are others, on the other hand, who, in order to justify their inertia, give the world up for lost, since they see in it so many evils."

Was Pius X talking about us?

8

CATHOLIC UNION THEORY[1]

George G. Higgins

The February issue of *Fortune* magazine attempts to do the impossible—and almost succeeds. It attempts to analyze "the meaning of America" under the title, "U.S.A. Permanent Revolution." All in all, it is probably one of the more remarkable accomplishments in the record of contemporary journalism. In fourteen beautifully illustrated and more or less interrelated articles—prepared by members of the staff under the general supervision of Russell Davenport, former Managing Editor of *Fortune*—it comes as close to accomplishing its announced objective as anybody could reasonably expect.

Fortunately or otherwise, its objective is limited rather severely to the political, economic, and technological aspects of our national tradition and does not concern itself, except indirectly and in passing, with the religious and moral issues of American culture. Nevertheless the project is carried off remarkably well—due allowance being made for the particular social philosophy of the publisher and board of editors and for a couple of infelicitous references to things Catholic.

In this most unusual issue of the nation's most respectable business periodical there is one article which particularly held our attention—the article on the U.S. labor movement. And there is one particular sentence in this article which has kept us guessing ever since we read it.

---

1. This text constitutes Higgins's column "The Yardstick, Catholic Tests of a Social Order" for release the week of February 19, 1951.

Labor Not "Class Conscious"

One of the principal conclusions of the article is this, that the American labor movement "is not 'working-class conscious'; it is not 'proletarian' and does not believe in class war." Just to add to the discomfiture of John T. Flynn et al., the article adds insult to injury by taking the position that this distinctive characteristic of the American labor movement is even more apparent in 1951 than it was at the turn of the century. "Never," it is said, "have left-wing ideologies had so little influence on the American labor movement as they have today." This conclusion, incidentally, we hope to have reproduced on a little card to be forwarded without comment to the many solicitous correspondents who write to tell us— sometimes in anger, sometimes in sorrow—that the editor of the *Yardstick* is being unpriestly in defending a "Socialist" labor movement. Sure we cannot be expected to be more anti-Socialist than *Fortune,* than which there is no more authentic or more highly respected spokesmen for the top leadership of the American business community.

And now for that mysterious, enigmatic sentence which has so intensely aroused our curiosity. "If there is an ideological influence in American labor today," the article states, "it is Catholic union theory —spread by a growing number of labor priests and Catholic labor schools and of considerable importance in several C.I.O. unions as well as in the building trades of the A. F. of L."

What Does It Mean?

Is this intended as a criticism or a gracious compliment—or merely a casual, non-committal statement of fact? And what does it mean? What is this "Catholic union theory?" Is it the theory that unions (and employer organizations) ought to become constituent parts of "industry councils," charged with the responsibility—under adequate government surveillance—of regulating the various industries according to the norms of social justice? If so, why did the editors insert such a sweeping generalization about the building trades? The building trades have reasonably good unions, in our opinion, but we had not been told that they were particularly aware of the industry council theory or that they were doing very much to put it into practice.

But if this "Catholic union theory" doesn't refer to the industry council proposal, what can it possibly mean? Perhaps the editors will clarify their meaning later on. Meanwhile we can only hope that the sentence does refer to the industry council theory, for the American labor movement badly needs an "ideology" as *Fortune* itself appears to suggest at the very end of the article.

We can be very grateful, indeed, the editors conclude, that the working people of the United States have turned their back on the Marxist interpretation of history and have gradually fashioned a distinctively American type of unionism. But "it is not enough for labor to define its beliefs and aims in Sam Gompers' famous answer to the question as to what labor wants: 'More.'"

MAJOR CHALLENGE

Given the strong unions of 1951—in contrast to the struggling little crafts of Gompers' generations—this very over-simplified and very un-philosophical theory of unionism can all too easily lead to the class struggle and the acceptance on the part of American working people of a "proletarian ideology." American union leadership, the article concludes, is faced with a major challenge at the half-way point of the twentieth century: to develop "new and positive policies that will institutionalize the worker's stake in the business enterprise and his responsible citizenship in capitalist society."

If you haven't choked to death on all those big words, ask yourself if this doesn't mean that union leaders ought to be aiming at a gradual growth into a system of industry councils. I don't think the editors of *Fortune* would altogether agree with you if you were to answer, "Yes," but then again I am not so sure. I really don't know what they think about "Catholic union theory." I don't even know how they would define it, for their rather casual reference to the subject, as we have already indicated, is tantalizingly brief and non-committal.

Be that as it may, I did like their February issue on "the meaning of America." I liked it very much—particularly the article on labor. I recommend the article very highly.

9

THIS MATTER OF RELIGIOUS FREEDOM

John Courtney Murray, S.J.

There has been considerable speculation about the reasons for the postponement of a doctrinal decision on religious freedom at the last session of the Council. (It provoked the famous "Day of Wrath," November 19.) The question is not, of course, the classical one: "Who done it?" This question is probably unanswerable, as often happens in Rome. The real question concerns the reasons, motives and feelings that lay behind the doing. It can be answered at least up to a point. First, however, it is necessary to give a brief sketch of the contents—the theme, methodology and argument—of the third draft *Declaration on Religious Freedom* submitted at the last session.

The *Declaration* made a simple and straightforward affirmation, namely, that coercion in religious matters—worship, observance, practice, witness—is, in principle, to be repudiated as offensive to the dignity of man. Primarily in view was legal coercion exercised by government; also in view were other forms of compulsion, direct or indirect, brought to bear by institutions or forces within society. In positive terms, the *Declaration* affirmed the free exercise of religion in society to be a basic human right that, in any society pretending to be well-ordered, should be furnished with a juridical guarantee so as to become a civil or constitutional right. Religious freedom, therefore, was clearly stated to be a juridical notion. Moreover, freedom here has the sense of "freedom from." It is an immunity in a twofold sense. First, no man is to be forcibly constrained to act against his conscience. Second, no man is to be forcibly restrained from acting according to his conscience.

From the historical point of view, religious freedom in the sense of immunity from coercive constraints came to be recognized as a human right even during the post-Reformation era of confessional absolutism, as it is called. The principle was gradually established that even the absolutist prince may not compel a man to act against his conscience or punish him for reasons of conscience. The doctrine of religious freedom as an immunity from coercive restraints was, however, first effectively proclaimed in the First Amendment to the Constitution of the United States. It was considered to be an integral element of the doctrine of limited constitutional government. The *Declaration* affirmed religious freedom in both of these senses. The affirmation was doctrinal.

At the same time, the *Declaration* recognized that religious freedom, like other human and civil freedoms, is exercised within society and may therefore be subject to limitation. Two principles of limitation were stated. The first was the general moral principle of personal responsibility, which requires that all civil rights be exercised with a sense of responsibility toward society and its common good, toward the state and its just laws and authority, and toward one's fellow men, who are equally persons and citizens. The second principle was that the exercise of religious freedom may in particular cases be subject to restraint by state intervention. As the criterion for this intervention, the Declaration posits the traditional jurisprudential norm, the necessities of the public order.

The public order is that limited segment of the common good which is committed to the state to be protected and maintained by the coercive force that is available to the state—the force of law and of administrative or police action. The public order thus comprises a threefold good—the political good, which is the public peace; the moral good, which is proper custody of public morality as determined by minimal and generally accepted standards; and the juridical good, which is harmony among citizens in the exercise of their civil rights. By this criterion, the exercise of religion is to be free unless, in some case, it seriously disturbs the public peace, violates public morality or results in infringement of the rights of others. The possibility of abuse of this broad criterion was obviated, as far as possible, by the inclusion in the *Declaration* of the basic principle of the free society, namely, that there is to be as much freedom as possible, and only as much restriction as necessary.

Furthermore, the *Declaration* articulates the concept of religious freedom in its corporate sense, in its application to religious communities, the family, and voluntary associations for various purposes. In its content, this corporate concept exhibited substantial agreement with the concept elaborated in official statements of the World Council of Churches. In particular, the *Declaration* recognized the right of religious communities to immunity from coercive interference, both in the conduct of their own internal affairs and in the bearing of public witness to their faith.

In accord with its basic premise, namely, that religious freedom is a juridical notion, the first section of the *Declaration* evolves and affirms the concept from the standpoint of reason and justice. In the second part, it affirms the harmony between the contemporary juridical notion of religious freedom and the revealed doctrine of the Church. Two doctrines are immediately relevant: 1) the freedom of the Church, both as a spiritual authority and as a spiritual community in its own right, and 2) the necessary freedom of the act of Christian faith. Thereafter, a brief section seeks to uncover the roots of religious freedom in the inspired words of God, the Scriptures.

The *Declaration* concludes with a pastoral exhortation to the faithful. It reminds them both of their duty of fidelity to Christian truth in its integrity and also of their duty of respect for human freedom in the pursuit and embrace of religious truth. The final paragraph is addressed to men and governments at large; it urges the rightness, value and necessity of religious freedom in the world of today.

The method followed by the *Declaration* in approaching its subject is governed by historical consciousness. The starting point is not abstract or ideological, but factual and historical. The initial appeal is to the fact that today man is growing more and more conscious of his own dignity, personal and civil. The *Declaration* does not lay as its premise the abstract truth of human dignity and then undertake to deduce from it the affirmation of religious freedom as a human right. In the general matter of human rights, this procedure is both logically perilous and also unconvincing. The truth of human dignity is as old as Christianity, and in a sense, even older. The new thing today, and the thing that matters for the argument, is the newly common human consciousness of this truth. Glenn Tinder, in his recent and remarkable book, *The Crisis of Political Imagination*, rightly asserts that mankind has reached a historical climax. Today,

> the free and transcendent character of the person has dawned more fully in the civilized consciousness than ever before in history. During approximately the past two thousand years, the irreducible reality and the final value of each individual have been among the fundamental premises of western civilization. But it has taken a very long time for a

deep and widespread awareness of these principles to develop. Man
was sanctified in myth and thought. But in his social relations he was
often openly and deliberately degraded.

Given, today, man's new consciousness of his dignity, this contradiction is no longer tolerable. Man demands civil liberties that he may
lead in society a life worthy of a man. And this demand for freedom
from coercion is made with special force in what concerns religion.
Hence it is that a juridical guarantee of religious freedom is contained
in the constitutions of all civilized states today.

This approach to the subject from the standpoint of historical consciousness has three major advantages. It avoids the fallacy of a false
"objectivism," as if truth could somehow be divorced from the possession of truth. It also avoids the pragmatist and positivist fallacy, which
would regard today's demand for religious freedom as no more than a
brute fact in the face of which one must simply give way. On the contrary, the *Declaration* accepts the present-day emergence of the human
self into the clear light of consciousness as the term of a genuine intellectual and moral progress in man's understanding of his nature. The
consequent demand for religious freedom therefore appears as an exi-
gency of man's own true nature, as the truth about man's nature has
historically penetrated into consciousness. Hence the *Declaration* can
affirm the validity of the demand—the validity of religious freedom
as a human right of man today. No shadow of opportunism or expediency clouds this argument. It frankly recognizes that progress has
taken place in the understanding of an ancient truth, in itself and in
its implications for social and civil life.

There is no need to set forth here, in detail, the grounds that the
Declaration advances for its affirmation of religious freedom. They are
metaphysical (the integrity of human person), moral (the nature of
religion and the role of conscience in religious life), political (the limits
of governmental competence) and legal (the nature of human law).
Suffice it to say that it would be difficult to raise serious objections
against the case made. One might indeed say that the case is incom-
pletely made. It was not, however, the intention of the *Declaration* to
make the case with all completeness. As a conciliar utterance, the *Declaration* was content to indicate the structure and lines of an argument
and to leave its further development to philosophers and theologians.

In sum, the *Declaration* would seem to commend itself, not only to
Catholics, but to all men of good will, by the solid substance of its affirmation, by the correctness of its method, and by the strength of its

reasoning. Why then the postponement of conciliar decision, which seemed to some to suggest the existence of doctrinal doubts or pastoral difficulties?

The suggestion has been made that "they" were to blame—meaning, of course, the Roman Curia. But the suggestion is too facile. It would be more adequate to say that a series of interrelated factors was at work.

In the first place, in its method and doctrine, the *Declaration* rejected the theory of religious tolerance and the related theory of governmental competence in religious matters that began to be developed in the post-Reformation era, assumed form in the 19th century, and subsequently became the received opinion among canonists. This theory rests on the abstract juridical maxim that error has no rights and on the correlative abstract political maxim that government is to repress error whenever possible and tolerate it only when necessary, as a concession to circumstances of religious pluralism. This theory was presented by a few conciliar Fathers. It impressed the assembly chiefly by its archaism. It obviously stands in dependence on a sociological situation, not so much of religious unity as of religious illiteracy. It also rests on the concept of government as paternal in character, charged with a duty toward the religious welfare of the "illiterate masses," to use the phrase of Leo XIII. It was not considered necessary at the Council to refute the theory; it was sufficient quietly to bid it good-by. Certain adversaries—as Santayana pointed out—are better treated thus. In any case, the theory was seen to be irreconcilable with the exigencies of the personal and civil consciousness at its contemporary height. Nevertheless, the classical theory of tolerance still has adherents, who are few indeed but tenacious of their view. They would represent the hard core of opposition to the draft *Declaration*. At that, they oppose, not so much the institution of religious freedom as such, but rather the affirmation of progress in doctrine that an affirmation of religious freedom necessarily entails.

The second factor was probably of greater significance. The advocates of religious freedom were divided among themselves. This has happened not seldom within the so-called "Progressive" majority of the Council. To understand the division, one would have to note the difference in methodology and focus of argument between the first two drafts of the *Declaration* and the third draft.

The first two drafts followed a line of argument common among French-speaking theologians. The argument began, not in the order of historical fact, but in the order of universal truth. The truth is that each man is called by God to share the divine life. This call is mediated to man by conscience, and man's response to it is the free act of faith. The essential dignity of man is located in his personal freedom of conscience, whereby he is truly a moral agent, acting on his own irreducible responsibility before God. Thus religious freedom was conceived to be formally and in the first instance an ethical and theological notion. The effort then was made to conclude, by inference, to the juridical notion of religious freedom—man's right to the free exercise of religion in society. The trouble was that this structure of argument seemed vulnerable to the advocates as well as to the adversaries of religious freedom. It is not obvious that the inference from freedom of conscience to the free exercise of religion as a human right is valid. Nevertheless, many French-speaking theologians and bishops considered their view to be richer and more profound. They were therefore displeased by the third draft *Declaration*, which relinquished their line of argument in favor of a line more common among English- and Italian-speaking theorists.

This line, as I have indicated, addresses the problem where it concretely exists—in the legal and political order. It considers religious freedom to be formally and in the first instance a juridical notion, whose validity, however, is to be established by a convergence of theological, ethical, political and legal argument. To the French-speaking school, this view of the matter seemed "superficial" (I heard the adjective often). This division of opinion was not, indeed, regarding the affirmation of religious freedom as a human right, but rather the manner of making the case for the affirmation. None the less, the division of opinion itself somewhat affected the climate of the Council. And the root of it—the new methodology adopted by the third draft—lent color to the complaint, made by the opposition, that the Fathers had been confronted with a "new schema" which should not be voted on before discussion.

A third factor was a confusion that begot a fear. The *Declaration* dealt with religious freedom as a constitutional issue, a problem in the juridical order of civil society. But in the minds of some, this issue was confused with another—the presently sensitive question of freedom and authority within the Church. This confusion gave rise to a vague fear that a conciliar declaration in favor of religious freedom would somehow be misinterpreted by the faithful and either cause trouble of conscience or possibly even undermine the authority of the Church. This confusion of two altogether separate issues was lamentable, and the ensuing fear was irrational. Fear, however, though it rarely furthers good purposes, is a potent weapon. Postponement of the issue could have been made to seem a good idea.

The decisive factor remains to be noted. In the end, a doctrinal decision on religious freedom was postponed for a year because it had already been postponed for some two hundred years. The remark may seem paradoxical. In the 19th century, the Church did indeed make a doctrinal decision on the notion of religious freedom that was advanced by Continental laicism. Its premises were the absolute autonomy of the individual conscience and the juridical omnipotence of the state. The notion itself implied that man is free from any dependence on God. It also implied that the state is the power superior to the Church, competent to make a theological judgment on what the Church is and to determine by legislation what role the Church is to play in society. As everybody knows, the thesis was that the Church is to play no role in society. It contended that religion is a purely private matter. The Church condemned this notion of religious freedom and its premises. The condemnation, however, left the real issue of religious freedom untouched. Only a historically urgent, but theoretically false, issue had been decided. The real issue was not faced by the Church until Vatican Council II. Even then, however, the conciliar Fathers and their theologians were not entirely prepared to face it. The reason was that free discussion of the real issue had been inhibited within the Church by the power of the Holy Office. The fact was well known and widely lamented. We have now come to lament also its consequences, the failure to develop a consensus within the Church. This can be done only through free discussion.

The failure was more lamentable because religious freedom is not the most important issue before the Council, nor the most difficult, except insofar as it raises the issue of development of doctrine, which is the issue underlying all issues at the Council. More noteworthy is the fact that religious freedom is not the most urgent issue in the world at large today. On the contrary, despite deplorable violations of the principle of religious freedom today, the principle itself is accepted by the common consciousness of men and civilized nations. Hence the Church is in the unfortunate position of coming late, with the great guns of her authority, to a war that has already been won, however many rear-guard skirmishes remain to be fought. An argument about religious freedom might almost be called a distraction from the real issues at the moment.

I felt obliged to be critical of the view taken by my French-speaking friends on the narrow issue of religious freedom. On the other hand, I entirely share the preoccupations that gave rise to their view. I mean the need to go to the depths of the religious problematic of our age, of which atheism is an important integral part, not only as a personal conviction but as a social force. I mean also the need to center all attention on the problem to which Leo XIII pointed at the deepest and most enduring level of his doctrine. It concerns, broadly, the problem of religious truth in its relation to human society in its full sweep.

The state can and should do no more than guarantee freedom of religion. It remains for religion itself, by the force of its own truth alone, to recover its public standing and its social influence in an industrial society to which religion has become largely irrelevant and even insipid. Leo XIII had to be content with an effort to inaugurate a dialogue between the Church and the rulers of society in his time, who were estranged from religion. Today, the estrangement has spread throughout society itself, so as to profoundly affect the human person as such, whose religious consciousness is necessarily social and historical. Today, as Paul VI has pointed out, the problem is to broaden the dialogue until its ever widening circles embrace the whole of humanity and include all human concerns, both personal and social. It is to be hoped that the Council will quickly conclude its distracting debate on religious freedom, finish the Church's long unfinished business, and get on to the deeper issue of the effective presence of the Church in the world today.

10

THE ENCYCLICALS AND SOCIAL ACTION: IS JOHN A. RYAN TYPICAL?[1]

Francis L. Broderick

Near the end of an intense busy career devoted to social reform, John A. Ryan casually searched for the label that best described his public position. He shied away from "liberal" and "conservative"—liberal because of its ambiguity, conservative because of its flagrant inaccuracy. "Progressive" attracted him for a moment—it allied him with the right people, and it suggested the forward-looking optimism that characterized most of his public statements from 1894 to 1945. Yet he settled finally on "papalist."[2] The tag, meaning an orthodox commitment to the mind of the Holy See, was apt both because of the use he made of the encyclicals to promote Catholic concurrence in American social reform and because of the period in which he worked. In Monsignor Ryan's lifetime, few if any Americans had a comparable claim on the title "papalist." After his death even fewer would be inclined to invoke the claim.

While still a seminarian in 1894, John Ryan came across Leo XIII's encyclical *Rerum novarum*. In it he found the standard Catholic denunciation of socialism and the standard reaffirmation of private property as a natural right. At the same time, Leo stated unequivocally that a

---

1. This paper was read as the presidential address at the forty-ninth annual meeting of the American Catholic Historical Association in New York on December 29, 1968. Mr. Broderick is chancellor of the University of Massachusetts at Boston.

2. Francis L. Broderick, "But Constitutions Can Be Changed . . . ," *Catholic Historical Review,* XLIV (October 1963), p. 393.

laborer had a right to enough of the world's goods to allow him to exist in "reasonable and frugal comfort." The state was obliged to guarantee that right, he said, "whenever the general interest of any class suffers, or is threatened with evils which can in no other way be met . . . ."[3] For Ryan these affirmations meant simply that if the state allowed the "greed and usurpation of . . . 'Plutocrats'" to destroy jobs, the state had a positive obligation to find jobs for every worker.[4] In the following decade, his great book, *A Living Wage* (1906),[5] in an argument now so familiar as to be redundant, translated man's natural right to share in the earth's bounty into an assertion of man's right in an industrial society to a living wage, enough to allow him to live with his family in decency. The worker's right rested on his dignity as an individual, Ryan argued, and that dignity undoubtedly included the right to marry and to provide a decent home for a family. Ryan insisted, therefore, upon a familial living wage as a matter of justice. With this book Father Ryan launched three decades of struggle for a legally guaranteed minimum wage. Always there as backup for his argument was *Rerum novarum* which, he said, had converted the living wage from an implicit to an explicit principle of Catholic ethics.

Well along in Ryan's polemical career, *Quadragesimo anno* (1931) reinforced his argument for distributive justice—a "great vindication" of Ryan, a former rector at Catholic University called it[6]—and suggested occupational groups of workers and employees guided by the state as the most effective device for meeting the demands of social justice. Ryan thought he saw Pius XI's occupational groups realized in the National Recovery Administration, and he served joyously in the NRA in 1934–1935 and mourned its demise in 1935. As late as 1942 he was rejoicing that Philip Murray of the CIO seemed to have caught the spirit and flavor of *Quadragesimo anno* in his post-war proposals.[7]

Ryan's credentials as a papalist remain good even outside industrial reorganization. In 1930, for example, he denied that compulsory legal sterilization for eugenic purposes was intrinsically evil and, in all circumstances, morally wrong; he believed that sterilization of the mentally diseased for the protection of the community was licit.[8] The

---

3. "Five Great Encyclicals" pamphlet (New York, 1939), pp. 1–30 *passim.*

4. *Northwestern Chronicle,* March 2, 1894.

5. John A. Ryan, *A Living Wage: Its Ethical and Economic Aspects* (New York, 1906).

6. Ryan, *Social Doctrine in Action* (New York, 1941), p. 242.

7. Ryan, "Catholic Social Teaching," MS. of Speech, August 25, 1942, in the John A. Ryan Papers, Catholic University of America, Washington, D.C. Hereafter, Ryan papers.

8. Ryan, "Moral Aspects of Sterilization," pamphlet (Washington, 1930), p. 7.

following year, after Pius took the opposite view in his encyclical on Christian marriage, Ryan withdrew completely from his position, now averring that Catholics were no longer morally free to choose from among the many conflicting opinions expounded by Catholic theologians.[9]

In a more famous situation, he refused to "minimize" the implications of Leo XIII's encyclical *Immortale Dei* ("The Christian Constitution of States"), and he found himself saying that "The State should officially recognize the Catholic religion as the religion of the commonwealth" and that "constitutions can be changed, and non-Catholic sects may decline to such a point that the political proscription of them may become feasible and expedient."[10] Even after these statements embarrassed both Ryan and Alfred E. Smith in the election of 1928,[11] Ryan substantially stood by them when he revised *The State and the Church as Catholic Principles of Politics* in 1940. By this latter date, to be sure, he hoped that somebody would reopen the whole question of church and state[12] (as his friend John Courtney Murray was about to do). But his own position did not depart from the orthodoxy of papal declarations.

To an extent that he sensed but never explored, Father Ryan adapted papal statements; when he could, he made a point of not letting himself get boxed in by Rome. Even in his earliest book, *A Living Wage,* he refused to accept an official interpretation of *Rerum novarum* when an important curial official equivocated on a crucial point: Cardinal Tommaso Zigliara said that the obligation to pay a familial living wage did not exist in strict justice. Ryan stiffed at the opinion's lack of clarity and conclusiveness.[13] Thereafter, he always assumed the encyclical's support when he spoke of the familial living wage. After 1931, Father Ryan made similar tactical use of *Quadragesimo anno:* in exchange for giving occupational group systems prominence in his program, he assumed that Pius had underwritten substantially all that Ryan had ever stood for. When other Catholic social thinkers with strikingly different, even conflicting, programs doubted Ryan's exclusive franchise and claimed the papal mantle for their variant

9. Ryan to R. S. Bellperch, February 3, 1931, Ryan papers.

10. Ryan and Moorhouse F. X. Millar, *The State and the Church* (New York, 1922), pp. 34, 38.

11. Broderick, *Right Reverend New Dealer* (New York, 1963), pp. 170–185.

12. Ryan to Philip Burnham, April 1, 1941, Ryan papers.

13. Ryan, *A Living Wage,* p. iii.

views, Ryan said rather airily, as he did to Charles E. Coughlin, that he knew the social encyclicals better than his critics.[14]

He had played a similar tactical game with *Immortale Dei*. He stated the traditional argument on the state as the ally of the Church in its full vigor. At the same time he tried to remove the sting of Leo's unpalatable dicta by making the danger so remote that both ortho-doxy and the American separation of church and state were made se-cure. Leo's injunctions about a Catholic nation applied to states that were more Catholic than Spain, Ryan said, and both expediency and formally ratified constitutions protected existing nations against Catholic intolerance. Surely "the great majority of our fellow citizens" would not let an event that might happen "some 5000 years hence" affect their attitude towards Catholics.[15] Ryan had many publics in mind: His religiously conservative critics would watch him for mini-mizing. His anti-Catholic critics would watch for equivocation or— what was even more damaging to the Church—for Leo's position accurately presented. His best friends did not want him to concede too much or to say too little. Ryan felt that he met the problem neatly, and he held to this opinion even after the searing turbulence of 1928. Revising the book in 1940, he did not retreat. Orthodoxy was the cru-cial keystone of his campaign for social justice; he was not going to leave his orthodoxy exposed by equivocating about a subordinate field like political theory.

The role of papalist served Monsignor Ryan well. Tactics aside, *Rerum novarum* was, indeed, a remarkably progressive document. Coming as the sequel of many decades of Roman conservatism, it brought the Church abreast of western European industrial condi-tions, and it spoke for the need of the working classes that had aban-doned the Church in droves as a response to its heedlessness. Now Ketteler and Manning had an ally further up the line, and Catholic reformers everywhere had an authoritative voice in their chorus.

Nowhere was the need more acute than in the United States. The Church in America, probably too undeveloped to be guilty of the charge of modernism, or "Americanism," was in no position to break fresh ground in social philosophy. Struggling to reconcile itself to an America with long traditions of anti-Catholicism, the Church was singularly vulnerable to the argument that any tampering with

---

14. Ryan, "Roosevelt Safeguards America," in *Seven Troubled Years* (Ann Arbor, 1937), p. 299.

15. Ryan, *The Church and the State,* p. 39.

laissez-faire was un-American, socialistic, and on both counts wrong. In such a climate Father Ryan found that *Rerum novarum* legitimized ideas that may well have come to him from Patrick Ford, Henry George, and Ignatius Donnelly. For a long time he had few associates. Only gradually, and in part because of a generation that he helped to train, could he buttress his position with American Catholic sources instead of saying slyly that he was about as radical as Leo XIII. The "Bishops' Program of Social Reconstruction" (1919),[16] which he wrote, was a major breakthrough. Despite its origin in a tiny committee of bishops and despite its chaotic randomness, it looked to uncritical outsiders like a coherent forward-looking Catholic position. Later Ryan's activities at the Social Action Department of the National Catholic Welfare Conference carried the same illusion of official endorsement. Then finally, after Catholic votes for Roosevelt made social reform defensible, the bishops' statement on "The Church and the Social Order" (1940)[17] endorsed every major reform but one that Ryan had called for in three decades of work and study. (The exception was the child labor amendment.) By that time, papalism was no longer necessary.

Nor would papalism win new life. The New Deal opened a continuing era of social reform that made old debates about socialism obsolete. The Catholics' early primacy in anticommunist hysteria helped to erase the old hyphenate sensibilities, and the election of 1960 brushed away the hurt of 1928. The pontificate of John XXIII gave new confidence to independent Catholic thought—*Pacem in terris* was warmly welcomed and approved, but it protected no one's orthodoxy, for the John A. Ryans of the postwar era spoke with the confidence and the independence that brought fulfillment to Father Murray's last years. Nothing in the legislative history and the subsequent reception of *Humanae vitae* suggests a reversal of the trend, for, ironically, the papalism that cloaked John A. Ryan may leave his successors curiously naked.

---

16. Reprinted in John Tracy Ellis (ed.), *Documents of American Catholic History* (Milwaukee, 1956), pp. 611–629.

17. NCWC Administrative Board, "The Church and the Social Order," in Raphael M. Huber (ed.), *Our Bishops Speak* (Milwaukee, 1952), pp. 324–343.

11

Episcopal Teaching Authority on Matters of War and Economics

James Heft

American Catholic Church historians emphasize that from the foundation of the Republic, Catholic bishops made a distinction between the spiritual authority of the pope, to which American Catholics were subject, and the temporal matters, in which they were free to do whatever was necessary for good citizenship. In 1826, Bishop John England told Congress that American Catholics wished to be just like their fellow citizens except in matters of religion.[1] In 1960, John F. Kennedy assured a group of nervous Protestant clergymen that his own Catholicism would in no way influence the exercise of his duties as president. Religion and politics would be kept separate. Or, as it was put on the eve of the 1980 presidential election by the title of an editorial that appeared in the *New York Times*, "Private Religion, Public Morality."

But times have changed considerably, especially in the last few years. Both England and Kennedy would be forced to rethink their statements now that the American Bishops have published a pastoral letter on the morality of nuclear war and are currently preparing one on the economy. The public reaction has been intense and disparate.[2] Among Catholics, some are thrilled by what they perceive as a new style of leadership, one marked by humility and courage and the free admission of its fallibility. Others are appalled that the leadership of

---

1. David J. O'Brien, "American Catholics and American Society," in *Catholics and Nuclear War*, p. 18, ed. by Philip J. Murnion (Crossroads: New York, 1983).

2. See "Notes on Moral Theology: The Bishops and the U.S. Economy" by David Hollenbach, in *Theological Studies*, 46 (1985), p. 102.

their Church is teaching through an episcopal conference when it has no authority to do so. Still others believe that although the conference may issue letters, they should only outline principles, leaving their application to those with the competence to apply them. Finally, some few are disappointed in the tentative character of the conference statements, and would have preferred clear and binding statements, the sort that would have enhanced, they believe, the authority of the bishops.

The purpose of this paper is to reflect on three points: first, the teaching authority that bishops may legitimately exercise on matters of morality that have to do with war and economics; second, the kind of teaching authority that episcopal conferences may exercise in such matters; and third, the ecclesiological significance of the process the American bishops have engaged in to draw up these pastoral letters. In other words, using more technical language, I will consider what bishops can teach about authoritatively, that is, the object of teaching authority; then the way in which bishops in national conferences can teach, that is, the subject of teaching authority; and finally, the role of the *sensus fidelium* in the formulation of authoritative teaching.

1. About What Can Bishops Teach Authoritatively?

In their 1983 pastoral letter on war and peace, the U.S. Bishops explained that they would "address many concrete questions concerning the arms race, contemporary warfare, weapons systems and negotiating strategies." But they immediately added:

> We do not intend that our treatment of each of these issues carry the same moral authority as our statement of universal moral principles and formal Church teaching. Indeed, we stress here at the beginning that not every statement in this letter has the same moral authority. At times, we assert universally binding moral principles (e.g., non-combatant immunity and proportionality). At still other times we reaffirm statements of recent popes and the teaching of Vatican II. Again, at other times we apply moral principles to specific cases (par. 9).

They then proceeded to explain that when they apply moral principles, they make "prudential judgments" based on specific circumstances which not only can change, but which people of good will can interpret differently. While admitting that their moral judgments in such specific cases (e.g., their treatment of "no first use") therefore do not bind in conscience, the bishops nevertheless ask that they be given "serious attention and consideration" (par. 10).

I shall limit myself to asking one question about these carefully nuanced statements of the bishops: at what level of authority are "universally binding moral principles" taught? In other words, could a person for good reasons dissent from such a "universally binding moral principle"? Put in another way, could a Catholic support the saturation bombing of civilian populations believing that such a tactic would in the long run save more lives? Put in still another way, can "universally binding moral principles" be taught infallibly, in which case no dissent may be possible without sacrificing one's identity as a Catholic Christian?

The first conciliar discussion of the object of pastoral teaching authority took place at the Council of Trent (1545–1563) where the role of the bishops was said to include the preaching to their people of the faith that must be believed and put into practice. The bishops used the phrase *res fidei et morum,* which, according to Francis Sullivan, "indicates that while some matters of faith are simply to be believed, others are to be both believed and put into practice."[3] At Trent, the Gospel was described as *"fontem omnis et salutaris veritatis et morum disciplinae."* Thus, the Gospel is understood as the source of all saving truth and *disciplina morum* is understood best not as "moral discipline," as a literal translation would have it, but as instruction or teaching *(disciplina)* about *morum* or practices, which includes how we are to live and act and worship as Christians.[4] At Trent, *disciplina morum* included more than teaching about morals; it included as well matters of custom and ecclesiastical and liturgical discipline. Thus, the phrase *res fidei et morum* is best translated as "matters pertaining to (Christian) faith and practice."[5]

A more thorough discussion of the object of episcopal teaching authority took place at Vatican I (1869–1870). There it became clear in the discussion about the object of papal infallibility, that is, about matters of faith and morals, that there existed both a direct and an indirect object. In the official *expositio,* Bishop Gasser, in the name of the deputation of the faith, explained it this way:

---

3. Francis A. Sullivan, *Magisterium: Teaching Authority in the Catholic Church* (Paulist Press, New York, 1983), p. 128.

4. Maurice Bevenot, "Faith and Morals in the Councils of Trent and Vatican I," in *Heythrop Journal,* 3 (1962), pp. 15–30.

5. Sullivan, p. 128. He explains that he insists "on the word 'Christian' to bring out the fact that for Trent, not only the 'salutary truth' but also the *disciplina morum* has the Gospel as its source."

> As I said before, since other truths, which in themselves may not be re-
> vealed, are more or less intimately bound up with revealed dogmas,
> they are necessary to protect, to expound correctly and to define effica-
> ciously in all its integrity the deposit of faith. Truths of this nature be-
> long to dogmatic facts insofar as without these it is not possible to
> protect and expound the deposit of faith, truths, I repeat, that do not be-
> long directly to the deposit of faith, but are necessary for its protection.[6]

According to Gasser then, infallibility extends first to those truths
which are revealed, and then to those which are not directly revealed,
but which are necessarily connected to revelation. The bishops of
Vatican I had disagreed over the precise content of the indirect object
of infallibility. They had agreed as to how those truths should be connected. Some of the bishops wanted the secondary object defined as
"those things connected with the deposit of revelation," but others
objected that this was too vague and could be interpreted to include
almost anything. Gasser explained that it included only those truths
necessarily connected to revelation. He noted the teaching of theologians that infallibility concerned only revealed truths, while other
definitions were only "theologically certain."[7]

Vatican Council II (1962–1965) did not attempt to clarify further
the secondary object of infallibility (see *Lumen Gentium*, art. 25), and
since the Council the only official statement to touch upon the matter
was *Mysterium Ecclesiae* of 24 June 1973 which restated the secondary
object of infallibility in slightly different terms: "things without which
the deposit cannot be properly safeguarded and explained" *(sine quibus
hoc depositum rite nequit custo diri et exponi).*[8] Sullivan concludes his
discussion of this matter in this way:

> While the fact that there is a secondary object of infallibility is held by
> most Catholic theologians to be certain, there is by no means unanimity
> with regard to what is contained in this object. I think it would be fair
> to say that many manuals of ecclesiology prior to Vatican II reflected
> the broad description of the secondary object as "truths connected with
> revelation." The current trend would be to limit this object to what is
> strictly required in order that the magisterium might be able to defend
> and explain the Gospel.[9]

---

6. Mansi. 52:1226.

7. Mansi. 52:1316–1317. See also Gustav Thils, *Infallibilité pontificale: Source, conditions,
limites* (Gembloux: H. Duculot, 1969), p. 246; also Sullivan, p. 133.

8. AAS, 65 (1973), p. 401.

9. Sullivan, p. 134.

Another way in which theologians have taken up this question is to ask whether the magisterium is able to teach infallibly about questions of natural law. After examining relevant portions of Gasser's official commentary on the texts of Vatican I, and after comparing a relevant portion of a schema proposed at Vatican II for the document on the Church with the final approved text, and after analyzing portions of the minority report of the commission of experts appointed by Pope Paul VI to study the question of birth control, Sullivan concludes that particular norms of natural law are not the object of infallible teaching.[10] Catholic theologians have come to this conclusion not only because of the particular complexity of the moral problems facing us today, but also because the Gospel often provides light rather than specific solutions for which Christians, as well as others, must search long and hard.[11] Finally, if the particular norms of the natural law are not to be included within the framework provided by Vatican I for the object of infallible teaching, basic principles of the natural law are, even though it "does not seem that any such moral principle has ever been solemnly defined."[12]

In the light of these considerations, I now return to my original question. What conclusions can be drawn? Can "universally binding moral principles" be taught infallibly? If Sullivan is correct, the answer would seem to be yes, but only if we are talking about basic principles of natural law, and specifically about those which have been revealed to us "for the sake of our salvation." The United States bishops illustrate what they mean by "universally binding norms" by citing as examples the principles of non-combatant immunity and proportionality, principles that require in their application the evaluation of complex specific circumstances, evaluations which in many instances could be legitimately disparate. This fact alone would seem

10. Sullivan, pp. 140–147. For a spirited argument against Sullivan's conclusion and for the possibility of defining infallibly particular norms of natural law, see Germain Grisez, "Infallibility and Specific Moral Norms" in *The Thomist* 49 (1985), pp. 248–287. Grisez argues that adultery and abortion could be infallibly condemned. His disagreement with Sullivan concerns the teaching on contraception. Our concern in this article, of course, is moral principles that have to do with war and economics.

11. Sullivan, p. 151.

12. Sullivan, p. 149. Sullivan explains: "Catholic moralists generally agree that those basic norms of the natural law which have also been revealed to us 'for the sake of our salvation' could be infallibly taught, either by solemn definition or by the universal ordinary magisterium" (p. 149). I suspect that moral theologians would have as difficult a time agreeing upon a list of basic and particular norms of natural law as dogmatic theologians would have in agreeing upon a list of infallibly defined dogmas.

to rule out the possibility that these principles could bind consciences, at least in their application, in the way in which basic principles of the natural law could bind. I will leave it to the moral theologians to enumerate and distinguish between basic principles of the natural law which could be infallibly taught, and of the natural law which can not. The very fact that moral theologians have not done this indicates the difficulties inherent in formulating moral principles that can be defined infallibly. Moreover, it would also be necessary to show that these principles, even before their application, have been revealed to us "for the sake of our salvation." No dogmatic theologian has, to my knowledge, ever attempted to demonstrate that.

2. WITH WHAT KIND OF TEACHING AUTHORITY CAN EPISCOPAL CONFERENCES TEACH?

I have just established that particular norms of the natural law, the sorts of norms which would be most often employed in discussions about the morality of war and economic justice, can not be a part of the secondary object of the infallible magisterium. I now turn to my second question: with what kind of authority can episcopal conferences treat matters of war and economics? It is commonly held in Catholic ecclesiology that the teaching authority of the hierarchy may be exercised in one of two ways: on the one hand, in an "extraordinary" way when a doctrine is defined by an ecumenical council, or by a pope speaking *ex cathedra*, or, on the other hand, in an "ordinary" way when a doctrine is taught by an individual bishop in his local church (see *Lumen Gentium*, article 25). The authority of teaching, *mandatum docendi*, is exercised legitimately therefore in either an extraordinary or an ordinary manner.

When the American bishops went to Rome in 1983 to discuss their pastoral on the morality of nuclear war, Cardinal Ratzinger said: "A bishops' conference as such does not have a *mandatum docendi* [a mandate to teach]. This belongs only to individual bishops or to the college of bishops with the Pope." Compared to the teaching prerogatives of individual bishops, Ratzinger said that "national conferences have no theological base."[13] Moreover, he stated that such conferences are merely practical expedients that run the danger of undercutting by bureaucracy and anonymity the personal teaching authority of individual bishops.

13. See *The Tablet*, December 8, 1984, p. 1223; also see *Newsweek*, December 31, 1984, p. 63.

Several points need to be made in view of the remarks of Cardinal Ratzinger. First, Vatican II acknowledged and encouraged the establishment of limited expressions of collegiality. At the end of Article 23 of *Lumen Gentium*, for example, it is stated that modern episcopal conferences can contribute fruitful assistance in the development of a deeper collegial sense.[14] Articles 37 and 38 of the *Decree on the Bishops' Pastoral Office (Christus Dominus)* underscore the importance of episcopal conferences by likening them to the synods, provincial councils and plenary councils that achieved so much good in the early Church. Concerning the teaching authority of episcopal conferences, article 753 of the new Code of Canon law states:

> "Although they do not enjoy infallible teaching authority, the bishops in communion with the head and members of the college, whether as individuals or gathered in conferences of bishops or in particular counsils, are authentic teachers and instructors of the faith for the faithful entrusted to their care."

Article 753 appears in the section of the code that deals with the Church's teaching function. There is, therefore, in recent official statements of the Catholic Church, a theological base for episcopal conferences exercising a legitimate role as authentic teachers.

There is also strong historical precedent for episcopal conferences that teach with authority. Particular councils have contributed in significant ways to the development of doctrine. One needs only to recall, among many possible examples from the early Church, that the provincial council of Carthage issued in 418 the first decrees on the subject of original sin, and that the Council of Orange condemned in 529 semi-Pelagianism, and from more recent history, that the episcopal conferences of Latin America have issued important statements at Medellin in 1968 and at Puebla in 1979. In view of this, it would be difficult, in the opinion of Avery Dulles, "to defend the view that there is no teaching authority between the universal magisterium of the popes and ecumenical councils, at the one extreme, and that of the

---

14. Article 23 of *Lumen Gentium* speaks of episcopal conferences as helpful ways to develop a "collegiate spirit" *(collegialis affectus)*, a phrase that has led, in the words of Charles Murphy, to a distinction between "effective and affective" collegiality: "'effective' referring to the exercise of supreme power in strictly collegiate acts; 'affective' describing more of an atmosphere of mutual co-operation, assistance and love among the bishops" (see "Collegiality: An Essay Toward Better Understanding," in *Theological Studies,* 46 [1985], p. 40).

individual bishop in his own diocese at the other."[15] After explaining
that episcopal conferences do not, according to Vatican II, exercise a
magisterium in the strict sense, Archbishop James Hickey of Washington, D.C., spoke about the impact of the teaching of episcopal conferences while addressing a meeting of the American bishops at Collegeville in June of 1982:

> . . . one would have to be quite blind and deaf to reality if he denied
> that the statements of episcopal conferences do have an effective impact
> on the pastoral life of local dioceses and beyond. How many have not
> relied on the pastoral letters of episcopal conferences to find pastoral
> solutions to burning moral issues? How many times are priests and
> people not referred to the teaching of our conference and of other con-
> ferences? Many of the pastoral letters of conferences play an important
> role in the life of the Church. We have to admit, then, that the confer-
> ence offers a most effective vehicle nationally for our teaching office.[16]

It is of course important that national episcopal conferences avoid
nationalism which would weaken the unity of the universal church.[17]
Moreover, they are not to substitute for the voice of the individual
bishop, but rather to strengthen it by providing a coherent framework
within which complex issues may be addressed more effectively.[18]

15. Dulles, "Bishops' Conference Documents: What Doctrinal Authority?," in *Origins*, Jan. 24, 1985, Vol. 14, #32, p. 530. Since Ratzinger's statements in December of 1984
concerning episcopal conferences, Dulles and a few other theologians have cited
Ratzinger's article published twenty years ago in the first volume of *Concilium* (Paulist
Press, 1965) on "The Pastoral Implications of Episcopal Collegiality" in which the then
young German theologian and peritus of Vatican II argued for a more effective exercise
of collegiality through episcopal conferences.

16. Sullivan, pp. 121–122.

17. Henri de Lubac, among others, has written about this danger. See his *Particular
Churches and the Universal Church* (San Francisco: Ignatius Press, 1982). Dulles notes that
in this regard "a test case arose in 1983, when several national hierarchies were simultaneously preparing divergent statements on war and peace. The Holy See intervened
and called an international meeting at which some of the problems were thrashed out
before the American pastoral was put into final form. Even so, however, there were significant differences of approach between the American, French and German statements" (*Origins*, art. cit., p. 533). In an article published a few months earlier, Dulles
remarked that "the issuance of diverse statements by different hierarchies may be an
excellent way to initiate dialogue with a view to reaching an ultimate consensus" ("The
Teaching Authority of Bishops' Conferences," in *America*, June 11, 1983, p. 454). Concerning the differences of approach among the pastorals on the American, French and
German Bishops on war and peace, see my article, "Do the European and American
Bishops Agree?," in *The Catechist*, October, 1984, pp. 20–23.

18. Bishop James Malone, "The Intersection of Public Opinion and Public Policy," in
Origins, Nov. 29, 1984, vol. 14, #24, p. 388. In a recent personal letter to me, Archbishop

It should be clear then that episcopal conferences do have solid historical and theological bases. It is also clear that they exercise a legitimate and authentic teaching authority. One question, however, remains: in the strict sense, do they have a *mandatum docendi*? Some theologians, including Cardinal Ratzinger, have answered negatively, and have based their response on what they maintain is a strict reading of the documents of Vatican II and the new code of Canon Law. They state that episcopal conferences are not given the capacity to engage in "truly collegial acts," acts that are given only to the pope united with the bishops in a council, or to all the bishops dispersed throughout the world but acting in union with one another and the pope.[19]

In response to such an argument, it needs to be remembered that one of the rules for the strict reading of any official document of the Church is never to assume that an answer has been given by a text to a question which was not raised when the text was formulated. At Vatican II there was no discussion of whether episcopal conferences had a *mandatum docendi.* The Council encouraged the establishment of episcopal conferences. Now that they have been established and are having a definite impact on the life of the Church, the question of whether they have a *mandatum docendi* naturally arises. The question is an open one. If one bishop teaching in union with other bishops and the pope has a *mandatum docendi,* it seems to me reasonable that even more so an episcopal conference which teaches in union with other bishops and the pope should have a *mandatum docendi.* An episcopal conference does not, of course, have "the authority proper to the whole episcopal college together with the pope."[20] Nevertheless, as canon 753 of the new Code states, the bishops, individually or gathered in conference, are "authentic teachers and instructors of the faith for the faithful entrusted to their care." Indeed, we may come to conclude that episcopal conferences exercise a *mandatum docendi* situated somewhere midway between that exercised by the individual bishop and that exercised by the bishops and pope gathered in council.

Pilarczyk explained that the authority of episcopal conferences "is a kind of joint but voluntary one, that is, each bishop must somehow make his own that which the Conference produces. To support such a theory, I point out that during one of my first meetings, when we were discussing capital punishment, one bishop got up and said that he believed in the appropriateness of capital punishment, and that if the Conference took a position against it he would publicly oppose that position in his see. Moreover, the ethical guidelines for Catholic health care facilities demand promulgation by the individual bishop in his diocese" (quoted with permission).

19. See, for example, Charles Murphy's recent article in *Theological Studies* (note 14).
20. Sullivan, p. 122.

3. THE EXPANDED ROLE GIVEN TO THE *SENSUS FIDELIUM*

The establishment in the last twenty years of both episcopal conferences and the international synod of bishops has created promising
forms of collaboration among the hierarchy. One of the most significant dimensions of the way in which the U.S. episcopal conference
has chosen to work is the process it used to draft the pastoral letter on
nuclear war and is using again to draft its letter on economics. The
committees responsible for drafting these letters have consulted a
wide variety of people. Preliminary drafts were made public so that
criticisms could be made and suggestions offered with a view to
preparing a second draft which again would be criticized and discussed before submission for a final vote—article by article—to the
members of the episcopal conference. Several comments should be
made about this process. I shall limit myself to three: first, the way it
indicates a new role for the laity; second, the way it calls for more
persuasive teaching; and third, the way it points out the importance
of non-infallible teaching.

Without ever defining what infallibility actually is, the bishops of
Vatican I did say that it was the same infallibility that belongs to the
Church as a whole. We know that the consultation of the laity
through their bishops played an important role in the definition of the
two Marian Dogmas.[21] The bishops of Vatican II made it even clearer
that the infallibility of the pope and bishops had to be related to the
sensus fidei possessed by the entire people of God:

> The body of the faithful as a whole, anointed as they are by the Holy
> One (cf. 1 Jn. 2:20, 27), cannot err in matters of belief. Thanks to a super-
> natural sense of the faith which characterizes the People as a whole, it
> manifests this unerring quality when, "from the bishops down to the
> last member of the laity," it shows universal agreement in matters of
> faith and morals. For by this sense of faith which is aroused and sus-
> tained by the spirit of truth, God's People accepts not the word of men
> but the very Word of God (cf. 1 Th. 2:13). It clings without fail to the
> faith once delivered to the saints (cf. Jude 3), penetrates it more deeply
> by accurate insights, and applies it more thoroughly to life.[22]

It is important to note the four effects of the *sensus fidei* mentioned
in the article: (1) the people accept the Word of God for what it really

---

21. James Heft, "Papal Infallibility and the Marian Dogmas," in *Marian Studies*, 33
(1982), pp. 59–63; reprinted in *One in Christ*, 18 (1982), pp. 309–340.
22. *Lumen Gentium*, article 12.

is; (2) they adhere to the true faith without ever falling away from it; (3) they are enabled to penetrate more deeply and elucidate more clearly that revelation; and (4) they are able to apply the Word of God more thoroughly to life. When we consider the issues of the morality of war and economic justice, it should be evident that the competencies of the laity must play a central role in the shaping of these teachings, especially if these teachings are going to include applications. It also seems evident that the bishops responsible for overseeing ("episcopacy") the drafting of such documents will need to depend upon the competencies of the laity to grasp more clearly and with greater insight the ways in which the Gospel is to be applied to these modern complex matters.[23]

Closely related to the *sensus fidei* is the *sensus fidelium*. If the *sensus fidei* is more of a subjective quality of believers, the *sensus fidelium* carries a more objective meaning which refers not to the believers but to what they believe. The importance of the *sensus fidelium* was pointed out by Newman when he showed how it was precisely the laity who had faithfully clung to the truth in the face of the Arian crisis. It is the recognition of the importance of that same *sensus fidelium*, that moved another English cardinal, George Basil Hume, to speak on 29 September 1980 at the International Synod of Bishops on the Family about the necessity of consulting the laity on such matters. He explained that the prophetic mission of husbands and wives is based on their experience as married people "and on an understanding of the sacrament of marriage of which they can speak with their own authority." Both their experience and their understanding constitute, the Cardinal suggested, "an authentic *fons theologiae* from which we, the pastors, and indeed the whole Church, can draw."[24]

Many theologians who write today about consulting the laity write also about the way in which teachings acquire authority through their reception.[25] There is a tendency in our democratic society to reduce the

---

23. *Lumen Gentium,* article 37.

24. G. B. Hume, "Development of Marriage Teaching," in *Origins,* Oct. 16, 1980. Vol. 10, #18, p. 276.

25. On the idea of reception, see Yves Congar, "La 'reception' comme realite ecclesiologique," *Revue des sciences philosophiques et theologiques,* 56 (1972), pp. 369–402; Aloys Grillimeier, "Konzil und Reception. Methodische Bemerkungen zu einem Thema der ökumenischen Diskussion," *Theologie und Philosophie,* 45 (1970), pp. 321–352; Edward Kilmartin, "Reception in History: An Ecclesiological Phenomenon and Its Significance," *Journal of Ecumenical Studies,* 21 (1984), pp. 34–54; and Margaret O'Gara, "Infallibility in the Ecumenical Crucible," *One in Christ,* 20 (1984), pp. 325–345.

matter of consulting the laity to the taking of a majority vote or the settling for the least common denominator. At the other extreme is the perception common among non-Catholics, and unfortunately among not a few Catholics as well, that papal and episcopal statements acquire their authority only because popes and bishops make them, and not also because the statements are true. Neither democracy nor autocracy exemplifies the process by which teaching acquires authority in the Catholic tradition. There is rather a subtle but important interplay, yet to be sufficiently worked out by theologians, between on the one hand, formal (who says it) and material authority (what is said), and on the other hand, the way in which the acceptance of a teaching affects its authority. Suffice it here to say that important insights into this complex matter will be found in a deeper grasp on the nature and function of the *sensus fidelium.*

A second new emphasis in the Church is the need for more persuasive teaching. There has been in the last 25 years a shift away from an emphasis upon formal authority to one on material authority.[26] This becomes all the more necessary when we are dealing with moral matters that depend to a considerable extent upon the interpretation of the natural law, such as is the case with matters of war and economics. As Sullivan explains, "When the (moral) norm itself is said to be discoverable by human reasoning, it would be a mistake to rely

---

26. Not all members of the Church represent the shift from formal to material authority. In an article entitled "The Sources of Conscience" that appeared in the *Notre Dame Magazine* (vol. 13, Winter 1984/85, pp. 20–23), James Burtchaell has pointed out the irony of how Archbishop (now Cardinal) John O'Connor and Governor Mario Cuomo, as well as Geraldine Ferraro, all agree completely on the source of authority for their quite different stands on abortion: both depend on formal more than material authority. The bishop sees his obligation as pastor discharged when he reiterates the official Catholic teaching on the matter. He once referred the entire matter to a higher authority: "So Geraldine Ferraro doesn't have a problem with me. If she has a problem, it's with the pope." Burtchaell comments: "The Archbishop gives the global impression that within the Catholic Church, moral edicts are officially asserted by bishops. The bishops formulate doctrines to which, as a matter of loyalty, all Catholics are expected to conform, and fail to do so at their peril." Governor Cuomo says essentially the same: namely, that to be a Catholic is to believe the core dogmas of our faith, one of which condemns abortion. As a Catholic, one might accept that Church law. Burtchaell explains: "The Church does not have a law on abortion, anymore than it has a law on embezzlement or a law on gossip or a law on child abuse. It does have a wisdom on these matters. And that wisdom, if it has any sense behind it, should be accessible to others whose grounding is not in our faith." And again: "Any moral conviction that is taken on faith alone is no conviction at all, but only a sectarian mystery that should not be let outside to roam the streets and threaten people."

too heavily on merely formal authority in proposing it for acceptance by thinking people."[27] The more people are consulted, the more the final result embodies the wisdom of the community, the more likely it is to be accepted by that community.

A third aspect of the new situation in the Church in North America is the discovery of the value of fallible teaching authority. In the past, most Catholics expected their bishops and the pope to speak infallibly or to remain silent. The new dialogical mode of proceeding employed by the American bishops in drafting their most recent pastoral letters openly calls for help and expects to learn a good deal through the process. The bishops in using this method have stated that some of their conclusions may be wrong and expect and respect divergent opinions on matters of application. This mode of operating is perplexing for those who prefer their bishops to speak in absolute ways or to remain silent. We all need to recognize that in many of the most important areas of our life we must rely upon discernment rather than infallibility to indicate for us the right way to live. In 1967, the German bishops put the matter well:

> . . . human life, even at a wholly general level, must always be lived by doing one's best according to one's lights and by recognised principles

27. Sullivan, p. 165. To ask for more persuasive reasoning in areas of morality related to the natural law is not to demand proof, nor is it to assume that what the natural law requires in particular cases is always obvious. Note the sobering remarks of Fr. Bede Griffiths, o.s.b.: "Is it not time for the Catholic Church to reconsider the respect which is due to the pronouncements of the Roman magisterium on matters which are outside the sphere of divine revelation? The Pope has declared that the morality of contraception is a matter of natural law, that is, of natural reason. It is obvious that neither the Pope nor the Roman Curia has any monopoly on natural reason, and in this matter the majority of theologians and educated lay people disagree with his view. In the same way, the Pope has said that the present system of nuclear deterrence is 'morally acceptable' under certain circumstances, whereas many would hold that it is totally unacceptable under all circumstances. These are but two instances in which there is disagreement about the application of the natural law at the present time. In the past there have been many occasions on which the Roman magisterium has been proved to have been wrong on matters of politics and economics and science and history and morality. Even in matters which concern the Bible and the liturgy, which come nearer to the sphere of divine revelation, the Roman magisterium has had to admit that it was mistaken. Above all, on the question of the relation between the different Christian churches and between Christianity and other religions, it has proved to have been seriously mistaken. To confuse such pronouncements with statements which belong properly to the sphere of divine revelation, on which the Church has a real claim to speak with authority, can only lead to discrediting the Catholic Church in the eyes of other Christians and of the rest of the world" (*The Tablet*, "Letters to the Editor," September 1, 1984, p. 850).

which, while at the theoretical level they cannot be recognised as absolutely certain, nevertheless command our respect in the 'here and now' as valid norms of thinking and acting because in the existing circumstances they are the best that can be found. This is something that everyone recognises from the concrete experience of his own life. Every doctor in his diagnoses, every statesman in the political judgments he arrives at on particular situations and the decisions he bases on these, is aware of this fact. The Church too in her doctrine and practice cannot always and in every case allow herself to be caught in the dilemma of either arriving at a doctrinal decision which is ultimately binding or simply being silent and leaving everything to the free opinion of the individual. In order to maintain the true and ultimate substance of the faith she must, even at the risk of error in points of detail, give expression to doctrinal detectives which have a certain degree of binding force, and yet, since they are not *de fide* definitions, involve a certain element of the provisional even to the point of being capable of including error. Otherwise it would be quite impossible for her to preach or interpret her faith as a decisive force in real life or to apply it to each new situation in human life as it arises. In such a case the position of the individual Christian in regard to the Church is analogous to that of a man who knows that he is bound to accept the decision of a specialist even while recognising that it is not infallible.[28]

The bishops can not afford to remain silent about matters on which they can not speak infallibly. How specific they should become in what they say may well be debated.[29] Whether they should speak at all should be obvious from what has been written here.

28. Sullivan, pp. 156–157.

29. I agree with Brian Benestad (*The Pursuit of a Just Social Order: Policy Statements of the U.S. Catholic Bishop, 1966–1980* [Washington, D.C.: Ethics and Public Policy Center, 1982]) who distinguishes between social teaching and policy statements, and recommends that the bishops limit themselves to the former unless it is clear that only one policy is consistent with the Gospel. Avery Dulles, who agrees with Benestad on this matter, puts it this way: "When they [the bishops] issue politically controversial statements, they tend to divide the Christian community along political lines and to marginalize persons whose faith and morals are above reproach. In their peace pastoral the bishops attempted to distinguish between their doctrinal teaching and their policy judgments, but this distinction was overlooked in much of the discussion. Generally speaking, I believe, the episcopal conference should devote itself primarily to teaching, leaving the concrete applications, where these are not obvious, to lay persons regularly engaged in secular affairs. Where they do feel obliged to make specific policy statements, they should clearly identify them as such" (in *Origins*, Jan. 24, 1985, Vol. 14, #32, p. 533).

4. Conclusion

I have concluded that bishops can teach infallibly only on the basic principles and not the particular norms of the natural law. I noted that it is commonly agreed that no such basic principles of the natural law have ever been infallibly defined. Secondly I concluded that episcopal conferences have in fact had powerful impacts through their teaching activity, and have in the process recreated in the Church a variety of expressions of collegial cooperation and activity. And while the question of whether they ought to have a *mandatum docendi* remains open, I have argued that in fact they should. Finally I have described three new developments in the interaction between the hierarchy and the laity: a more important role for the laity, an emphasis on more persuasive teaching and a deeper appreciation of the value of non-infallible teaching authority. These developments are, of course, causing a good deal of confusion within the Church, something not unexpected when there is a change in the way of doing things. With the new initiatives of the bishops and the greater involvement of the laity addressing issues that in fact constitute the structures of everyday life for all citizens, the *sensus fidelium* will be called upon more than ever to penetrate the Gospel and apply it more thoroughly to life as it is actually experienced and lived.

12

AIMS AND MEANS OF THE CATHOLIC WORKER[1]

The aim of the Catholic Worker movement is to live in accordance with the justice and charity of Jesus Christ. Our sources are the Hebrew and Greek Scriptures as handed down in the teachings of the Roman Catholic Church, with our inspiration coming from the lives of the saints, "men and women outstanding in holiness, living witnesses to Your unchanging love." (Eucharistic Prayer)

This aim requires us to begin living in a different way. We recall the words of our founder, Dorothy Day, who said, "God meant things to be much easier than we have made them," and Peter Maurin who wanted to build a society "where it is easier for people to be good."

When we examine our society, which is generally called capitalist (because of its methods of producing and controlling wealth) and is bourgeois (because of a prevailing concern for acquisition and material interests, and its emphasis on respectability and mediocrity), we find it far from God's justice.

In *economics*, private and state capitalism bring about an unjust distribution of wealth, for the profit motive guides decisions. Those in power live off the sweat of another's brow, while those without power are robbed of a just return for their work. Usury (the charging of interest above administrative costs) is a major contributor to the wrongdoing intrinsic to this system. We note especially how the world debt crisis leads poor countries into great deprivation and a dependency from which there is no foreseeable escape. Here at home, the number of hungry and homeless and unemployed people rises in the midst of increasing affluence.

---

1. This article originally appeared in *The Catholic Worker* (May 1987).

In *labor*, human need is no longer the reason for human work. Instead, the unbridled expansion of technology, necessary to capitalism and viewed as "progress," holds sway. Jobs are concentrated in productivity and administration for a "high-tech," war-related, consumer society of disposable goods, so that laborers are trapped in work that does not contribute to human welfare. Furthermore, as jobs become more specialized, many people are excluded from meaningful work or are alienated from the products of their labor. Even in farming, agribusiness has replaced agriculture, and, in all areas, moral restraints are run over roughshod, and a disregard for the laws of nature now threatens the very planet.

In *politics*, the state functions to control and regulate life. Its power has burgeoned hand in hand with growth in technology, so that military, scientific and corporate interests get the highest priority when concrete political policies are formulated. Because of the sheer size of institutions, we tend towards government by bureaucracy; that is, government by nobody. Bureaucracy, in all areas of life, is not only impersonal, but also makes accountability, and, therefore, an effective political forum for redressing grievances, next to impossible.

In *morals*, relations between people are corrupted by distorted images of the human person. Class, race and sex often determine personal worth and position within society, leading to structures that foster oppression. Capitalism further divides society by pitting owners against workers in perpetual conflict over wealth and its control. Those who do not "produce" are abandoned, and left, at best, to be "processed" through institutions. Spiritual destitution is rampant, manifested in isolation, madness, promiscuity and violence.

The *arms race* stands as a clear sign of the direction and spirit of our age. It has extended the domain of destruction and the fear of annihilation, and denies the basic right to life. There is a direct connection between the arms race and destitution. "The arms race is an utterly treacherous trap for humanity, and one which injures the poor to an intolerable degree." (Vatican II)

In contrast to what we see around us, as well as within ourselves, stands St. Thomas Aquinas' doctrine of the Common Good, a vision of a society where the good of each member is bound to the good of the whole in the service of God. To this end, we advocate:

- *Personalism*, a philosophy which regards the freedom and dignity of each person as the basis, focus and goal of all metaphysics and morals. In following such wisdom, we move away from a self-centered individualism toward the good of the other. This is to be done by taking personal responsibility for changing conditions, rather than looking to the state or other institutions to provide impersonal "charity." We pray for a Church renewed by this philosophy and for a time when all those who feel excluded from participation are welcomed with love, drawn by the gentle personalism Peter Maurin taught.

- *A Decentralized Society* in contrast to the present bigness of government, industry, education, health care and agriculture. We encourage efforts such as family farms, rural and urban land trusts, worker ownership and management of small factories, homesteading projects, food, housing and other cooperatives—any effort in which money can once more become merely a medium of exchange, and human beings are no longer commodities.

- *A "Green Revolution,"* so that it is possible to re-discover the proper meaning of our labor and our true bonds with the land; a Distributist communitarianism, self-sufficient through farming, crafting and appropriate technology; a radically new society where people will rely on the fruits of their own soil and labor; associations of mutuality, and a sense of fairness to resolve conflicts.

We believe this needed personal and social transformation should be pursued by the means Jesus revealed in His sacrificial love. With Christ as our Exemplar, by prayer and communion with His Body and Blood, we strive for the practices of:

- *Nonviolence.* "Blessed are the peacemakers, for they shall be called children of God." (Matt. 5:9) Only through nonviolent action can a personalist revolution come about, one in which one evil will not be replaced simply by another. Thus, we oppose the deliberate taking of life for any reason, and see every oppression as blasphemy. Jesus taught us to take suffering upon ourselves rather than inflict it upon others and He calls us to fight against violence with the spiritual weapons of prayer, fasting and noncooperation with evil. Refusal to pay taxes for war, to register for conscription, to comply with any unjust legislation; participation in nonviolent strikes and boycotts, protests or vigils; withdrawal of support for dominant systems, corporate funding or usurious practices are all excellent means to establish peace.

- *The works of mercy* (as found in Matt. 25:31-46) are at the heart of the Gospel and they are clear mandates for our response to "the least of our brothers and sisters." Houses of hospitality are centers for learning to do these acts of love, so that the poor can receive what is, in justice, theirs: the second coat in our closet, the spare room in our home, a place at our table. Anything beyond what we immediately need belongs to those who go without.

- *Manual labor* in a society that rejects it as undignified and inferior. "Besides inducing cooperation, besides overcoming barriers and establishing the spirit of brotherhood (besides just getting things done), manual labor enables us to use our body as well as our hands, our minds." (Dorothy Day) The Benedictine motto "Ora et Labora" reminds us that the work of human hands is a gift for the edification of the world and the glory of God.

- *Voluntary Poverty.* "The mystery of poverty is that by sharing in it, making ourselves poor in giving to others, we increase our knowledge and belief in love." (Dorothy Day) By embracing voluntary poverty, that is, by casting our lot freely with those whose impoverishment is not a choice, we would ask for the grace to abandon ourselves to the love of God. It would put us on the path to incarnate the Church's "preferential option for the poor."

We must be prepared to accept seeming failure with these aims, for sacrifice and suffering are part of the Christian life. Success, as the world determines it, is not the final criterion for judgment. The most important thing is the love of Jesus Christ and how to live His truth.

13

Lay Movements in the United States Before Vatican II

Gary MacEoin

Lay Catholics in the first quarter of the 20th century who had ideas about playing an active role in church life were well advised to keep their ideas to themselves. Centralized decision-making and authoritarian control of expression characterized the institution worldwide. Papal condemnation of "Modernism" in 1907 was followed by a Code of Canon Law (1917) that straitjacketed belief and practice, silencing not only the laity, but the clergy too.

In the United States the silence was particularly profound. After the crushing of lay trusteeism in the 19th century, clerical control had become absolute, a condition reinforced by the limited educational level and limited English of many of the immigrant faithful. The clergy joined the laity in silence after Pope Leo XIII's condemnation of "Americanism" in *Testem Benevolentiae* (1899).

Other than in nonideological groups, such as the Knights of Columbus and the Catholic War Council (quickly coopted by the bishops as the National Catholic Welfare Council), no lay voice was heard until the 1920s, with *Commonweal* magazine as the first major initiative. Conceived in New York by an all-male group (four priests, nine laymen) in 1922, it first appeared in 1924. Its thrust was intellectual, and particularly in its early years it appealed primarily to the rather small group of the highly educated. Indeed, it was far from typical of Catholicism on the East Coast in its first decade. Except for Canadian editor in chief Michael Williams, the members of the first group were graduates of Harvard, Yale and other prestigious secular universities.

Several were descendants of the Catholic aristocracy of early Maryland and saw themselves so linked to that stream of Catholicism that they called themselves the Calvert Associates, after the first Lord Baltimore. Mr. Williams belonged for some years to the colony of "advanced thinkers" founded by ardent Socialist Upton Sinclair.

It was in Chicago, Minnesota and elsewhere in the Midwest that lay, middle-class Catholics first began to find a voice and a social identity. There seems no doubt that St. John's College, Collegeville, Minn., played a decisive role in this awakening. German Benedictines had been in Minnesota since 1856, and at St. John's the liturgical movement took on an American form and became a vehicle for a social action movement. Here the key person was Virgil Michel, o.s.b., for whom liturgy meant community, a concern for others. He inspired the first efforts to rediscover the church as the People of God, not a dominant hierarchy dictating to passive masses, but Christianity as God's call to all of us to renew the face of the earth. A vigorous opponent of racism, he supported organized labor, the agrarian movement, cooperatives and distributism. Father Michel was first editor of *Orate Fratres* (later renamed *Worship*) in 1926.

From these beginnings came many of the major movements of the 1930s and 1940s. The Catholic family movement, known as the Cana Conference, began in St. Louis, Mo., in 1941. It defined its purpose as to consider "not so much spiritual things as things spiritually," that is, to integrate the mundane aspects of family life within a 20th-century mentality both American and spiritual.

Cana was soon complemented by the Christian Family Movement, which started as a Catholic Action group for men in Chicago but soon developed as an organization for married couples. It followed the "see, judge, act" technique of Young Christian Workers, focusing on social action, the family and cultural, political, economic and national life. By 1963, 40,000 couples were actively participating in small groups in the United States and Canada, and an equal number worldwide.

The Midwest was also the first American home of The Grail, another movement that pioneered in liturgical experimentation. A Jesuit, Jacques van Ginneken, who believed women had a special mission to save the world from masculine power and greed founded it in Holland in 1921. Brought to the United States in 1940 by Lydia van Kersbergen and Joan Overboss, it settled on a farm near Cincinnati. Grailville's Holy Week liturgical celebrations quickly became famous.

What many regard as the decisive event in creating a unique style of lay Catholic involvement occurred in 1933, when *Commonweal* managing editor George N. Shuster sent a French hobo, philosopher, poet and social visionary named Peter Maurin to visit Dorothy Day, then a freelance writer for *Commonweal* and other Catholic publications. The first fruit of this meeting was the monthly *The Catholic Worker*, an eight-page "call to perfection" founded on faith and $57, and first sold by volunteers on New York streets at a penny a copy on May Day 1933. Circulation in a few years would reach to 150,000. Thus began the prophetic Catholic Worker movement with Dorothy Day's plea for personal commitment and practice of the works of mercy and justice complementing and reinforcing the cerebral insights of *Commonweal* academicians and scholars.

Dorothy Day came from an extreme left-wing background similar to that of *Commonweal*'s Mr. Williams, and her leading helpers—in addition to Peter Maurin—included Russian-born Baroness Catherine de Hueck, who founded the first Friendship Houses and later in Canada started the now worldwide Madonna House apostolate.

The next dynamic insertion into the U.S. Catholic scene also came from two outsiders, an Australian lawyer named Frank Sheed and his wife Maisie Ward, member of an aristocratic English Catholic family. This sociologically strange but amazingly successful combination made its reputation in England in the 1920s by combining soapbox defense of Catholic faith and morality at London's Hyde Park Corner with a whole new style of Catholic book publishing—open, questioning, challenging, intellectually honest. Their project, though apparently defined quite independently, was remarkably similar to that being simultaneously developed by *Commonweal* on the other side of the Atlantic. Speculative theology was practically nonexistent. Instead, they set out with Jacques Maritain to rediscover Thomas Aquinas, with E. I. Watkin to compare Eastern and Western mysticism, with Christopher Dawson to place the church in the history of culture and culture in the foreground of history.

Like Michael Williams and Dorothy Day, Frank Sheed had Socialist credentials as the son of a militant Marxist. Though theologically conservative, and the first layman ever to receive an honorary papal doctorate in theology, he always retained a Marxist interest in social issues. His *Communism and Man* (1936) was used in Communist study circles and praised by George Orwell. Sheed insisted that the church's social action should be as thoroughgoing as that of the Communists, and far more compassionate. "Short of that," he said, "it didn't matter how theoretically superior the church might be; the search for justice would simply pass it by, or trample it down."

In 1933 Sheed & Ward decided to add the United States to its empire, setting up a soapbox on Wall Street and publishing offices nearby, and for more than 30 years Frank Sheed and Maisie Ward were the leaders in fashion and excitement in Catholic book publishing. Frank Sheed plugged his books by giving innumerable lectures in seminaries and colleges. Maisie Ward became a familiar figure in the New York Catholic Worker House on Mott Street (later on Chrystie Street) and among the down-and-outs on Dorothy Day's farms. The Sheed home was a meeting place for an interracial group formed by the flamboyant Baroness of Friendship House. Sheed & Ward also published Eddie Doherty, who married the Baroness and took her off to Canada.

What these outsiders were offering proved to be exactly what the Catholic mainstream wanted. The Catholic worker movement caught on like wildfire, with Chicago the second major center in a process that gradually swept the entire country and captured the world's imagination. In the English Catholic Social Guild started an English edition of *The Catholic Worker*. Ireland, also, though suffering a double depression in the 1930s—the world economic collapse coming on top of British discriminatory tariffs against Irish beef in a dispute over the interpretation of financial clauses of the Anglo-Irish Treaty of 1922—felt the Dorothy Day spell. My mother, in a West of Ireland village, managed to scrape together, from time to time, a few pennies to help her feed her Bowery bums.

When I lived in Trinidad in the 1940s, Dorothy Day was well known there. My first pilgrimage on reaching New York in 1947 was to the Catholic Worker House to continue a discussion, already begun by correspondence, about the poetry of a young black Trinidadian. Similarly, when years later a sociologist friend from Bergen, Norway, came to visit me in New Jersey, I had to take him to talk to Dorothy at the farm on the Hudson. There was an immediacy of faith about her that fascinated all of us. As Robert Coles, the psychologist, explains it, "For Dorothy Day, just yesterday was when Jesus walked Galilee."

Catholic Worker activists quickly began to infiltrate *Commonweal* and Sheed & Ward. They were typically from Catholic working-class backgrounds, most of them Irish at first, with some seminary or Catholic college education. From Chicago, John Cogley and Jim O'Gara came to *Commonweal*, having first started *Today* as a national Catholic publication aimed primarily at college students. Joined by William Clancy, son of a Detroit auto worker, they revealed the presence of grass-roots intellectuals in the Catholic community.

From these beginnings a rash of movements mushroomed in the late 1940s—liturgical, interracial, pacifist. In the Catholic Worker mind-set, many of them were challenging the too comfortable concubinage of the Catholic establishment with what people were beginning to call the consumer society. What they disliked, Wilfrid Sheed has written, "was a land of sleek pastors in box seats seated jowl-by-jowl with fat cats voted 'layman of the year'—the understanding being that 'the business of the laity is business.'"

The Midwest appreciation of liturgy was slow to reach the East Coast. Abigail McCarthy recalls how startled President John F. Kennedy was when, in 1961, the congregation in the Cathedral in St. Paul, Minn., broke out into a strong-voiced *Missa recitata*. One could go to Mass every Sunday in any Eastern city and never have such an experience. I recall my own excitement at the first dialogue Mass in which I participated. It was the center piece of the marriage ceremony of Patricia McGill, daughter of the Irish radical novelist and a Sheed & Ward employee, and Owen McGowan, who owned a Catholic bookstore in Fall River, Mass. It was all in Latin, of course, which we read from our bilingual missalettes. The subsequent reception was held in the parish hall, the simple fare appropriately served on bare tables. It was the first time I ever saw a nun—still in full regalia—dance. I believe it was the Rev. George B. Ford, unofficial Catholic chaplain to Columbia University in New York City, and an early influence on Thomas Merton, who presided at the Eucharist.

Enthusiasm found many expressions. Helene E. Froelicher, an immigrant from Switzerland, a 13th-generation descendant of Ulrich Zwingli of Reformation fame, and a convert, decided to do something about the Sunday sermon. It was a logical commitment for one raised with the Reformed reverence for the Word. In 1937, for her Crusade for More Fruitful Preaching and Hearing of the Word of God, she assembled an advisory board of 250 priests and an episcopal board of 24 bishops and archbishops. Pope Pius XI endorsed the effort enthusiastically. Impressive as was the response, I regret I have not yet found the parish church that consistently demonstrates the results.

The number of women in leadership roles in the lay apostolate is striking. Dorothy Day, Carol Jackson, the Baroness, Eileen Egan of Pax Christi, Maisie Sheed and the Grail members are just the best known. They deserve to be reverenced as precursors of today's Catholic feminism, even though they found it prudent to keep the low profile that convention expected of women. Mrs. Froelicher, for example, always signed her letters "H. E. Froelicher," leaving bishops and priests comfortable in their assumption that her daring initiatives demanded male intelligence.

A Catholic Daily Newspaper, the *Daily American Tribune,* was already appearing in Dubuque, Iowa, and had been since 1920. Although it survived until 1942, its impact on the national scene was only relative. The concept was revived by a group headed by Robert G. Hoyt, and an eight-page daily tabloid, the *Sun Herald,* began publication in Kansas City in October 1950. Chicago had been the first choice of its sponsors, but the authorities in that archdiocese, and in two or three other dioceses, were opposed. It told its readers that it would be "heavily analytical, concerned less to record events than to discover their meaning." Inadequate financing and reader support forced it to fold in June 1951.

Mr. Hoyt, however, refused to give up: If not a daily, then a weekly, the *National Catholic Reporter.* It arrived on the scene as Vatican Council II began, immediately caught its spirit and has grown with it through the years. The National Catholic Reporter's impact on Catholic thinking in the United States has been enormous. Back in the 1960s I wrote a weekly column widely syndicated in the diocesan press in the United States and Catholic publications in several other countries. When I dropped it and started to contribute to N.C.R., I discovered that two paragraphs there brought more feedback than 600 words in 35 diocesan weeklies.

Before the advent of N.C.R., probably the most influential organ of the counterculture was *Integrity,* inspired by Carol Jackson (alias Peter Michaels), an educated convert, and executed principally by Ed and Dorothy Willock. It denounced labor-saving devices and dressing up for church on Sunday, but it also had intellectual structure and content. Its roots were in Catholic England of the 1930s, Hilaire Belloc and G. K. Chesterton's distributism and Eric Gills' cult of a commune of both manual and intellectual labor. Although *Integrity* survived for only 10 years, from 1956 to 1966, it did have considerable impact in its time.

Attitudes of the clergy toward these lay movements tended to be negative. Some priests were nearly always involved, but generally they kept a low profile. John Cogley once said that, during his years at the magazine (1949–54), "*Commonweal* was largely ignored by the clergy—neither wooed nor openly denounced." Its experience with Francis Cardinal Spellman was fairly typical. When Cardinal Spellman was named Archbishop of New York, *Commonweal*'s lead editorial promised him "loyalty and devotion." When he died 28 years later, *Commonweal* commented that the editors had difficulty in writing about him. "Apparently he made an indelible impression on those who met him. Neither he nor his office ever contacted us about anything, either to praise us or blame us. He let us alone and we more or less let him alone."

Many of the movements were provided with a forum for their ideas by *Jubilee* magazine, brainchild of Edward Rice, Robert Reynolds, Robert Lax and other friends of Thomas Merton at Columbia University. It was conceived as a cooperative enterprise, and 351 stockholders bought 400 packages of preferred stock for $100 each before publication. I still hold my now worthless package for sentimental reasons.

Describing itself as "a nationally distributed pictorial magazine about the church and its people," *Jubilee* provided a mix of think pieces and conventional devotion. Rice had a genius for achieving sophisticated visual effects with limited resources. For years I taught small magazine production at Columbia University's School of General Studies, and I dissected *Jubilee* for my students to show what is possible on a limited budget. There was substance, too: John LaFarge, s.j., Bishop Joseph Blomjous of Tanzania, François Mauriac, Christopher Dawson, Romano Guardini, Jacques Maritain, Dorothy Day, Joseph Cardijn, Dom Helder Camara, Yves Congar. A distinctive feature was a long report in most issues from a different part of the world. Peter White's "Letter from Vietnam" came in 1956 at a time when few in the United States could find Vietnam on the map.

Several *Jubilee* contributors take us into the 1960s and the incredible change of climate caused by Vatican II. The dreams of the liturgists and the hopes of the social reformers had come true in a church that had broken legalistic chains. In the United States, nevertheless, many bishops and priests had difficulty in adjusting. When *Jubilee* started to raise such then-taboo subjects as contraception, mandatory clerical celibacy and pastoral solutions for divorced Catholics who wanted to remarry, it was banned from many church racks. Squeezed by a sharp circulation decline, it changed hands in 1967 and disappeared a year later.

Commonweal, on the other hand, maintained its prestige and influence through the changes. I think Edward S. Skillin, still active as its publisher in his mid-80s, provided the correct explanation when he told me: "We thought that many of the things we advocated were achieved—at least on paper—at the council: liturgical reform and use of the vernacular, an ecumenical approach, emphasis on social justice, greater responsibility and status for the laity."

Catholic book publishing was also transformed. The changed perception of the church caused by Vatican II persuaded general publishers to move massively into the Catholic market. I was hired for a year by Crowell, Collier and Macmillan to help integrate two of the Catholic houses they had acquired, Bruce and Kenedy. The general publishers, however, had made two miscalculations. Their sales people did not know how to reach the specialized Catholic market. Besides, that market was changing. Book-buying priests and religious were moving to inner cities and other small-group activities, and the books they were buying were not the pre–Vatican II back lists. So rather than integrator, I became an undertaker. It was a year on which I prefer not to dwell, especially because by 1969 the computer was making the decisions, a computer not in one's own office but in the remote headquarters of the television network that had swallowed the publishing house.

Although similarly affected by the changes in the Catholic book market, Sheed & Ward survived. Already past 70, Frank Sheed was anxious to pass on a firm that had never provided a living for him (he paid his own way by lecturing). His only concerns were that all debts be paid, that those who had invested in Sheed & Ward be repaid and that the Sheed & Ward imprint should under new ownership maintain the quality standards he had established.

I represented an unidentified client in negotiations that lasted more than a year. The problem was that my client needed to know the exact state of the finances, and the finances of publishers tend to be tangled skeins. We finally unraveled the skein, and Sheed & Ward became part of Universal Press Syndicate whose editor in chief had worked earlier for Sheed & Ward before becoming managing editor of *Ave Maria,* and later of the *National Catholic Reporter.* Jim Andrews, the most fantastically creative editor I ever knew, and a man of absolute integrity and generosity, wanted nothing more than to be known as the one who followed Frank Sheed as head of Sheed & Ward. His premature death from a massive heart attack ended that dream. After a few years in limbo Sheed & Ward was acquired by the *National Catholic Reporter,* where it is still in good hands.

As for the Catholic Worker movement, it acquired further stature and support as a result of the council. Its extreme pacifist stand, which had earned it widespread enmity during the Spanish Civil War, World War II and into the 1950s, now became an asset. Dorothy Day was a well-known figure in Rome during the council, as a lobbyist for her causes. It was my privilege to dine with Eileen Egan and her at a trattoria on Via della Conciliazione as she ended a 10-day fast that had convinced the council fathers to insert a paragraph in *Gaudium et Spes* calling for the total banning of war. Dorothy's ideas and ideals have survived her. In Catholic Worker houses across the United States and abroad, thousands inspired by her live the Beatitudes and the works of mercy voluntarily.

Well, that takes me past the council and to the start of a radically different church experience, for both clergy and laity. However different, nevertheless, it would not be what it is were it not for the prophets and unsung workers who laid the solid foundations.

14

FEMINISM AND SHARING THE FAITH: A CATHOLIC DILEMMA

Elizabeth A. Johnson, C.S.J.

THE DILEMMA

A brief vignette reported in the press last year illustrates the dilemma that I will grapple with this evening. A woman had reached the point in her spiritual journey where she felt called to become a member of the Catholic Church. As she went through the RCIA (Rite of Christian Initiation of Adults) program, however, certain church teachings struck her as being offensive to the dignity of women. Her growing awareness of women's second class status in the church was buttressed by several small incidents, most likely not even noted by the clergymen involved. In the end, with sadness, she left the RCIA program for the good of her own soul.

This woman haunts me. Her turning toward the Catholic community, with all the personal hope this involved on her part and all the richness being offered on the church's part, and then her turning away again due to a problem which is not a figment of her imagination but a very real bias: these turnings resonate deeply in the psyches of many, especially women. They define a critical dilemma.

On the one hand, at the heart of Christian faith is the good news of salvation coming from God in Jesus. Graced by divine mercy in their own hearts and lives, the community that follows Jesus (and that is commonly called the church) has a mission to witness to this treasure, to share it with fellow human beings to the ends of the earth. They are called to participate with the Spirit of God in making salvation effective in all dimensions of life.

On the other hand, despite this good news, the Catholic community in the course of history has developed institutional structures and theologies that are profoundly sexist. The official church today not only promotes the priority of men in theology, law, and practice, but justifies such male dominance with the claim that this is the will of God. Whether made known by natural law or revelation (arguments differ), it is according to God's gracious pleasure that male rule be the norm in the church.

Herewith the Catholic dilemma, illustrated in that one sad story of the woman and the RCIA program. Why would any justice-seeking woman or man want to join a group like this? Why do women stay in a community like this? And how can we continue with integrity to share the gospel with the next generation or with persons in the wider society when our own community's institutional structures and official attitudes are pervaded by sexism and therefore harmful to the well-being of women and men? Such questions, being asked by many in the church today, cannot be taken lightly. They come from a profound experience of disappointment, grief, anger, and, even if passingly, despair.

This lecture will wrestle with this dilemma in three points. First, I will describe world feminism in general as the background against which this dilemma arises; next, I will explore, as the crucible of the dilemma, Christian feminism with its assumptions, critiques and hopes; and finally, as a way through the dilemma, I will propose three Catholic strengths that may sustain persons in the struggle for a more just church, one converted from sexism toward a community of the discipleship of equals.

WORLD FEMINISM

Feminism, in a generic sense, is a worldview or stance that affirms the dignity of women as fully human persons in their own right, critiques systems of patriarchy for their violation of this dignity, and advocates social and intellectual changes to bring about freeing relationships among human beings and between human beings and the earth.[1]

The engine that drives feminism is women's experience of being marginalized, with all the suffering this entails. The concept of being marginal has become a key category for interpreting women's experi-

---

1. For excellent introduction and background, see Sandra Schneiders, *Beyond Patching: Faith and Feminism in the Catholic Church* (NY: Paulist, 1991).

ence. It identifies women as accessories to men rather than as key players or active subjects of history in their own right. "To be in the margin," writes African-American theorist Bell Hooks, "is to be part of the whole but outside the main body."[2] It is not an unnecessary place but a place of systematic devaluing. Being there signifies being less, being overlooked, not having as much importance, not being able to shape symbols or decide significant matters for the whole community.

The fundamental system that casts women as a group into this marginal position is known as sexism. In Margaret Farley's generic description, sexism is "the belief that persons are superior or inferior to one another on the basis of their sex. It includes attitudes, value systems, and social patterns which express or support this belief."[3] It is thus a prejudice. Like racism which assigns an inferior dignity to some people on the basis of their skin color or ethnic heritage, sexism views women as essentially less valuable than men on the basis of biological sex. It labors mightily to set up structures and attitudes that keep women in their "proper" social "place." In both *isms* bodily characteristics are made to count for the whole essence of the human person so that the fundamental dignity of the person is violated.

In civil society women experience the harmful effects of sexism in multiple ways:

- For most of recorded history women have been denied political, economic, legal and educational rights. In no country in the world are these yet equal to men in practice.

- According to United Nations statistics, while forming more than one-half of the world's population, women work two-thirds of the world's working hours, own one-tenth of the world's wealth and one-hundredth of the world's land, and form two-third's of the world's illiterate people. Over three-fourths of starving people are women with their dependent children.[4]

- Subordination on the basis of sex is intertwined with subordination on the basis of race and class. Poor women of color,

2. Bell Hooks, *Feminist Theory: From Margin to Center* (Boston: South End Press, 1984) ix. Rebecca Chopp, *The Power to Speak: Feminism, Language, God* (NY: Crossroad, 1989) 15–18 and 115–124 offers a fine analysis of marginality.

3. Margaret Farley, "Sexism," *New Catholic Encyclopedia* (NY: McGraw Hill, 1978) 17:604.

4. "World's Women Data Sheet" (Washington, DC: Population Reference Bureau in collaboration with UNICEF, 1985); and *Report of the World Conference to Review and Appraise the Achievements of the United Nations Decade for Women: Equality, Development and Peace* (NY: United Nations, 1985).

subordinated to poor men of color who themselves are already socially marginalized, are the oppressed of the oppressed.

• To make a dark picture even bleaker, women are bodily and sexually exploited, physically abused, raped, battered and murdered. The indisputable fact is that men do this to women in a way and to a degree that women do not do to men. Sexism is rampant on a global scale.

Feminism is the worldview that brings these situations to consciousness. It articulates the suffering women endure as a result. It analyzes these situations to reveal the pattern of male dominance that underlies them and makes them possible. It criticizes and resists this pattern as unjust. It embraces alternative worldviews more inclusive of women and the earth. It promotes changes in attitudes, theories, laws, and structures to bring about more wholeness of life. The dynamic of the whole movement is creating a change in consciousness that is irreversible. For those who enter into this worldview, it becomes as unthinkable to return to the endorsement of women's subordination as to return to slavery.

Make no mistake about it: feminism today is a powerful, worldwide phenomenon. It is part of the surge toward emancipation of oppressed peoples occurring in the twentieth century. We have seen colonized nations push against imperial rule; people of color demand equality under the law; economically poor people cry out for economic justice; young people quest for recognition as persons against inherited authorities; subjugated peoples claim their freedom in revolutions both velvet and bloody. Now women too are rising up and claiming their human worth in the face of congealed layers of prejudice. Since women are present although with marginalized status in every social group and nation, the very process of their taking their lives in their own hands and seeking mutual rather than subservient relationships with men signals a radical transformation of human society.

CHRISTIAN FEMINISM

As long ago as 1963, Pope John XXIII took note of women's emerging consciousness in his encyclical *Pacem in Terris*. He named this a distinctive "sign of the times," along with the rise of the working class and the emergence of new nations:

> It is obvious to everyone that women are now taking a part in public life. This is happening more rapidly perhaps in nations with a Christian

tradition, and more slowly but broadly among people who have inherited other traditions or cultures. Since women are becoming ever more conscious of their human dignity, they will not tolerate being treated as inanimate objects or mere instruments, but claim, both in domestic and public life, the rights and duties that befit a human person.[5]

The Second Vatican Council picked up this thread in its "Constitution on the Church in the Modern World" under the rubric of the essential equality of all persons and the demands this entails for social justice. The bishops wrote:

> True, all persons are not alike from the point of view of varying physical power and the diversity of intellectual and moral resources. Nevertheless, with respect to the fundamental rights of the person, every type of discrimination, whether social or cultural, whether based on sex, race, color, social condition, language, or religion, is to be overcome and eradicated as contrary to God's intent.[6]

Keeping the focus on women, it is clear that this pastoral constitution is teaching that discrimination based on sex is contrary to God's intent. In theological terms this means it is sinful. In the next sentences, the Council goes on to give examples of discrimination, all taken from the experience of women:

> For in truth it must still be regretted that fundamental personal rights are not yet being universally honored. Such is the case of a woman who is denied the right and freedom to choose a husband, to embrace a state of life, or to acquire an education or cultural benefits equal to those recognized for men.[7]

In the mind of the Council, these words were aimed at society. But what about the church itself? If a woman in the church is denied the right and freedom to embrace a state of life because of her sex, is this not discrimination which should be overcome and eradicated as contrary to God's intent? Christian feminism argues the logic of this, while the church's official rhetoric posits an essential difference between church society and civil society to prevent such a conclusion from being drawn.

The Second Vatican Council influenced Catholic women enormously. The concept of the church as people of God, the call of the

---

5. John XXIII, *Pacem in Terris* #41; reprinted in Joseph Gremillion, ed., *The Gospel of Peace and Justice* (Maryknoll, NY: Orbis, 1976).

6. Vatican II, *Gaudium et Spes* #29; in Walter Abbott, ed., *The Documents of Vatican II* (NY: America Press, 1966).

7. Ibid.

whole church to holiness, the revaluation of the dignity of the laity—
all of these teachings entail new roles and identity for women. Perhaps
it was providential that the Council's teaching arrived in North America in the 1960s just as feminism in civil society was gaining a newly
strong foothold. In hindsight it is clear that it was the confluence of
these two streams, civil and religious, that created the torrent that is
Christian feminism in North America today.

Christian feminism is a worldview or stance that affirms the equal
human dignity of women, criticizes patriarchy for violating this dignity, and advocates change to bring about more just and mutual relationships between women and men and human beings with the
earth—and does so based on the deepest truth of the gospel itself. Its
assumptions, criticisms, and goals are drawn from the message and
spirit of Jesus the Christ encountered from the perspective of women's
experience.

Assumptions

Christian feminism fundamentally affirms that Christian doctrine
regarding the human person applies to women equally as to men. It
therefore claims that women are equally created in the image and
likeness of God, redeemed by Christ, sanctified by the Holy Spirit,
called to a life of faith and responsibility in this world, and destined
for glory with God forever. In the light of women's ownership of this
basic Christian doctrine, Christian feminism develops a criterion for
what is true, good, and beautiful. Theories, attitudes, laws, and structures that promote the dignity of the female human person are sal-
vific and according to the divine will; theories or structures that deny
or violate women's dignity are contrary to God's intent. For Christian
feminism, women's flourishing is crucial to the truth of the gospel.[8]

These assumptions, while not very radical at first hearing, signal
that at a deep core of their being Christian women are turning away
from sexism and turning toward something being powerfully shown
to them in religious experience: their inclusion in human dignity before God and in the mystery of salvation wrought in Christ. I would
argue that this existential NO to sexism coupled with a YES to one's
own female self as God's beloved creature is an axial event in the history of spirituality. Happening among circles of women on every con-
tinent, it is an experience that cannot be denied, nor can the resulting

---

8. For a more detailed explanation of this criteria, see Rosemary Radford Ruether,
Sexism and God-Talk: Toward a Feminist Theology (Boston: Beacon, 1983) 18–20.

consciousness be reversed.[9] In face of this religious experience, any institutional authority that argues for the propriety of male dominance loses its moral power.

Critiques

From this stance Christian feminism sees that sexism pervades not only civil society but also the church. For most of ecclesial history women have been subordinated in theory and practice at every turn.

Until very recently in Christian theology women have been consistently defined as mentally, morally and physically inferior to men, not created in the image of God in their own right (Augustine), defective mates (Aquinas), even a temptress and degrading symbol of evil (Tertullian). Their minds have been characterized as less rational than those of men, their wills weaker and more open to temptation, and their sexuality degraded and its use demeaning. Left to their own devices women would not have so defined themselves, but the official voice of theology was exclusively male.

Recently this sexist anthropology has been recast to overcome its more blatant inequity, but inequity nevertheless remains. The present pontiff's encyclical on the dignity of women, for example, argues strongly that women and men are both equally created in the image of God as human persons, both have rational souls. But then, using a basic notion of complementarity, he argues that women have a special nature that defines their dignity and vocation. This nature is one that is oriented to "the order of love":

---

9. Latin America: Elsa Tamez, ed., *Through Her Eyes: Women's Theology from Latin America* (Maryknoll, NY: Orbis, 1989); and Maria Pilar Aquino, *Our Cry for Life: Feminist Theology from Latin America* (Maryknoll, NY: Orbis, 1993).

Asia: Chung Hyun Kyung, *Struggle to Be the Sun Again: Introducing Asian Women's Theology* (Maryknoll, NY: Orbis, 1990).

Africa: Denise Ackermann, ed., *Women Hold Up the Sky: Women in the Church in South Africa* (Pietermaritzburg: Cluster Pub., 1991), and Virginia Fabella and Mercy Amba Oduyoye, eds., *With Passion and Compassion: Third World Women Doing Theology* (Maryknoll: Orbis, 1988).

Europe: Elisabeth Moltmann-Wendel, *A Land Flowing with Milk and Honey: Perspectives on Feminist Theology* (NY: Crossroad, 1986).

The multicultural diversity of religious feminism in the United States beyond Anglo-Christian scholarship is exemplified by Ada Maria Isasi-Diaz, *En la Lucha: In the Struggle: An Hispanic Women's Theology* (Minneapolis: Fortress, 1993); Delores Williams, *Sisters in the Wilderness: The Challenge of Womanist God-Talk* (Maryknoll, NY: Orbis, 1993); Judith Plaskow, *Standing Again at Sinai: Judaism from a Feminist Perspective* (San Francisco: Harper and Row, 1990).

> In God's eternal plan, woman is the one in whom the order of love in
> the created world of persons takes first root. . . . The bridegroom is the
> one who loves. The bride is loved: It is she who receives love, in order to
> give love in return. . . . When we say that the woman is the one who
> receives love in order to give love in return, this refers not only or above
> all to the specific spousal relationship of marriage. It means something
> more universal, based on the very fact of her being a woman. Woman
> can only find herself by giving love to others.[10]

By nature, then, women are pre-ordained to social roles of loving, nurturing, and caring for life, while their capacity for thought and active leadership are counted of little worth. This obviously translates into the domestic and private spheres of life being defined as women's proper domain. In the context of patriarchy where public laws, symbols, and structures are shaped by men, such a dualistic anthropology of "woman's special nature" simply ensures women's continuing secondary social status and dependence upon men. In an ironic twist, it also credits women with being more capable of living out Jesus' great commandment of love, but this seems not to be noticed by the promoters of such dualistic anthropology.

Not only theology and corporate memory marginalize women, but church practice likewise effects their exclusion. They may not receive all seven sacraments. Thus they may not preach or preside in the liturgical assembly, or mediate God's grace in officially sacramental ways. The effect is to make women dependent on a male clergy for such mediation of God's grace. In a word, women are excluded from centers of significant ecclesial decision-making, law-making, and symbol-making, and prevented from exercising public, institutional-leadership roles. Awareness of this subordination has created a crisis over the eucharist for many women. As Rosemary Radford Ruether expresses it, women come to the table to be nourished by the word of God and the bread of life, only to leave still starved because what has been powerfully ritualized is their own subordination.[11]

Christian feminism argues vigorously that, even for the church, sexism is contrary to God's intent. Such second-class citizenship disparages the image of God in women, profanes our baptism, distorts the relationship between the sexes, and damages the community that is the church.

10. John Paul II, "Dignitatis Mulieribus," (On the Dignity and Vocation of Women), *Origins* Vol. 18: No. 17 (October 6, 1988) #29–30.

11. Rosemary Radford Ruether, *Women-Church: Theology and Practice* (San Francisco: Harper and Row, 1985) 4.

Goals

What Christian feminism hopes for is a transformed community. Cooperating with the Spirit of life, feminism hopes so to change unjust structures and distorted symbol systems that a new community in church and society becomes possible, a liberating community of all women and men characterized by mutuality with each other, care for the weakest and least powerful among them, and harmony with the earth. This is a vision of the church as a community of the discipleship of equals,[12] that is, as a community shaped according to the reign of God preached by Jesus, rather than one modeled on imperial Rome or the divine right monarchies of the age of absolutism.

THE DILEMMA INTENSIFIED

Let me point out, lest anyone think we are dealing here with superficial matters, that the deepest questions raised by Christian feminism are of universal import. Who is God? Is God a male ruler who wills male supremacy? Or a triune mystery of love beyond all imagining who wills the genuine equality of women and men in community and who, as a result, can be referred to in female and cosmic imagery? Are women deficient human beings or really created in the image and likeness of God? What is salvation? Is Jesus Christ a Savior of all or a tool of patriarchal oppression? Does baptism really recreate women in the image of Christ, or does its effect not quite take when the recipient is female? Is the church to be forever sexist, or can it be redeemed from sexism to become a more just community of disciples?

Vatican II taught the idea that the pilgrim church on its way through history is continually in need of reform and increased fidelity to its own calling.[13] Thus, we may look upon Christian feminism as a blessing, not only for women, and not only for women and men together, but for the church itself. In Anne Carr's lovely phrase, in the midst of the history of sexism, feminism comes as an offer of "transforming grace" to the church, an offer to repent and become a living community of justice and peace.[14] In faith and struggle feminist women and

12. This term, coined by Elisabeth Schüssler Fiorenza, *In Memory of Her: A Feminist Theological Reconstruction of Christian Origins* (NY: Crossroad, 1983), has become a symbol of Christian feminist hopes.

13. "Decree on Ecumenism," #5–6. See Karl Rahner "The Sinful Church in the Decrees of Vatican II," in his *Theological Investigations* (NY: Crossroad, 1982) 4:270–94.

14. Anne Carr, *Transforming Grace: Women's Experience and Christian Tradition* (San Francisco: Harper and Row, 1988).

men are growing the church into a new moment of the living tradition, one more reflective of God's gracious design for our salvation. However, and terrifyingly, grace may always be refused.

The continuing refusal of the institutional church today to be converted from its ancient sexism makes it, in the eyes of many, an obstacle to faith, that is, a motive not to believe. This is in contrast to the old apologetics where a motive for the credibility of the faith was said to be the church itself. As a result a number of women are leaving the church, some to live out their call to ordained ministry in other Christian bodies; others simply to find a more inclusive community in which to pray and raise their children; still others to seek the divine in worship that honors the feminine. Having taught some of these women, and presently being friends or colleagues with others, I know their stories, resonate with their pain, and greatly respect their decisions. At the same time, my own path and that of others keeps on winding through the Catholic community itself.

There is need to articulate reasons for this. And so we return to our dilemma. Why remain in the church? How, with integrity, share the faith with others?

The force of these questions was brought home to me several years ago when I was giving a lecture on feminist theology on the campus of U.C.L.A. A young woman student in the audience, whom I had noticed listening intently, stood to ask whether I worshipped the goddess. In response I asked whether she thought that praying to divine mystery in female images such as mother, Holy Wisdom, or feminine Spirit within the contours of the following of Jesus was tantamount to worshipping the goddess. When she replied "No," I could say in truth that then I did not worship the goddess.

But we were not finished yet, for then she asked "Why not?" Here was a question I had never really articulated. To gain time to think (!), I asked if she worshipped the goddess. When she answered affirmatively, I asked why. She named respect for the body, connection with the earth and nature's cycles, and sisterhood with other women as her reasons. Saying that these were precious values and that the Christian tradition had not given them priority, I asked quietly if her worship of the goddess turned her to the poor or motivated her to have compassion on the most abandoned. Her negative answer opened the door to my own attempt at response: I still followed the Way of Jesus, I offered, for it turns you toward the nearest neighbor in need, without denying the values that she so beautifully affirmed.

And so we conversed, tentatively and respectfully probing one another's stances for the truth that might lie there. I still remember the intense silence in the auditorium as this genuine conversation took place. It was not a matter of one-upmanship but of common search in which all present seemed to be charting their own steps on a vitally important issue. In retrospect I think my intuitive response about care for the oppressed was to some degree inadequate. Not only do many worshippers of the goddess have strong concern for justice but many Christians, in reality, do not, despite the gospels and contemporary Catholic social teaching. Ever since, I have been thinking about how to articulate the values of Christian faith within a feminist consciousness.

Catholic Strengths

As a way to deal with this dilemma, not to resolve it but to struggle with it, I would like to identify in Catholicism today three dynamic strengths that together add up to a rich religious possibility for one's life when interpreted through feminist consciousness. My experience in ecumenical dialogue and with the splendid witness and theological scholarship of so many Protestant and Orthodox Christians has led me to immense admiration for them, so in no way is this intended to suggest that other Christian churches are lacking these strengths. Rather, it is the way these factors are combined in the Catholic church that gives this group its particular character. The three strengths are these: the gospel, the community, and the imagination.

First, the gospel. The community that is the Catholic church continues to keep alive the liberating, compassionate power of the gospel. We continue to hear from the scriptures of God's gracious intent to heal, redeem, and liberate all peoples and the cosmos itself. The Jewish scriptures connect us with divine presence through proclamation of the exodus from slavery to freedom, the covenant and the law; through the prophetic word against injustice that promises release; and through the wisdom word about creation that points to divine ways in the world of nature and everyday life. The Christian scriptures release the power of the Spirit through the "dangerous" story of Jesus the Christ—his way of relating to people against all social stigmatizing, his challenge to follow, his death and resurrection releasing mercy and hope for all. In other words, if the core of the gospel were missing, there would be no point to remaining in the church or inviting others to share the faith. But I find it still there.

Particularly heartening is the angle of vision opened up on the scriptures and their traditioning process by feminist interpretation.[15] Thanks to this reading we can see ever more clearly that Jesus-Sophia, in the name of God, gives the world a new pattern of love, hope, and meaning by embodying and teaching a new way of relating to each other. Not domination-subordination but the inclusive, mutual connections of sisters and brothers should characterize the community of disciples.

Furthermore, feminist biblical hermeneutics highlights Jesus' attitude toward women, his outreach toward women in need, his inclusive table community, the influence of women upon him, the witness of his women disciples. These disciples, key among them Mary of Magdala, provide the moving point of continuity in the gospel story. Having accompanied him as disciples around Galilee, they followed him when he set his face toward Jerusalem and were present at all the important events of his last days. They kept faith with him even to the bitter end. It is simply not true to say, as so many do, that all of his disciples abandoned him during the crucifixion; the circle of women disciples kept vigil by the cross as a sacrament of God's own seemingly absent fidelity. The women disciples, according to the gospels, helped to bury Jesus. Thus knowing where the tomb was, they were the first to experience the risen One and receive the apostolic commission to "go and tell." The fire of the Holy Spirit was poured out on women and men alike in the upper room. Accordingly, the participation of women in ministry in the early years of the church was not an aberration but an expression of a new worldview learned from Jesus the Christ.

The egalitarian character of the Jesus movement was eventually coopted by patriarchy, although it did not go down without a fight. But the revolutionary realization that women are equally made in the image of God, are restored by Christ in the power of the Spirit, and are capable of responsibility commensurate with this surfaces again and again in Christian history. Thus there is a critical and transforming tradition stemming from the gospel itself that can add impetus to the conversion of the church today from sexism. The institutional church has already changed its long-held stances regarding the religious correctness of slavery and contempt for the Jews. It is now time for the living tradition to grow away from the subordination of

15. Carol Newsome and Sharon Ringe, eds., *The Women's Bible Commentary* (Louisville, KY: Westminster/John Knox Press, 1992); Letty Russell, ed., *Feminist Interpretation of the Bible* (Philadelphia: Westminster, 1985).

women. The gospel carries this message as a subliminal text even in the midst of sexism.

Second, the community. The Catholic people is an ancient and universal community of all sorts of folks, connected through time and space. The connection with believers throughout the ages as expressed, for example, in the "Litany of the Saints" gives us deep historical roots. In addition to community through time, there is also community through space given the wide geographic spread of Catholicism. The Catholic church is probably the major world institution that crosses the lines of first, second, and third worlds, linking together populations in western and eastern Europe, North and South America, Asia, Africa, and Australia. There are close to one billion of us, peoples of various cultures but with a shared faith, sacred memory, and symbol system, struggling to be faithful and make sense of our lives. This vast network becomes wonderfully real when you travel to different countries.

Being a Catholic means being joined with all of these people. I find particular delight in discovering so many women in different countries forming networks of mutual help, moving forward with actions to promote the dignity of women according to the possibilities of their own culture. In North America there are feminist Catholics and Catholic feminists of all stripes, women pastoring parishes, women in justice and peace movements, theologians of multi-cultural hues, the Women-Church movement (a strategy for spiritual survival and prophecy). In India there is Virginia Saldanha with her circle of friends heading up the first Women's Desk for the Diocese of Bombay. In Ireland there is the publication entitled "Womanspirit: A Journal of Feminist Spirituality" coming out of Dublin. In Brazil there is Ivone Gebara committed to being a voice for the voiceless as she connects the issues of poverty, sexism, and ruination of the earth in Recife. In South Africa there is the artist Dina Cormick creating images of the divine creator in the likeness of women of color—to name but a few. Being a Catholic means being joined in a community of faith with all of these women, along with so many other women and men working for justice and peace around the world.

Obviously, I have here made a distinction between the church as institution and the church as community. I have also given theological and existential priority to the latter, a move well fought over and taken by the Second Vatican Council.[16] And yet we also need the institution

---

16. Herbert Vorgrimler, ed., *Commentary on the Documents of Vatican II* (NY: Herder & Herder, 1967) 1:105–137.

to link and unite such disparate local churches. The feminist vision maintains that the institution need not be sexist in order to fulfill its purpose.[17] Catholic women's experience of community in some places gives a foretaste already of what a renewed church could be.

Third, the imagination. The Catholic church offers a rich heritage of sacraments, sacramentals, prayers, spiritual writings, practices, and guides. Today there is a deep hunger for God and the things of the spirit abroad in our land. Many people are tired of life being so materialistic, superficial, meaningless. Catholicism has what David Tracy calls an analogical imagination which notices the presence of grace in and through the everyday world.[18] With this sacramental sense of things, the Catholic tradition unlocks the religious dimension of life. Its diverse spiritual traditions provide a feast for the soul, delineating paths that flow toward the ideal of simplicity and peace. Ambiguity inheres even here, however, as much classical spirituality denigrates the body with its passions and thus, in an androcentric framework, women. In accord with the foundational sacramental imagination, however, emergent feminist spiritualities attend to women's ways of being in the world, pouring the search for the transcendent into a path that cherishes the body, sexuality, and the earth. In forging new patterns of wholeness feminist spiritualities draw from deep wells in the Catholic tradition while they comfort, challenge, and empower women to resist the debilitations of religious sexism.[19]

These three strengths—gospel, community, and spirituality—in their particular combination in the Catholic community provide, I think, light in the darkness and give some warrants for remaining in the church and for sharing the faith with others. As these strengths operate, they interact with the sufferings that women bear in their membership, along with the sufferings of men sensitive to injustice being done to women, to become a powerhouse of energy to resist sexism in the name of the deepest truths that we profess.

17. Letty Russell, *Church in the Round: Feminist Interpretation of the Church* (Louisville, KY: Westminster/John Knox Press, 1993); and Mary Hines, "Community for Liberation: Church," in Catherine LaCugna, ed., *Freeing Theology: The Essentials of Theology in Feminist Perspective* (San Francisco: Harper, 1993) 161–84.

18. David Tracy, *The Analogical Imagination: Christian Theology and the Culture of Pluralism* (NY: Crossroad, 1981).

19. Joann Wolski Conn, ed., *Women's Spirituality: Resources for Christian Development* (NY: Paulist, 1986); Paula Cooey, Sharon Farmer, Mary Ellen Ross, eds., *Embodied Love: Sensuality and Relationship as Feminist Values* (San Francisco: Harper and Row, 1987); Katherine Zappone, *The Hope for Wholeness: A Spirituality for Feminists* (Mystic, CT: Twenty-Third Pub., 1991).

Conclusion

During the Viet Nam War a bumper sticker appeared in reaction to anti-war protests: "America, love it or leave it." I thought at the time what a stupid sentiment that was. If you really love something, you do not abandon it to its errors but try to make it better. Anguished over that war for moral reasons though I was, the idea of becoming a citizen of a different nation had little appeal. Better to demonstrate, to lobby, to teach, to cast votes, to pressure the government with its deceit and tunnel vision to end the hated thing, for the good of our own country as well as for the Vietnamese people. Similarly today, to struggle for the conversion of the institutional church from sexism locally, nationally, and internationally seems to me worthwhile. Though the errors of the official leadership regarding women are in many instances egregious, stubbornly so, even a small change for the better can affect a community that is world-wide. This in turn can have profound impact on society, even for generations yet unborn.

I would like to end as I began, with a story, this time one with a hopeful ending. It was recounted to me in a letter from a friend in South Africa. To understand the setting, you should know that Phokeng is a black township, that Father Gerard is its pastor, and that "to supply" is priest-language for saying Mass on Sundays in a place where one is needed. I quote:

> Let me tell you about some feminist theology in action! I have been going to Phokeng to supply for Gerard while he is away. Two weeks ago I noticed an altar server (male) going up to a young woman in the communion line and speaking to her. She left the line and went back into the pew. After Mass I inquired and was told that since Father Gerard's absence, they (meaning the men of the parish council) had decided that women and girls should cover their heads as a mark of respect when receiving communion. No hat, no communion. I vented my anger with those I was talking to, and decided I would have to do something about the situation on my next visit.
>
> Last Sunday I was in the parish again. I noticed all the women wearing hats, berets, or veils (called doeks), even Maggie Bopalamo, former detainee in Bophuthatswana, lecturer at a teachers' college, a leader in the parish community. After communion and the communion prayer, I went up to a young woman in the front pew who was wearing a blue hat with white ribbons. I asked if I may borrow it. Then in full vestments I put the hat on my head. Laughter. I adjusted the hat here and there and asked how I looked. More laughter.
>
> Then I opened the Bible and read from Galatians 3:27-28. Because we all drink of the one Spirit, "there is neither Jew nor Greek, neither

slave nor free, neither male and female, for all are one in Christ Jesus."
Rapt attention. On the basis of this equality, I said, it seems all the men
will have to wear their heads covered as well. Next week I want to see
all the men with hats on if they want to go to communion, and promised that I, too, would celebrate Mass wearing a hat. The women
cheered and shouted "Viva" and clapped and danced.

I had found the gap and went right through it, speaking about discrimination against women in the church. More cheers from the women.
This empowered me even more and I went on. More dancing. Finally, I
said that the reason given why women should cover their heads was to
show respect, but the only respect the gospel demanded was not visible
to the eye: it was in the heart of a person. The women left the pews,
went into the aisles dancing. Gradually some of the men joined in as
well, and of course, yours truly! It was a wonderful teaching moment.

After some ordinary news and chat, my friend finished his letter by
hearkening back to the township story, ending with this blessing: "May
all women all over the world leave their pews, get into the aisles, and
dance their way to freedom and full partnership in the church!" With
such moments breaking out all over the world, the Catholic dilemma
of feminism and sharing the faith begins to be lit up by hope.

15

UNDER THE CROSS AND THE FLAG: REFLECTIONS ON DISCIPLESHIP AND CITIZENSHIP IN AMERICA

John A. Coleman, S.J.

I invite you to eavesdrop as we inspect several scenarios. An expectant crowd of 400 citizens—approximately a third of them Latino, a third black and a third white—have gathered in a crammed school cafeteria in East Oakland, Calif. A block away, the nearby main artery, East 14th Street, a lively if somewhat run-down commercial thoroughfare, teems with shoppers. Yet we also see, in every few buildings, boarded-up storefronts. Over the East 14th Street skyline looms a large abandoned Montgomery Ward store, closed for business now for over 10 years. It occupies a full square block. The crowd we are seeing has come together to try to reclaim that building for a local community development scheme.

At 7:30 P.M. sharp the meeting begins. At one table in the front of the cafeteria sits the pastor of St. Elizabeth's Church and his parishioners, neighborhood residents. At a table opposite, the local city council representative and the head of Oakland's Office of Economic Development and Employment have taken their seats, knowing full well that they are about to be "pinned" in a community-organizing action. The group will press them to commit their energies to pressuring Montgomery Ward to donate the land and building for a neighborhood redevelopment scheme. These savvy political types have heard before the slogans of the community organizers: "We voted for you, now we are going to hold you accountable."

The meeting begins with a woman leading a prayer-reflection in Spanish and English. "How beautiful it is to meet here, united and working together as a community. In preparing this reflection, I thought about how we must have faith, a faith that leads us to action. God has given us a place and asks us what we are going to do with it. Part of the place God has given us is this street and that huge building that has been unused for 10 years. We want to make this place something that serves everyone, something for the community."

A prayer follows. Then another leader turns to address the civic officials: "We're tired of promises—none of them fulfilled. We want action. We ask city officials to work with us to put pressure on the Montgomery Ward Corporation to develop it or tear it down. We have faith we can make this happen—and there are more than 400 of us here!" At the end of the evening, the crowd leaves with a sense of accomplishment. Both public officials have made a commitment to the community. They have agreed in public to a specific timeline for putting the Montgomery Ward building to a new community use.

Next, let us channel-surf a bit to watch scenario No. 2. It is Holy Week. A consortium of local Bay Area Pax Christi chapters have organized a pilgrim walk from Richmond, Calif., to the Lawrence Livermore Laboratory (where nuclear weapons are designed) 30 miles away. Each day they have stopped at some preordained site to dramatize symbolically the forces that make for violence in our society. Today, half-way in space and time to the civil disobedience planned for Good Friday at the Lab, they drag the large cross to their fourth Holy Week station of the cross. They stand in front of a gun shop in Berkeley and call on passersby to enact gun control measures to reduce gun violence in our society. The language and symbols they use are deeply religious.

We channel-surf a third time and find ourselves in Eagle Butte, S.D., on an Indian reservation. The annual Habitat for Humanity Jimmy Carter Jamboree has just finished in the hot July sun. Nearly 2,000 Americans, young and old, have come from around the country to build low-cost homes in a marathon house-building cooperative venture. Few of the volunteers know that, until the last minute, only half of the aluminum siding needed for the 30 houses being built had arrived. Agitated efforts by the organizers unloading the siding until 2:00 A.M. allows the group to launch on schedule the work they have come to do. Thirty new homeowners, doing what Habitat calls their "sweat equity," work side by side with professional and middle-class volunteers helping to erect what will be their own homes. Later, these homeowners will in turn expand that self-interested sweat equity to join Habitat to build houses for other homeowners.

Each morning this week on the reservation, the day's work begins with morning prayer and devotions. Hymns and prayers start off a day of what Millard Fuller, the founder of Habitat, likes to call "the theology of the hammer." At the end of the process, each new home will be officially dedicated and the homeowner will be given a Bible. One of the Habitat executives from headquarters in Americus, Ga., reflects on what he sees taking place: "I am looking at the way I carry out my Christianity as a way of expressing my citizenship. The liberal press tries to say to us, 'Wait a minute, you have to put your religion over here.' We don't have freedom of religion today, we have freedom from religion. They put freedom in such a box that, if anything even approaches religion, then it can't be citizenship."

These three scenarios could be duplicated in other locales. For example, representatives of Bread for the World, a Christian lobbying organization based in Washington, D.C., work to support legislation intended to alleviate world hunger at home and abroad. They alert local members around the country to activate their phone trees to get fellow members to write, phone or wire their congressional representatives to save legislation providing help for poor women and infant children through the Women, Infant and Children nutrition program. Each June, on lobby day, Bread for the World escorts members from corridor to corridor to visit their senators and representatives to find out just where they stand on legislation aimed to combat hunger.

These variant scenarios remind us that it is not just the Christian Right that translates its vision of discipleship into a more public political arena. Nor does the Christian Right represent the only faith-based political movement that is growing and having an impact. Congregation-based community organizing groups in this country have millions of members. Frances Moore Lappé and Paul DuBois have written a book, *The Quickening of America,* about the citizenship-revitalization movements around the nation that already have renewed our democratic citizenship and gained a voice for ordinary Americans. Almost every second group they refer to has a name like Valley Inter-Faith, Joint Ministry Project or Shelby County Inter-Faith, names that link them to churches. Bread for the World, for its part, currently aims to boost its membership by about 6,000 to reach a membership base of 50,000. Pax Christi is holding its own in memberships, at a time when other secular peace movements have atrophied because of the end of the cold war.

How do Christians of various stripes think of their common citizenship? What designs or hopes do they have about the *res publica*? Is it legitimate for Christians to fuse, as they do, their discipleship and citizenship language? Or is this a kind of Christian imperialism that dishonors the equal respect due to those of no belief or of different belief? Should Christians impose gag rules on themselves about using their faith language when they engage in common citizenship pursuits? These are some of the questions I want to raise.

I. Six Paradenominational Groups

My basis for answering these questions will not be simply theoretical or abstract. For the past four years, I have been part of a research team interviewing hundreds of Americans involved in paradenominational groups engaged in citizen activism or education. We have gone around the country to research sites in the South, Midwest, East and Pacific and Mountain regions. We have transcribed reams of transcripts from nearly 300 formal interviews with reflective and thoughtful citizens who have talked to us about how they see the contours of citizenship in this country, what they are doing to improve the communal climate of our culture, what motivates them to give time and money to volunteer efforts to change our country, how they see the tensions and complementarity between their Christian identities— what we in the research project call discipleship—and their common identities as citizens in a pluralistic society.

The New Form of Public Church

I was first led to focus on paradenominational groups because of the research of a Princeton sociologist, Robert Wuthnow, who notes how such groups have been growing apace. He alleges that the new religious special interest groups may "be the ones that increasingly define the public role of American religion." Such groups, religious in orientation although not agents of any one church or denomination, in Wuthnow's words "combine the best of both worlds. Like churches they delimit the services they try to provide. And like sects, they are for the most part relatively small groups of like-minded people who share the same concerns. But unlike churches, they do not all try to provide the same (or a full range of) services. Unlike sects, they require relatively limited engagement."

Wuthnow's data derives principally from individual aggregate statistics. He makes no careful inspection of such paradenominational groups to find out how they actually operate, whom they recruit, what relation they have to individual congregations and parishes and how they picture their ideal image of the public church.

My research focuses on groups that are national in character and that also have local grass-roots memberships. We did not want purely paper groups or national lobbying organizations without local units. We also wanted our analysis to represent the range of Christian America: mainline Protestant, Catholic, evangelical and black Protestants. Two of our groups include Jewish respondents in the sample.

The Sample

In the end, we determined to study the following six groups:

1. *Habitat for Humanity.* Founded by an evangelical person but drawing widely from the whole range of religious and secular America, Habitat builds low-cost housing as a non-profit organization. It is the 17th-largest home builder in America.

2. *Pico.* The name, an acronym for The Pacific Institute for Community Organizing, is now a misnomer, because Pico has affiliates all over the country. It is the second-largest (after The Industrial Areas Foundation) church-based community organizing group in the United States. Founded by a Jesuit, John Baumann, Pico helps give ordinary Americans a voice by mobilizing and equipping them with citizen skills; it brings together the moral vision of the churches with participant democracy to revitalize urban neighborhoods and demand better police protection, improved schools and economic development.

3. *Bread for the World.* As already indicated, this is a large hunger-lobby group that also engages in education and research on hunger issues. Founded by a Lutheran pastor, Art Simon, Bread draws strongly from a mainline Catholic and Protestant base.

4. *Pax Christi USA.* Pax is a Catholic peace education and activist organization that tries to affect both the Catholic Church and our Government. It is open to membership by non-Catholics. Pax Christi was chosen, among other reasons, in order to include in our study a more radical version of citizenship-activism, since a number of its members engage in civil disobedience.

5. *Focus on the Family.* This evangelical ministry, based in Colorado Springs, was founded by the well-known radio family pundit and

best-selling author, Dr. James Dobson. Focus itself engages in public policy and is affiliated with public interest groups at the state and national level that lobby for family-related legislation and policy, e.g., taxation, vouchers, home schooling, protection of heterosexual marriage and divorce legislation. Focus and its affiliates also galvanize local church members into greater political involvement through its grass-roots Community Impact Forum. While a number of Focus affiliates have loose alliances with the Christian Right, Focus spokespersons distance themselves somewhat from the hard Christian Right and foster a moderate image.

6. *The African Methodist Episcopal Church.* We sampled four large megachurches of the A.M.E., the oldest historic black church in America. For example, Bethel, the site we studied in Baltimore, manages the high school equivalency program for that city. The congregation in Los Angeles we focused on—First African Methodist Episcopal, familiarly known as FAME—spearheaded the community development renaissance after the communal uprisings at the time of the Rodney King trial and has spawned dozens of non-profit spin-offs. We were determined to include a sample from the black churches in our study since few American churches do as good a job as the black churches do wedding discipleship to citizenship.

I am now writing a book about these six case studies. Here I want to present some of the most important conclusions from our study.

II. Religion Generates Social Capital

One important research finding points to the inordinate amount of "social capital" generated by churches. Social capital—a term made famous by the Harvard University political scientist Robert Putnam—points to features of social life, such as networks of mutuality and norms of trust, that enable participants to act together more effectively to pursue shared objectives. To the extent that social capital serves a bridging function—where norms, networks and trust link substantial sectors of the community and span underlying social cleavages—social cooperation is enhanced and serves broader rather than narrower interests.

Putnam links social capital (which, in a now classic essay "Bowling Alone in America," he claims is diminishing in an America where more people bowl than ever before but in ever fewer leagues) to conventional political participation. While social capital is not the same as political participation, it leads to it and maximizes it. People connected to networks of communication and mutuality are more likely to vote and engage in volunteer civic activity. No institution in America generates as much social capital as the churches. People who are active in them are more apt to volunteer time and money to the institutions of civil society—first of all, of course, to the churches themselves, which garner the preponderant share of such volunteer activity, but also to non-church civic activity.

The churches regularly and straightforwardly act as communication networks that foster civic voluntarism. As one of the main students of voluntarism in America puts it, "Religious organizations tell people of opportunities to serve, both within and beyond the congregation itself, and provide personal contacts, committees, phone numbers, meeting space, transportation or whatever it may take to help turn good intent into action."

The sociological evidence linking religion to social capital seems overwhelming. According to a survey conducted by *The Nation,* two-thirds of those active in social movements in America draw principally on religious motivation for their involvement. Two-thirds, as well, of all small support groups in America are directly connected with churches and synagogues. Brian O'Connell, the president of Independent Sector, claims, "A very large part of the non-profit sector's service to society is performed by religious institutions." From soup kitchens to non-profit, low-cost housing alternatives, from AIDS hospices to shelters for the homeless and services to immigrants, the religious sector takes up the slack where government programs fall down.

Churches represent the lion's share of the so-called thousand points of light. Americans give seven times as much to churches as to political campaigns and several times as much as they give to secular charities. People are more likely to give time and money, even to secular efforts, if they are church members.

Resources for the Public Order

In their book *Voice and Equality,* a massive study of political and civic voluntarism in America, Sidney Verba, Kay Schlozman and Henry Brady argue that religion significantly increases the democratic potential in the United States. Along with workplace and non-political civic organizations like the Rotary Club, churches offer four important resources that increase the likelihood and effectiveness of both civic and political involvement:

- They train people in transferable skills, such as giving a speech, organizing a meeting, writing a memo or raising money—skills that can then be translated back into politics.

- They provide dense networks from which civic activists can be recruited. People respond better to requests for activity when asked by a friend rather than a stranger.

- They give people a sense of efficacy in a local setting, which in turn increases the chances that they will feel that they actually can have some real impact in the political arena.

- They give information and cues about politics. They also expose people to political messages in settings that are not explicitly political.

The workplace has a built-in bias toward providing these civic and political advantages to the affluent and well-educated. Those who already have, receive even more. Managers, rather than ordinary workers, are routinely asked to organize meetings, write memos and give speeches. The same is true of nonreligious civic organizations. Churches compensate by making our democracy more representative.

Verba, Schlozman and Brady conclude: "Only the religious institutions provide a counter-balance in this cumulative resource process. They play an unusual role in the American participatory system by providing opportunities for the development of civic skills to those who otherwise would be resource poor. It is commonplace," they continue, "to ascribe the special character of American politics to the weakness of unions and the absence of class-based political parties that can mobilize the disadvantaged—in particular the working class—to political activity in America. The mobilizing function often performed elsewhere by unions and labor or social democratic parties, is more likely to be performed by religious institutions." Indeed, a blue-collar worker in America is more apt to be given opportunities to practice civic skills in church than in a union, "not because American unions are particularly deficient as skill builders, but because so few American blue-collar workers are union members and so many are church members."

Community Organizing

It was not by chance that community organizing groups in America turned to churches as an essential anchor of their activity. Community organizers came to see that no other resource—neither neighborhoods

nor other civic institutions—could rival churches in providing the networks of solidarity and trust on which they depend in building their
community organizations. As Paul Bryant, a Southern Baptist pastor
in Pensacola, Fla., told us: "I say that really, you take the churches out
of this part of town, there's no voice for the people. You really don't
have anyone else speaking for the people and with the people."

Denise Collazo, an Oakland, Calif., community organizer in the
Pico network, put it this way: "In most neighborhoods people don't
know each other anymore. It's not like before, where you knew
everyone and everyone's business and their kids and everything.
Neighborhoods have changed in the past 30 years. But in the church
most people have known each other for all their lives. Their kids have
been raised with each other, so I think just the level of relationship
that you have to start with is bigger and broader with the churches.
The ante is upped significantly when you are with a church. If someone you've been going to church with for 15 years comes up to you
and says, hey, we're working on this project with the Oakland Community Organization and it's something that would really interest
you, you're going to take that much more seriously than if some organizer comes knocking on your door. And I think," she went on, "that
with church-based organizing, you have the power of the pulpit.
You've got those pastors, who are seen by the politicians as powerful;
that in itself makes you more powerful. Then I think one most important thing is that it's value based, giving us the ability to talk about
why we are doing what we do, and looking at the Bible and specific
stories we all know. We have all heard or have all been sort of brought
up hearing and using these examples as the reason why we do this."

Horizontal Religion

We need to be nuanced when speaking about the social capital
found in parishes. First, not every form of religion carries social capital. Robert Putnam, for instance, in his study of civic voluntarism in
Italy, *Making Democracy Work,* found a negative correlation between
religion and social capital.

Putnam's data from Italy force us to make a distinction between
types of religion. For example, there are those, like traditional Italian
Catholicism, that are intensely hierarchical in structure. They foster
vertical relations (between bishops and priests, and priests and people)
of passivity and subordination. Then there are religions, like congre-
gational forms of Protestantism and Judaism, and variant forms of
Catholicism, such as are found in post–Vatican II American parishes,

that nurture horizontal relationships of interaction between congregants in parish councils, finance and worship committees, lay leadership and small faith groups. *Voice and Equality* demonstrates that there is more social capital available in black congregations and Protestant churches than in the typical large Catholic parish.

Some religious units pay scant attention to the social capital they generate or do not know how to turn it into politically relevant social movements, civic service and voluntarism. Much of the social capital of some congregations remains frozen in the local unit, or is even isolated into separate pockets within the congregation, and therefore does not spill out into the larger society. And some congregations define themselves essentially as sanctuary havens from the heartless world. Not every congregation sees itself as having a civic, public mission.

In particular, as Robert Wuthnow claims, the local congregation may find that public debates about economics and civic matters inside the very heart of the church "can easily become polarized, taking on an aura of antagonism that runs against the grain of religious teachings about fellowship and reconciliation." Furthermore, there exists—as Gallup data repeatedly shows—a widespread and strong public dislike in America of religious leaders' playing too direct a role in politics.

Mutuality of Congregation and Paradenominational Groups

The congregation and the paradenominational organizations need each other to generate a public church in America, because most local congregations do not know how to use the social capital they generate. Sam Reed (a pseudonym), a major executive in the Pico network, puts it this way: "I would suggest that community organizing in the churches in which I am hired helps them learn how to make their institutions effective. I don't think that what the community organizing staff provides the church is beyond the self-interest of the institution itself. I don't think local congregations know how to make values real. I think they want to, but they don't know how." Norm Rodert, a pastor in Kansas City, Kan., echoes Reed. He says that community organizing, with its focus on building relationships and nurturing the skills of leadership, actually taught him for the first time how to be an effective pastor. The spillover was not just to society, but within the church itself.

Again and again, in our interviews with the community organizers, we heard how community organizing bridged groups within a parish or community. Thus, Mary Ellen Burton-Christie recounts how community organizing is the only aspect of her parish in which Hispanics and Anglos socialized and the two disparate social networks of the parish intersected. Pastor Bernard Yates of the Primitive Baptist Church in Pensacola told us that Pico was the first organization in Pensacola history to bridge the black and white churches.

Pico and the other paradenominational organizations both depend upon and add to the social capital they find in parish settings. These groups rely on pre-existing strands of community in society. But in many congregations, those strands exist largely in isolation from one another—as friendship cliques, service societies, lifestyle enclaves and many other "clumps" of individuals. Community organizing, when it speaks of reweaving the fabric of society, points to the ways it establishes cross-linkages among the many isolated strands of relationship within a congregation.

Congregations and paradenominational organizations relate in a symbiosis. The latter, we have found, are not good units for practicing discipleship, because they are so specifically focused and involve limited liability commitments. "I don't look to Habitat to fulfill basic religious needs; that's what the church is for" and "I always expect that we should bring our religious sentiments and beliefs with us to Habitat rather than vice-versa," were typical comments. Discipling—that is, taking seriously the Christian message and norms—either takes place in families or congregations or not at all.

Over and over again our respondents told us that they got involved in civic voluntarism mainly because of their religious motivation. They closely link their sense of discipleship with their citizenship. Torn Burke, a Pax Christi member from Virginia, says: "I am not a citizen exclusive of who I am as a member of my faith community." Even the civic participatory and self-interested strands in the community-organizing culture have been affected by the discipleship motif. Judy Reyes-Ortiz, a Pico leader, echoes this theme: "I really believe it's about relationship building and the community building and the grounding in faith that keeps us from getting too wild or too way out there. In other words, it keeps us from trashing people, our opponents. We have to respect their dignity, and that comes from the faith base."

What Paradenominational Groups Give to Congregations

"I tend to think of myself as living my life as a disciple and also as being a citizen," a Sioux Falls Habitat volunteer told us. "A good Christian can't be a bad citizen and a bad citizen can't be a good Christian," volunteered Ron Cioffi, founder of the New Jersey Pax Christi chapter. Yet the same people who told us that their sense of discipleship moved them to civic action, wax enthusiastic about how it was the paradenominational group, rather than the parish, that taught them how to put their faith into concrete action. A Bread for the World member in Albuquerque, N.M., told us, "I find more encouragement to exemplify my Christianity in Bread." A San Francisco Habitat executive catches the symbiosis between congregations and paradenominational groups: "Habitat is not a church but an outward sign of what we do and believe in the church." Precisely because of the widespread American taboo against introducing controversial political issues into the local congregation—even when they have religious and moral overtones—paradenominational groups serve local congregations by providing outlets for a social and public faith without dividing the congregation as such. Our respondents showed gratitude to their groups for providing them with a sense of efficacy, helping them "lean our weight on the side of an answer to chip away at a festering problem."

III. A CRITICAL PATRIOTISM

In our interviews we heard a litany of complaints about how our democratic process works or, often, doesn't work. Focus on the Family respondents lamented governmental encroachment on the family sphere, anti-family taxation and school policies. Many of them saw America as a post-Christian or pagan society. None of them wanted to impose a Christian hegemony on our pluralistic society, preferring what they called "winsome persuasion" to coercive measures. Pax Christi respondents focused their complaints on a culture of violence. Some in the Pax Christi sample (the Jesuit John Dear, for example) actually refuse, on principle, to vote since they think citizenship has been corrupted. Those we interviewed in Habitat lambasted the impersonality of government bureaucracy and the way the welfare state turns people into dependent clients. Like most Americans, our interviewees thought that government is mainly controlled by special interest groups that buy favors and dictate policy.

We specifically asked those we interviewed to tell us if they saw any tensions between discipleship and citizenship and, if so, where and how they might resolve them. Some readily pointed to consumerism, individualism and militarism as anti-Christian values. One Habitat informant exclaimed simply, "We are a nation in denial." Others could only entertain a hypothetical conflict. All, however, told us that in cases of real or imagined conflict between the two roles, they would want discipleship values to trump.

One major motif heard over and over again is caught in a Habitat volunteer's remark: "Especially as Americans we have such a huge chunk of the world's wealth. It's incumbent upon us to contribute to the rest of the world and help to lessen the disparity in wealth among countries." If I were critical, at all, of the conceptualization of citizenship we found in the interviews, it would be because of excessively localist, anti-Federalist sympathies and the relative blindness to the dangers posed to common citizenship not just from an over-regulatory state, but also from an untrammeled appeal to market metaphors.

Habitat especially needs to monitor what happens to its logic of a voluntary citizenship as more and more corporations send their executives to help build houses. We actually found some local executives debating the wisdom of dispensing with the volunteers, if that were the more cost-effective way to build houses! Clearly, respondents differed in their sense of the legitimate range and limits of governmental activity. Some—most strongly the Focus on the Family sample—would restrict the government to the barest minimum, night-watchman state. It is not that these Focus respondents were unfeeling toward the plight of the poor and the need for a safety net. They simply felt that the evangelical churches should get off their duffs to provide this safety net. We still need a national debate among citizens about just what is the legitimate range of governmental subsidiary aid to the institutions of civil society.

The bias toward localism was not unexpected. After all, Americans in poll data show that they trust government more the closer it lies to home, less when it is in the nation's capital. But when we asked those we interviewed about their citizenship, they told us, in the words of a Detroit Bread member, "We are citizens of the world and not just the United States." Millard Fuller, the founder of Habitat, echoes this theme. "I wear my citizenship in the United States very lightly because there is a citizenship greater than being a U.S. citizen. Jesus never had a U.S. passport. He was not a U.S. citizen, and I think my citizenship in the kingdom is infinitely more important than my citizenship in the United States."

Those who think that discipleship in the United States is reducible to a mere pallid civil religion of flag-waving would find precious little justification from our admittedly specialized sample of disciple-citizens. We found, instead, a healthy critical patriotism. Few were as eloquent as a Michigan grandmother, Helen Casey, of Pax Christi.

Casey puts her critical patriotism graphically. "If there are B-52s at Ritsmouth Air Force base equipped with nuclear weapons, and they are told to take off and go bomb some place, that's being done in my name, because it's a United States aircraft with United States soldiers on it and I'm a citizen of the United States. From that point of view, they are acting in my name. And I just wanted to state [through her civil disobedience at Ritsmouth] that I don't want to be any part of it. Not in my name. Don't do this in my name." Casey puts her critical patriotism in perspective. "My family, my sisters think I do nothing but criticize this country. Well, I always tell them, it's like you criticize your children, but that doesn't mean that you don't love them."

IV. RELIGIOUS LANGUAGE IN PUBLIC

The last issue I want to raise involves the appropriateness of using explicitly religious language in public citizenship activity. Some important American liberal philosophers—one thinks of the University of Nebraska philosopher, Robert Audi, and Harvard's John Rawls in his most recent book, *Political Liberalism*—have argued that religiously motivated people should engage in a species of what Audi calls "epistemic abstinence." In order to show equal respect for fellow citizens who are not believers, Audi argues, religious citizens, when addressing issues of public policy or supporting laws that coercively bind all citizens, should refrain from appeals to faith-based or sectarian language.

Audi goes so far as to state that it would be bad citizenship for a religious believer to vote for a religious rather than a secular reason. Audi articulates two principles of what he calls the duty of citizens: (1) the principle of secular rationalism states that "one should not advocate or support any law or public policy that restricts human conduct unless one has, and is willing to offer, adequate secular reason for this adequacy or support." (2) The principle of secular motivation states that one should be motivated by a secular rather than a religious reason when acting in one's capacity as a citizen.

The Nebraska philosopher thinks that most religious people also have secular motives. He seems to assume, too, that most religious reasons can be translated into secular accounts. Audi mainly bases his fear of religious argument on the anxiety that religion could be dangerously divisive in public. He remarks that "conflicting secular ideas, even when firmly held, can often be blended and harmonized in the crucible of free discussion; but a clash of gods is like a meeting of an irresistible force with an immovable object."

Several strong objections can be raised to this liberal case for gag rules on religious language in public. One points to the naive assumption that we can easily find secular warrants that will compel universal or large-scale assent in our pluralistic society. Another seems to be the rank injustice of arguing that religious people must give up their deepest selves, motivation and language whenever they enter the common arena of citizenship and be obliged to talk in someone else's language, motivation and motifs. Believers would be forced to pretend to be a kind of self they really are not.

For the disciple-citizens we interviewed, faith matters a great deal. They almost universally claim that it is the main motive-spring for their civic actions. Exclusive liberal philosophies that force the religiously devout to submit to gag rules before they will be allowed to act as legitimate citizens seem neither democratic nor liberal.

Especially when religion acts as a catalyst to bring into the public arena voters and citizens who heretofore have had no voice, it seems a cruel sort of equality to demand that believers must speak the philosopher's language before they have a right to speak at all. In our community organizing sample, religious language helped disenfranchised people to find courage and the voice to address their deepest citizenship concerns for the first time.

An Inclusive Liberalism

A much wiser way to deal with religious motivation and language swaying the actions of citizens would allow it access to the public arena without any demands that believers engage in some kind of "epistemic abstinence." Many of the people we interviewed knew very well how to employ more "secular" sounding language in the public when it seemed to them that the secular case (e.g., against nuclear weapons) would be likely to persuade more people. They also knew that almost every religious belief system accords some role to reason as an avenue toward truth. Religious believers, no less than secularists, hold an ideal of reason. Yet they may rightfully resent claims that they must remain silent about their more religious accounts.

A more inclusive liberalism might follow the advice of the university of Texas law professor, Sanford Levinson, who asks whether the search for criteria that would exclude certain types of discourse from the public square is misguided. Levinson appeals to a more inclusive liberalism when he puts the question this way: "Why doesn't liberal philosophy give everyone an equal right, without any version of engaging in epistemic abstinence, to make his or her arguments, subject to the prerogative of listeners to reject the arguments, should they be unpersuasive—which will be the case, almost by definition, with arguments that are not widely accessible or are otherwise marginal."

Ron Cioffi, during our Pax Christi interviews, reflected on the secular claims of some to exclude religious language from our common citizenship. His thoughtful response can conclude our reflections of discipleship-citizenship in America: "I can talk to them about the same values and the end-product in a language they would hopefully find more acceptable. And I would try to do that, and in the process I would also probably invite them to reflect on what it is about faith that nettles them so. And [I would argue] that whether one wishes to exclude all faith language in a secular setting or not, that faith language is indeed a reality in the lives of many people; and that it's better to face and deal with that dimension of reality than it is to try to hide it away, or ignore it, or try to suppress it. [I would oppose this gag rule] because it wars against my conception of who I am as a human person with God-given dignity and the right to speak and the right to share my vision. Not to force it, on others, but to share it with others, and at least to put it out there for consideration. While I could say I can speak in a secular way and be an advocate for reform and that kind of thing, it would be a sorrow to do that, because I would not be celebrating the depth and the richness from which my conviction grows and which is nourished every day."

16

THE PUBLIC LIFE AND
WITNESS OF THE CHURCH

Joseph Cardinal Bernardin

Let me begin by expressing my appreciation to Georgetown University, and particularly to Father Leo O'Donovan, president of this university, for inviting me to return here to reflect upon the public life and witness of the Catholic Church in the context of U.S. society and culture. Each time I have come to Georgetown, it has been in a Presidential election year, but I regard that as a secondary consideration. The church must reflect continuously on its public witness. That witness is rooted in religious and moral convictions, so the reflection must be theological in its foundation and then related to the issues of policy that shape the life of our society.

This afternoon, I seek to provide a "broad" interpretation of the church's public witness. It will be broad in two senses: First, I will address three large areas of intersection between the Catholic moral vision and U.S. society: 1) religion and politics, 2) economic choices and social justice and 3) the sanctity of life and U.S. culture. Second, in each area—politics, economics and culture—I propose to look not only at how Catholic teaching speaks to American society, but how these issues should be reflected upon in the internal life of the church itself.

Building upon the premise that theological principles should ground our thinking about the church's public life, I will rely principally upon a major teaching document for each area of my address, using the Second Vatican Council's "Declaration on Religious Liberty" for religion and politics, the U.S. Catholic bishops' pastoral letter *Economic*

Justice for All for justice and the economy, and Pope John Paul II's *The Gospel of Life* to address life and culture.

I. Religion and Politics: The American Style

The relationship of religion and politics is as old as the U.S. constitutional tradition. The nation was founded in great part by those who had experienced religious discrimination or who were wary of any close connection of religion and politics. Religious pluralism has been for this nation both a factual condition and a constitutionally protected characteristic of the society almost from its inception. Precisely because of its centrality to the U.S. political tradition, the issue of religion and politics requires constant intellectual attention.

Commentators have often noted an apparent paradox: Religion is kept strictly separate from the institution of the state, yet the U.S. public overwhelmingly thinks of itself as a religious people, with a very high percentage consistently affirming their religious convictions. The paradox is apparent because an argument can be made that careful distinction between religion and politics may be in fact our source of religious vitality. I suggest we think of the role of religion in our society in terms of three questions: church and state, church and civil society, and finally, religion and politics.

Separating Church and State

The church-state question is the central structural element in understanding the role of religion in U.S. society. For all its centrality, however, it is actually a quite limited issue. It is best, I think, to try to keep it both limited in its significance and clear in its content.

The church-state relationship governs how the institution of the state will relate to religiously based institutions in our society. To discuss, debate, or analyze church and state is not at all to engage the full range of religious conviction, commitment and engagement in our society. The church-state relationship is narrow, juridical and institutional in character. Governed by the First Amendment to the U.S. Constitution, it essentially affirms that religious communities should expect neither special assistance from the state nor any discrimination in the exercise of their civil and religious activity in society. This description of the meaning of the First Amendment does not attempt to exegete the court decisions that address specific dimensions of the law. It is, rather, a political interpretation of this standard element of our constitutional life.

From the perspective of Catholic teaching, embodied in the "Declaration on Religious Liberty," the political meaning of the First Amend-

ment is good law. It protects what the Second Vatican Council and
Pope Paul VI asserted was the basic requirement of church-state relations in any culture: the freedom of the church. Keeping secular and
religious institutions distinct in purpose and function, in fact, creates
space for the church to teach, preach and serve. Having the freedom
to function guaranteed by law allows the church—and any religious
community in this society—to define its ministry, pursue its religious
and civil objectives and demonstrate the transforming power of faith,
love and grace in society.

It is precisely when the church-state relations are clearly defined
in law that the second dimension of the role of religion in society becomes centrally important. The relationships, networks, institutions
and associations that lie "beyond the state" are neither created by the
state nor are they controlled by the state. The concept of civil society is
captured in the distinction between state and society that is pivotal in
the Western liberal tradition of politics and that both Jacques Maritain
and John Courtney Murray, s.j., used in building the case within
Catholicism for the right of religious liberty.

Engagement in Civil Society

Both external and internal events in the United States have refo-
cused scholarly attention and policy debates about the role and function of civil society. The collapse of Communism in Central Europe
and the former Soviet Union has yielded proposals from the West on
how "to shrink" the state and build the fabric of civil society. At the
same time, troubling trends in the United States on issues as diverse
as family life, education, citizen participation and general standards
of civility have concentrated attention on the quality and character of
our own civil society.

It is in the fabric of civil society that religious communities and institutions flourish. In terms of the U.S. political tradition, it is crucially
important to stress that the logic of church-state relations, which lays
stress on legitimate separation of secular and sacral institutions, should
not govern the logic of civil society. The logic of this relationship is *engagement*, not separation. In other words, to endorse a properly secular state, which has no established ties to any religious institution, does
not imply or mean that we should support a secularized society, one
in which religion is reduced to a purely private role.

Both Catholic social theory and U.S. constitutional principles support a substantive role and place for religion in the fabric of our society

and culture. The state will not and should not be the agent for advancing a substantive conception of religious values and principles in the life of the nation, but the state should not be hostile to the enterprise. Precisely because of the pervasive role of religious convictions among the citizens of our society, there is a legitimate place in our national life for these convictions to find expression.

Civil society is a sphere of freedom; it provides political and legal space for a multiplicity of actors and institutions to help form and shape the fabric of our national life and culture. In this sphere of freedom, religious institutions can exercise the full range of their ministries of teaching and service. Religious witness will only be as effective and as persuasive as the religious communities render it through the lives and work of their leaders and members. This is the meaning of being "free to function." We can demand this right, then we must meet our responsibilities.

While the constitutional framework that generates our place in civil society is clear enough, it is also clear that one finds in the debate about civil society today some voices that are less than comfortable with a vigorous role for religious institutions in our public life and policy debates. This may in part be due to the way some religious witness is undertaken. But it is also the case that some versions of civil society advance the logic of separation to the point where the public life of our society would lose its religious content.

If this happened, I submit, we would be a poorer culture and society. There is clearly no place for religious coercion or proselytism in our public life, but there is a broad area in which religious ideas and institutions can contribute to issues as diverse as strengthening the family, humanizing the drive of economic competition and defining our responsibilities as a nation in a very changed world.

Vision, Ministry and Citizenship

To those who are skeptical or simply opposed to a public role for religion, and to the community of believers upon whom lies the responsibility for religious witness, I submit there are three ways in which religious traditions can enrich civil society. The first is through religious vision and discourse. The Hebrew Scriptures tell us that, where there is no vision, people perish. A constant responsibility of religious communities is to enrich our public vision through the resources of ideas, values, principles and images that are the core of any great tradition.

In the Catholic tradition, I have tried to take the theme of the sacredness of the human person and develop its implications through a "consistent ethic" of life. The ideas supporting the consistent ethic have been cultivated in the Catholic moral tradition for centuries. But a convergence of forces arising from contemporary society threatens the sacredness of human life and creates a new context in which the ancient themes of an ethic of stewardship of life take on new relevance. Essentially, I have argued that we must systematically address a series of threats to life by building within civil society a shared vision of what human sacredness demands and how we install binding principles of restraint and respect in our personal codes of conduct and in our public policies.

The theme of a consistent ethic is only one way in which a religious tradition can enrich our public dialogue. I realize that part of the apprehension of some citizens, scholars and analysts is that religious convictions that are not universally shared will be thrust into our policy debates. I understand the concern, and I will return to it, but here I simply want to establish the point that a policy of *excluding* religious vision, discourse and insights from our search for coherent, just, viable public policies is a price too high to pay. Without vision, people perish; we need all the resources we can muster today in developing an adequate vision for our society.

But religion is not exhausted by ideas and vision alone. A second crucial contribution it can make to civil society is through the ministry and work of religious institutions of education, health care, family service and direct outreach to the poorest parts of our society. The web of religious institutions is a pervasive aspect of our social support system. I believe it is the time to think intensively about how a more extensive public-private pattern of collaboration could serve to extend the range of effectiveness of these institutions and at the same time use scarce public resources more efficiently in support of human needs.

Thirdly, perhaps the most effective, long-term contribution that religious communities make to civil society is the kind of citizens who are shaped, often decisively, by participation in a religious tradition. In Christian terms this is the link between discipleship and citizenship. Recent research, reflected in the work of Robert Putnam at Harvard University, as well as that of Jesuits John Coleman (see *America* 5/11) and David Hollenbach in the Catholic community, points to the way in which religious affiliation has a decisive impact on the kind of civic engagement of individuals, particularly engagement in the service of others.

In summary, my argument thus far has been in support of clear distinctions between church and state, in opposition to any exclusion of religion from civil society and in advocacy of a broad, deep, activist role for religious institutions in shaping our public life.

A Question of Style

There is a final piece of this argument, this one directed to the religious communities rather than civil society: the theme of religion and politics. My point here is that a proper understanding of both the logic of separation (church and state) and the logic of engagement (church and civil society) locates the church in the proper place for public witness. *How* religion engages the political order is a question of style, and style here carries major importance. Style refers to the way religious communities speak to the political process, and style also refers to the manner in which we engage others in debate and discussion.

One reason why some have apprehension about religious involvement in public life is the style sometimes employed by religious institutions or communities. My proposal, therefore, is that effective religious witness depends, in part, on our style of participation. Engagement in civil society must be characterized by commitment and civility; witness must be a blend of advocacy and restraint. I am hardly pressing for a timid or feeble religious voice! My concern, rather, is to establish from within religious communities standards of participation that will shape our public witness.

Allow me to use two examples. First, while I know there is a healthy debate on this topic among scholars, I am inclined to the view that our style of arguing a social position ought to distinguish among how we speak within the church, how we participate in civil society and how we address the state on law and policy. Within the church, the full range of biblical, theological themes that structure our belief should be used.

Within civil society, I also think that explicit appeal to religious warrants and imperatives is both legitimate and needed if we are to address some of the profoundly human themes that are at the heart of our policy debates. But when we address the state, I believe we should be ascetic in our use of explicitly religious appeals. Here we seek to shape law and policy that will obligate all in society. At this point we accept the responsibility of making our religiously grounded convictions intelligible to those who do not share the faith that yields these convictions.

Secondly, our style of religious witness should constantly be a testimony to the theological virtue of charity, which, in turn, produces the civic virtue of civility. Vigorous pursuit of our deepest convictions—even those involving life and death—should not involve questioning the motives of others, or their character. We should vigorously oppose conclusions we find unwise or immoral; we should vigorously pursue objectives that are essential for human life and dignity. But we should also be known for the way in which our witness leavens public life with a spirit of fairness, respect, restraint and a search for common ground among contending positions. As you know, I have recently called for a Catholic Common Ground Project, a process of conversation and collaboration on issues that divide us within the Catholic Church. I do so not only because I believe we need such an initiative to enhance our own community but also because I believe that the style of our internal life is part of our public witness and contribution.

II. JUSTICE AND THE ECONOMY: A CATHOLIC PERSPECTIVE

One example of public religious witness, which attracted much attention a decade ago, was the pastoral letter on the U.S. economy, *Economic Justice for All.* The 10th anniversary of the letter is being observed by a series of symposia, commemorations and efforts to reflect upon what the pastoral letter's teaching on justice says to us in the new condition of the 1990s. Since its publication 10 years ago, the U.S. economy has continued to experience deep and far-reaching change generated by broader global patterns of economic interdependence.

As bishops, we came to see in the 1980s that it was virtually impossible to isolate the U.S. economy for analysis apart from the global economy. Today that truth is even more evident. Obviously many aspects of our economic life are quite positive: We are in a period of sustained economic growth, the competitiveness of American workers and industry has been demonstrated convincingly, the unemployment statistics are modest if not satisfactory, and inflation has been contained.

These "macro" indicators of our economic life are crucially important, but they do not address crucial moral questions that must be part of our assessment of U.S. economic life. While we have demonstrated our ability to compete internationally, not all in our nation have survived the competition. Economic dislocation, downsizing of major industries and loss of jobs, threats to familial and personal economic security are experiences all too well known by significant sectors of our population. The dynamic of the global market does not address the human costs of global competition either here or in other countries. The dynamic of the market must be complemented by a broader framework of social policy that attends to the needs of those who lose in the economic lottery.

The pastoral letter *Economic Justice for All* sought to focus the attention of both church and civil society on those whom our economic life has left out, left behind and left alone. Catholic social and economic teaching is always concerned for the welfare of society as a whole and for the human dignity and human rights of each person; this systemic concern is exemplified in the concept of the common good. Within the context of a concern for all, however, there is a basic obligation to attend to the needs of the vulnerable—old or young, black or white, male or female. This is the religious mandate specified by the Hebrew prophets' call to protect "the orphans, the widows and the resident aliens." It is the contemporary theme in Catholic teaching embodied in "the option for the poor."

The striking fact is how accurately the prophets of 2,700 years ago speak to our life today: Secular sources of analysis identify women and children as the most vulnerable groups in our society. Recent legislation—at the state and national level—effectively eliminates basic social support and services for "resident aliens" in our midst, whether they are legal or undocumented immigrants in our society. While pertinent legal distinctions exist among these two groups, the moral tradition of the prophets affirms moral obligations that we have to both, and uniquely to their children. The voices of the prophets are too accurate for us to be satisfied by "macro" indicators of economic health. The poor are still with us, and there is nothing in the Hebrew and Christian Scriptures that tolerates complacency about their needs.

Health Care and Welfare

Two of our major socio-economic policy debates of the 1990s should make us think deeply about our societal contract, or conception of moral obligation among the citizens of this nation. Both the health-care debate of the early 1990s and the welfare debate of this past year point to deeper issues than either health or welfare policy. The health-care debate, large and complex as it was, contained a core element of the need to extend the social safety net to the 40 million citizens without basic coverage. The welfare debate, also complex in its elements, forced to the surface the question of whether any social safety net would be preserved at all. I should be clear: In highlighting the complexity of both policy issues, I acknowledge that health-care policy must address the exponential increase in health-care costs, the need to restructure parts of our delivery system and the need to strike a balance between competing objectives of quality of care and the kinds of care provided in the health-care system. I also acknowledge that reform of the welfare system is required for the good of all concerned: recipients, taxpayers and providers.

Even with these considerations squarely before us, however, both of the extended policy debates on these issues, in my view, failed to meet basic standards of responsible policy. The leading industrial democracy in the world failed to extend a minimum standard of health care to its citizenry as a whole, and it has effectively dismantled the most basic protection for children in our society. Both the prophets and the pastoral letter stand in judgment of these actions. If this society cannot protect its most vulnerable—our sick and our children—it must be because we cannot think and speak clearly to each other about fundamental moral imperatives. Even in a deficit-driven economic debate, the fate of the sick and the young hold primacy of moral standing. Yes, we have "changed" health care and welfare. But from the perspective of those for whom we bear moral responsibility, change does not equal reform. It looks more like abandonment.

The deeper issues behind health care and welfare involve not only our societal compact with each other; they also involve allocation of responsibility for social policy that meets both the standards of effectiveness and justice. On an age of issues—social policy, tax policy, the stability of families, the cultivation of key values in personal and public life—I fear we are carrying on fundamental debates in a style that does not match in depth the substance of the issues addressed.

Moral Role of the State

Running through most of our social policy debates is the discussion of the appropriate role of the state in our common life as a society. Catholic social thought is hardly statist in its premises or principles. The concept of "subsidiarity," a staple of Catholic social theory, explicitly requires that responses to social needs not start with the state. But subsidiarity does not yield a conception of the state that removes from it basic moral obligations not only for the general welfare but also specific moral duties toward those afflicted by illness, hardship, unemployment and the lack of adequate nutrition and housing.

My point is that it is not sufficient to carry on a discussion of the appropriate role of the state purely in terms of efficiency or size or "intrusiveness." These criteria are important but not significant if we omit a conception of what the state's moral role is in society. To speak of the state's moral role is not only to address the cultivation of moral standards; it also involves specific duties, often of a socioeconomic nature, which the state has to its citizens.

Critics of this position will say I am making an abstract argument about the state's responsibility without acknowledging that the state does not generate the resources for its socio-economic policies and programs; citizens do that. The critics are partially right; we cannot discuss the moral obligations of the state apart from a substantive analysis of the obligations we have to each other as members of civil society. To the critics I will grant the point, because I am convinced the deeper issue beneath our policy debates is precisely this question: how we conceive of our social bonds of obligation and responsibility, within families, beyond families to neighborhoods and ultimately to the national community of which we are a part.

A purely contractual view of our relationships is inadequate; it quickly reduces our obligations to those freely chosen, with no wider fabric of accountability. Contractual relations serve useful, limited functions, but we need a stronger fabric of social ties to undergird our life as a society. We require a sense of obligation to those we do not know, will never meet and yet bear a responsibility for, precisely because of their need and our capacity to share in meeting that need.

There are many ways to express this stronger sense of social responsibility; John Paul II and the pastoral letter rely on the concept of "solidarity." Solidarity implies a fabric of moral bonds that exists among humans because of a shared sense of personhood. Solidarity precedes subsidiarity. The first defines our moral relationship; the second regulates how we will fulfill the duty of solidarity. Social solidarity finds expression in several ways. It sustains personal relationships; it binds families in a common life of love and support; it initiates and supports private efforts of charity and social service. But it also helps to define the moral responsibility of the state and its citizenry.

Solidarity points toward the neuralgic issue of U.S. politics—taxation. Taxes are one way in which the state facilitates our responsibilities to each other. Tax policy is a secular issue, but it is rooted in moral obligations we have to one another. A fair tax policy, one which obliges each of us to play a role in sustaining the human dignity of all in our society, is a requirement of distributive justice. In Catholic teaching, paying taxes is a virtue. Taxes help us to meet our pre-existing obligations to the poor.

Public-Private Collaboration

In addition to establishing the basis for a just tax policy, Catholic teaching, I believe, has something critical to say to our contemporary debate about institutional responsibility and social policy. Over the last 60 years, three key ideas have characterized Catholic social teaching: subsidiarity, solidarity and socialization. They need to be held in tandem. Solidarity establishes the basis of common obligation; subsidiarity argues that private voluntary institutions are needed to fulfill our obligation, and socialization maintains that increased societal interdependence requires an activist state to meet the needs that private institutions cannot meet alone. I spoke earlier about the need for new patterns of public-private collaboration. To address the deeper issues of our social policy debate, we need to attend to these three concepts. We do have moral obligations to the vulnerable. So we should have an adequate public policy to guarantee that the orphans, the widows and the resident aliens are not left to the ravages of life.

As we seek to contribute to the societal debate about allocation of social responsibility, the role of our own social institutions becomes a crucial part of our public witness. Catholic schools, Catholic health-care systems and Catholic charities testify to our conviction that we have abiding social responsibilities. We live in a time of declining public resources and exploding public needs. Our institutions should not be used as an example that we do not need public engagement to meet social needs. But as we argue for a strong fabric of social programs to meet human needs, our institutions can seek to demonstrate the quality of care for human life which a vision of human sacredness cultivates.

Precisely because we already support a broad range of social institutions, and because we are also committed in principle to an active if limited role for the state, the Catholic community should be a creative and articulate participant in the much-needed debate in this society about the comparative advantage that public institutions of the state have on some aspects of social policy and the severe liabilities they have on other issues. Seeking a new relationship of public and private agencies in our society is an imperative of the first order. Such a discussion involves constitutional issues of church and state, societal issues of how best to structure civil society and empirical issues of operational effectiveness. It is a far-reaching argument, but it must be undertaken because today too many suffer from the lack of an effective and humane policy vision.

III. THE SACREDNESS OF LIFE:
RELIGION, CULTURE AND POLITICS

In this concluding section I return to the concept of the consistent ethic. Thus far in addressing religion and politics, justice and economics,

I have sought to reflect upon how we care for life in our midst, both personally and through public policy. Caring for life, supporting it and responding to basic human needs of nutrition, health, housing and education is an essential aspect of the consistent ethic. As I have indicated, I believe we have yet a substantial way to go in caring for the lives of the least among us. But in the contemporary U.S. context, caring for life does not exhaust our moral obligations. We now face in the 1990s profoundly threatening public issues where life is being taken without moral justification.

In proposing the consistent ethic over a decade ago, my purpose was to help create a dialogue about the full range of threats to life which modern society poses. I recognize the difference between the obligation of caring for life and that of defending life against attack. I recognize that the moral failure to care for life adequately is different from the moral crime of taking an innocent life. But I was convinced— and still am firmly convinced—that the overriding moral need in our society is to cultivate a conviction that we must face all the major threats to life, not only one or two. The consistent ethic precisely seeks to relate our moral analysis about different kinds of moral problems. It seeks to provide a framework within which individuals and groups, who begin with a concern for one moral dimension of life, can be brought to see the threat posed by other issues in our societies.

When we shift our focus in U.S. society from thinking about *caring* for life to *defending* life, there is hardly a better guide than Pope John Paul II's encyclical, *The Gospel of Life*. The Holy Father identified three issues—abortion, capital punishment and euthanasia—in his sweeping critique of what he described as a creeping "culture of death." Here again, even within the Catholic tradition these three issues have not been simply collapsed into one question. Capital punishment has not in the past been regarded as unjust killing in the way abortion and euthanasia have been. But the power of the papal argument is that it helps us to see that, today, different kinds of taking life should be systematically related. Faced with a need to build a societal consensus that respects life, Catholic teaching has clearly moved to restrict the state's right to take life, even in instances previously approved.

Capital Punishment, Abortion and Assisted Suicide

There is an inner logic to an ethic that respects life and a contrary logic in quick, frequent resort to solving problems by taking life. While not seeking to simplify complex human problems, I suggest we think carefully about our society, which annually sustains 1.5 million abortions, which is overwhelmingly in favor of capital punishment and which is now moving rapidly toward acceptance of assisted suicide. Each of these problems must be argued on its own terms. There are clearly distinctions among positions held across this spectrum of issues, but there is also a truth to be learned in relating these three questions. The truth is that respect for life will cost us something. To move beyond solutions to problems by taking life will require a more expansive care for life—at its beginning and its end.

I cannot plunge at this point into a detailed assessment of these three issues in our public life. But I do think that relating the experience we have had on abortion to the current debate about assisted suicide can be helpful. Once again, the deeper themes behind the specific choices are the most important ones. In both the abortion and the assisted-suicide debates, I am convinced that the basic picture one has of the social fabric of life is crucial to how one makes a moral judgment on the specific issues.

The abortion debate has been publicly framed as a "private choice." In both public debate and recent judicial decisions, assisted suicide has been argued in similarly "private" terms. Such a construction of these questions promotes the idea that social consequences are lacking in both cases. I am convinced that such a view is profoundly short-sighted.

To use assisted suicide as an example: It is undoubtedly a deeply personal issue because it touches upon life and death and a person's conception of whom they are accountable to in life and death. But it also directly affects the doctor-patient relationship and, through that, the wider role of doctors in our society. As has been noted by others, it threatens to introduce a deep ambiguity into the very definition of medical care, if care comes to involve killing. Beyond the physician, a move to assisted suicide and, perhaps beyond that, to euthanasia creates social ambiguity about the law. In civilized society the law exists to protect life. When it also begins to legitimate the taking of life as a policy, one has a right to ask what lies ahead for our life together as a society. There are deep psychological, social and moral questions at stake in how we conceive our social relationship to each other and particularly to the most vulnerable in our society—again the very young and the very sick become test cases.

After two decades of struggle over abortion, our society and our church now face a double challenge to *defend* life even as we continue to pursue ways to *care for* and *nurture* it. I remain convinced that our witness will be more effective, more persuasive and better equipped to address the moral challenge we face, if we witness to life across the spectrum of life from conception until natural death, calling our society to see the connection between caring for life and defending it.

Here again, there are implications for the internal life of the church. It is urgently necessary that we remain a voice for life—vigorous, strong, consistent. In the recent case of partial-birth abortion, the protest raised from within our church and by others was absolutely necessary. The procedure should not be allowed; it should have been stopped. There will undoubtedly be other cases, at both ends of life, when our voice, our advocacy, our legitimate efforts will be needed. But we also must continue to witness by deed to a conception of caring for life that seeks to invite the wider society to see the linkage between care for and defense of life. So I commend those who have been organized in support of single mothers, those who seek to provide a place for pregnant women of all ages to receive support and care, those who sponsor and serve in health care facilities and programs that care for the dying and sustain hope even in the face of a long, painful dying process. These efforts from within the church are essential to match the public witness of the church in society.

IV. Conclusion

As you are well aware, this has been a long lecture. In bringing it to a close, I will consciously change its tone and tenor. When I accepted Father O'Donovan's invitation, I undertook the assignment of giving a policy lecture suited for an academic audience. I have tried to fulfill that task. But I also thought at the time of the invitation that I would likely have several opportunities to contribute to the U.S. debate on religion and our public life, on the moral values of human dignity and the sacredness of human life.

As you are aware, I now face a very different horizon. In human terms, I have been advised my life span is now quite limited. This fact does not change any of the moral or social analysis that I have used in this address. But it does shape one perspective decisively. I have already said that, as a person of faith—of resurrection faith—I see death as a friend, not a foe; and the experience of death is, I am convinced, a transition from life to life—from grace to glory, as St. Augustine said.

These are my deepest convictions of faith, which has been rooted in God's word and confirmed by the sacraments of the church. But the experience I am now going through sheds new light on the moral order also. As a bishop I have tried, in season and out of season, to shape and share a moral message about the unique value of human life and our common responsibilities for it. As my life now slowly ebbs away, as my temporal destiny becomes clearer each hour and each day, I am not anxious, but rather reconfirmed in my conviction about the wonder of human life, a gift that flows from the very being of God and is entrusted to each of us. It is easy in the rush of daily life or in its tedium to lose the sense of wonder that is appropriate to this gift. It is even easier at the level of our societal relations to count some lives as less valuable than others, especially when caring for them costs us—financially, emotionally, or in terms of time, effort and struggle.

The truth is, of course, that each life is of infinite value. Protecting and promoting life—caring for it and defending it—is a complex task in social and policy terms. I have struggled with the specifics often and have sensed the limits of reason in the struggle to know the good and do the right. My final hope is that my efforts have been faithful to the truth of the Gospel of life and that you and others like you will find in this Gospel the vision and strength needed to promote and nurture the great gift of life God has shared with us.

17

"Economic Justice for All": Ten Years Later

Archbishop Rembert G. Weakland

In the Catholic tradition, anniversaries are meant to help us recapture the thrust of the events of the past and the spirit that animated them, to re-enkindle the same enthusiasm in us now, and then to assist us in projecting those same insights into the future. That so many celebrations have taken place this year on the 10th anniversary of the pastoral letter by the American bishops, *Economic Justice for All* (November 1986), is significant. The peace pastoral that preceded it was most important in its time, but on its 10th anniversary it engendered less interest since the threat of a nuclear buildup appears to be behind us. The economic pastoral, on the other hand, confronted issues less restricted to the times in which it was written and so seems to be even more important than 10 years ago. The situations that gave birth to it then have changed character somewhat but have not disappeared. Revisiting that letter 10 years later, therefore, has special importance.

I would like, first of all, to present some preliminary reflections about the letter. Then, under four distinct headings, I will proceed to ask myself what has changed in the world situation that would alter significantly the content of, or the approach to, the letter if it were to be rewritten now. In other words, I ask myself: What new emphases would be needed because of new situations? Although one could say that the principles of Catholic social doctrine do not change, nevertheless they are constantly being refined as they face ever-new situations. Thus, I would also ask myself what kinds of refinement would be needed now in that teaching that perhaps were not as necessary 10 years ago.

Preliminary Observations

The procedure for writing the two pastoral letters of the early 1980s was unique. The numerous hearings that preceded the first drafts brought many actors into play. That procedure gave breadth and scope to the letter that it could not have otherwise obtained. For an issue so complex the consultative process was most helpful. One of its finest features was also its ecumenical and interfaith dimension. Although the time commitment for bishops involved was extensive, I can personally confess it was well worthwhile. Some opposition came to that procedure from certain church quarters; namely, the fear was expressed that it could give the impression that the bishops were deficient in their knowledge of social justice and thus that their teaching authority would be diminished.

There is no reason to believe that the consultations gave that negative impression. On the contrary, most applauded the bishops for such openness and for listening to so many divergent views. If the letter were to be rewritten today, I am not sure that such a procedure would be engaged in. The energy might be lacking, as well as the enthusiasm and support on the part of all the bishops that was so essential to the undertaking. Yet the procedure itself used for both the peace pastoral and the economic pastoral letter remains one of the major contributions of the two letters to the process of church teaching.

The chief criticism against the letter from a pastoral point of view was that it was far too long. That criticism was valid in our society then and would be even more true now. It is clear to me now that we really tried to write three letters at one time and that it became totally unwieldy. We should have written a first letter that dealt only with the principles of social justice from a biblical and natural-law point of view. A second letter could have followed with examples of how those principles could be applied to several distinct areas. A third would have discussed the demands of the Gospel and social justice on our Christian lifestyle, including both the responses that the individual Christian as well as the church should give to the present economic situation.

We simply tried to do too much by including all these aspects in one letter. If we were to redo the letter today, I would suggest a series of at least three or even perhaps four letters, the last being a discussion of some of the alternative ways of looking at the present economic system, namely, an enlargement of the theme of cooperation found in Chapter Four of the original letter, a section that seems to have been forgotten in the discussion that followed.

If the letter were to be rewritten today, I feel certain that we would also have a different set of applications. As you might recall, the four sections of applications were: 1) Employment, 2) Poverty, 3) Food and Agriculture and 4) The U.S. Economy and the Developing Nations. We would probably go back to our original idea of doing something on natural resources and ecology and not on the more restrictive question of agriculture.

Some criticized the bishops for the sections dealing with the application of the principles, asserting that it would have been better if they had given only the principles and had left the application up to the experts in the field. As I see it now, I believe that the application sections were most important. The history of our Catholic teaching on social justice shows that it became more and more refined precisely through the attempts at application. Catholic social doctrine has not been at a standstill for these last 100 years. As different problems arose, it was necessary to delve more deeply into one or the other of the basic principles, thus increasing our knowledge and understanding of them. The teaching has grown and become more refined, I repeat, precisely because there were attempts to apply it to different problems at different periods of time.

For example, subsidiarity became an important way of looking at the relationship between government and economic initiative in Pius XI's encyclical *Quadragesimo Anno* (1931), but today the application of the principle of subsidiarity might be different and more refined because of our present circumstances and because it has become a commonly cited principle, with a different twist, outside of the Catholic tradition.

After these preliminary remarks, I would like to take up issues that I believe would change the character of the letter if it were written 10 years later. I would like to name and discuss some events that have occurred and how they would affect the discussion today. I would also like to mention shifts in attitudes that would have to be faced by the bishops.

I have grouped these reflections under the following four titles: 1) the fall of Communism and the reflection on church social doctrine since then, 2) the globalization of the economy, 3) the antigovernment sentiments in our American society and 4) domestic trends in the economy that are affecting American society as well as the world.

The Fall of Communism and Catholic Social Doctrine

Perhaps the most important event in the world in the last 10 years, i.e., since the economic pastoral letter was published in 1986, was the fall of Communism. Ten years ago the economic alternative of Communism was still much alive and, as an alternative that was attractive especially to third world nations, had to be reckoned with. Foreseeing this new situation, Pope John Paul II had written in 1991 that "it is unacceptable to say that the defeat of so-called 'Real Socialism' leaves capitalism as the only model of economic organization" (*Centesimus Annus,* No. 35).

Still, free-market proponents have assumed that the free-market system triumphed because of its inherent virtues. This single system now dominates the world. Even China has made an attempt to accommodate to it and enter world economic markets. Pope John Paul II pointed out that the fall of Marxism did not mean that the realities of marginalization and exploitation would disappear. In a prescient fashion he wrote, "Indeed, there is a risk that a radical capitalistic ideology could spread which refuses even to consider these problems, in the *a priori* belief that any attempt to solve them is doomed to failure, and which blindly entrusts their solution to the free development of market forces" (*C.A.,* No. 42).

Some had hoped that the fall of Communism would liberate economists to be more critical of the failures and problems of capitalism and free-market economic structures. Previously, any critique of capitalism was seen as support for Communist or socialist thinking. Unfortunately, openness to critique free-market economic structures has not come about as expected. It is now just taken for granted by many that capitalism won; therefore, the system itself must be fine.

For us who are concerned about the inner life of the Catholic Church this demise of Communism has had another repercussion that has become more and more visible in the last few years. There has been a definite weakening of interest in liberation theology. There seems to be no consistent voice from Latin America now advocating positions that 10 years ago were very strong.

Political changes in countries like El Salvador, Nicaragua and Guatemala have modified the concerns within the church in those countries as well. The challenges now being faced in Latin America deal with the pastoral question of the new religious movements, more evangelical in character and more inclined to promise their adherents the same prosperity as found in their American origins.

The question must be asked if liberation theology has spun itself out and if we are entering a new situation in those countries. In spite of Michael Budde's thesis that Latin America will remain very anti-capitalist and pose the vexing problem of a divided church, a capitalist one in the North and an anti-capitalist one in the South, it is not clear that this anti-capitalistic trend will continue in Latin America. I sense that, in spite of what the theologians have written about the popular church, the people in those countries want what people everywhere in the world want, namely, a higher standard of living like that which they believe is found in the United States.

The concept of a popular church that would be at odds with the official church does not seem to me to be a serious development that will now gain ground. The expansion of secularism seems to be the more likely threat as these nations come more and more into contact with our consumer culture. The fall of Communism affected not just the basis of sociological analysis that was used by some liberation theologians but seems to have taken the wind out of the sails of those predicting a church of the poor that would be more communitarian in character.

Perhaps the error of the liberation theologians was to propose as a biblical ideal a church of the poor when most people want to live at the same basic economic level as the rest of the developed world. Just as Americans vote by their pocketbook and not their religious convictions, so others seek most of all what they believe will raise their economic standards.

It is also clear that Pope John Paul II and others have given up any talk about a "third economic way." Just as Chapter Four of *Economic Justice for All* has been forgotten, so also any other alternatives, other than various combinations of a mixed economy, have not prevailed. The economic situation is so complicated with its global implications that alternatives do not seem feasible. One is just happy to get some light on the present rapidly changing picture.

RECENT PAPAL ENCYCLICALS

In these 10 years the teaching on economic justice has not been absent as could be seen by the passages quoted from Pope John Paul II's encyclicals. If the economic pastoral were to be rewritten today, the authors would have to examine carefully the two encyclicals that appeared in the meantime, *Sollicitudo Rei Socialis* at the end of 1987 to commemorate the 20th anniversary of Pope Paul's encyclical *Populo-*

rum Progressio (1967), and *Centesimus Annus* from 1991 to commemorate the 100th anniversary of Pope Leo XIII's *Rerum Novarum* (1891).

The difference in tone between these two encyclicals would pose an interesting exercise for drafters of a new pastoral letter. The first encyclical, you will notice, was written before the Communist bloc began to open up, the second after. The first has a sharper tone, similar to the encyclical of Pope Paul VI that it commemorated; the latter is more concerned about the fall of Communism, how it happened, why it happened and what could come after that fall.

Since the former dealt more with development of nations and was more concerned about the poorer nations, it tended to be more critical of present situations. The latter is more cautious, less clear and less challenging. Some feel that it tends to be more ambivalent and thus has lent itself to so many different interpretations. Proponents of free-market economy co-opted it at once, saw it as a victory for their position and attempted to interpret it to suit their own interests.

The Pope seems to have been aware of this confusion, somewhat irritated by the feeling that his document had been co-opted, and he tried to give his own spin to his own work in the famous speech at the University of Latvia on Sept. 9, 1993 (text in *Origins*, 23, pp. 256–8). He said in that academic milieu:

> Besides, Catholic social doctrine is not a surrogate for capitalism. In fact, although decisively condemning "socialism," the church, since Leo XIII's *Rerum Novarum*, has always distanced itself from capitalistic ideology, holding it responsible for grave social injustices (see *R.N.*, No. 2). In *Quadragesimo Anno* Pius XI, for his part, used clear and strong words to stigmatize the international imperialism of money (*Q.A.*, No. 109). This line is also confirmed in the more recent magisterium, and I myself, after the historical failure of Communism, did not hesitate to raise serious doubts on the validity of capitalism, if by this expression one means not simply the "market economy" but "a system in which freedom in the economic sector is not circumscribed within a strong juridical framework which places it at the service of human freedom in its totality" (*C.A.*, No. 42).

In any case, one would have to say that *Centesimus Annus* is a remarkable document because it reverses some of the earlier teaching of the popes in their condemnations of democratic political processes and because it approves of a kind of free-market system that meets certain criteria. It also seems to approve of the reforms of the welfare states that were in progress at that time in Europe, much to the pleasure of so many conservative economists and politicians. The letter is an important one, not because it breaks new ground, but because it gives a clear reflection of the reasons for the fall of Communism and some caveats about the capitalist system that alone rules now in the world. I am afraid, however, that it will not have the significance of some of the other encyclicals on social justice, because it is tied in too much to the historical moment right after the fall of Communism and is not forward-looking enough, not being sharp enough in critiquing the new situations that were bound to evolve. I was not surprised, for example, that the lineamenta (the preparatory outline) for the Special Assembly of the Bishops of the Americas cites *Sollicitudo Rei Socialis* much more frequently than *Centesimus Annus.*

The enemy, Communism, has disappeared. What we can learn from its demise is clear, but what have we yet to face is not so evident. The Pope was wise, however, to remind the countries of the former Soviet bloc about the perils of unbridled capitalism. Would that his wisdom had been listened to!

Conferences of Bishops

The bishops, if they were to rewrite their letter, would also have to look at another body of teaching, namely, the pastoral letters from conferences of bishops from around the world. These important documents could easily be forgotten; but, given the internationalization of the economy, they become important for all to read.

Last year the Jacques Maritain Institute in Rome finished a project of enormous proportions. For five years they examined the teaching of most of the local conferences of bishops on social justice. This body of teaching is enormous, as one could well imagine, but it again could be reduced to several overarching themes and concerns: the preferential option for the poor, the value of labor over capital, the disparity of wealth, and so on.

If Catholic social doctrine is refined by its continual application to current issues, then this body of teaching material is most important. I would like to cite in particular two recent documents of prime importance: *The Common Good and the Catholic Church's Social Teaching,* a pastoral letter of the bishops of England and Wales published in October 1996 in preparation for coming elections in that country, and *A New Beginning: Eradicating Poverty in Our World,* published by the Australian bishops in September 1996. This latter lengthy document is a unique attempt to treat the poverty issue on a worldwide basis and not just as a domestic problem.

As one looks at this whole body of teaching, one is immediately aware that the Catholic social tradition and its teaching have never been and still will not be comfortable with free-market economic solutions as such. Any attempt to "baptize," to "Christianize" the system ends in unreal expectations. There will always be a tension between the Bible and capitalism, the Sermon on the Mount and the market-place. The capitalist system is now accepted as a given in church documents since that is the world in which we all must live, but the defects and dangers in that system are also clearly pointed out. Ten years ago some had hoped that the American bishops would have condemned capitalism as intrinsically evil in itself. Pressure from South America pushed in this direction. The position of the Holy Father in *Centesimus Annus* is the one the American bishops had also assumed: The reality we live under is a free-market economic system, and we simply accept that fact. We must ask the question then: How can we avoid the negative aspects of that system so that it works for the largest number of people, and what are our responsibilities toward those who seem to be outside the system?

I have come to accept the reality that the church will always be uncomfortable with every economic system, with some, perhaps, more so than with others, because no system is perfect, and no system can meet all the biblical requirements. All systems, like human persons themselves, are imperfect, fallible. The attempts of the Enlightenment to create a rational system that would work in an automatic fashion for the benefit of all is an ideological utopia that now we can perhaps put behind us.

I have come to accept that I will always live in a world where human frailty will infect whatever economic system arises. It is not pleasant to have to admit that the prophetic stance of critiquing the human systems will never go away, but that is the realism we have learned. Every system will constantly need critiquing and controlling. Even practitioners of the free-market system like George Soros have arrived at the same conclusion. (See his article "The Capitalist Threat" in *The Atlantic Monthly,* February 1997.) At this moment, when so much is at stake in the internationalization of the economic free-market system because it affects the lives of everyone on this globe, such criticism is absolutely necessary.

This theme leads into my next section. The second clear change since the pastoral letter was written 10 years ago is certainly the rapid growth in the globalization of the economy.

THE GLOBALIZATION OF THE ECONOMY

Ten years ago we bishops knew of the growing internationalization of the economy. In fact, at the beginning of our discussions among committee members about the scope of the letter, some were in favor of making globalization the dominant theme in the undertaking. It was an enticing suggestion and would have made the letter more prophetic at that time. We knew that the internationalization of the economy was happening at a rapid pace and would continue to do so with even more rapidity in subsequent years, but we felt impelled to look first at the American economy because we sensed that such a critique was what the other nations of the world expected of us.

We compromised by making the international economic scene one of the four areas where we applied our principles, but it did not become the centerpiece of the letter itself. If the letter were to be redone today, globalization would have to be a central, not a peripheral, theme. The globalization of the economy is a fact now, not just a tendency. If it was difficult for us in 1986 to sum up in a single definition what capitalism in its different manifestations around the world was all about, it would be even more difficult today to describe all the nuances and idiosyncrasies of free-market economy in so many different cultures on this globe.

If one is to take seriously such works as Lester Thurow's *The Future of Capitalism: How Today's Economic Forces Shape Tomorrow's World* (1996) and William Greider's *One World, Ready or Not: The Manic Logic of Global Capitalism* (1997), the picture seems to be one of an enormous engine that is just rolling ahead at a most rapid pace, without clear goals and with no conductor. The pace defies an analysis that is clear and secure. There has been no single economist who has proposed a theory, a mechanism, that could pull it all together in a comprehensible way. The variables seem to be too many. This rapidly changing economic climate makes all the former modes of analysis and prediction almost impossible.

One of the changes that has become evident in the last 10 years in this globalization process has been the plight, if one could call it that, of economics as a science and of economists in general. The "dismal" science finds it more and more difficult to keep up with all the factors that must be brought into account if any kind of rational picture is to be obtained. The confusion among economists themselves would be one of the factors that might be annoying to bishops if they wanted to rewrite the economic pastoral letter today. Perhaps the flip side of the coin is that economists are now more and more aware of the human equation in their work and less inclined to rely on purely mathematical solutions.

One of the most trenchant and real criticisms brought against the economic pastoral of 1986 was that it did not treat of the relationship between wealth and power. That such a relationship existed was a truism, but it should have been explicitly studied. In this present period that theme has become more and more important as we see that some of the larger international corporations are economically more powerful than some of the countries where they do business.

We are all familiar with those lists that include the major international corporations and their worth in comparison to the G.N.P. of a whole series of nations. For example, Mitsubishi has more economic power than Indonesia; Ford is more powerful than Turkey; Wal-Mart is financially stronger than Israel. The question of nation-states also poses its own problems today, exacerbated by the breaking up of the old Soviet bloc and the ethnic exclusivity that one sees growing everywhere in the world.

Kenichi Ohmae noted this problem a few years ago in his book *The End of the Nation State: The Rise of Regional Economies* (1995). He stated that most government leaders thought that the borderless economy we are entering would not affect national sovereignty, but they were wrong. "The forces now at work," he wrote, "have raised troubling questions about the relevance—and effectiveness—of nation states as meaningful aggregates in terms of which to think about, much less manage, economic activity."

Moreover, the relationship between wealth and power poses specific problems also for those nations that are large and where there cannot be any talk of the demise of the nation-state. We all see how the question of wealth and power comes into play in election campaigns and sense a need, probably in vain, to try to regulate that use of power. George Soros's concern about the effects of unbridled capitalism on democracy is a serious one precisely because wealth is power. Concentrated wealth means concentrated power.

We have also seen that the globalization of the economy has only exacerbated the difference between the poorer and the richer nations. This question of global inequality—posed by every pontiff since the time of Pope Pius XII—will not go away. However one wants to analyze the question of economic dependency, the fact is that some players will be major economic and political forces in the world, while others will not have a chance but will remain dependent on the decisions of others.

The issues of justice and equality will be constantly raised in such a world. Because of these inequalities, especially in the labor market, we will continue to see waves of immigration on a large scale and problems maintaining safe borders. The other scenario proposed by some economists asserts that we will instead see a lowering of wages of unskilled laborers in the United States till they are the same as third-world wages. One aspect is sure in this globalization process: Labor is suffering most. Some predict that the situation is much like that at the turn of this century and will call forth a similar kind of re-action of social upheaval except, this time, on an international level.

If the bishops were to tackle again the question of an economic pas-toral letter, they would have to deal with this fluctuating situation and its consequences as the centerpiece of their endeavor. As this border-less economy moves ahead, they could not help but notice that labor has become just one more fragile factor in the big equation and that the church's position that it should not be the object of uncontrolled market forces is losing ground. The bishops could not now, as we did 10 years ago, deal with domestic poverty in the United States without analyzing its connection to growing poverty throughout the world.

Finally, in such a new world, they would have to ask the question already posed by Pope John XXIII about a world authority that could bring some kind of order into the chaos that is ensuing. To state that the markets themselves will bring that kind of order leaves most of us highly skeptical. Moreover, even if one assumes that the markets could effect such an order, the time needed to do so, as estimated by even the most optimistic capitalist theorist, would be so long that the human suf-fering in the meantime would be horrendous. One would have to ask again whose responsibility such poverty would be. Since so much of globalization of the economy is tied into the advances in technology, es-pecially information technology, countries without access to such means of information will be left out of the circle and remain dependent for as far as one can look into the future. It is not too soon to ask what that new world will look like with such disparate partners and new forces.

I feel sure the bishops, facing such a world, would repeat the basic moral principles they articulated in 1986. In this regard the times have not changed; the speed has just accelerated. The four principles enunciated in *Economic Justice for All* (No. 258) still remain as valid as the day they were written:

> 1. The demands of *Christian love* and *human solidarity* challenge all economic actors to choose community over chaos. They require a defi-

nition of political community that goes beyond national sovereignty to policies that recognize the moral bonds among all people.

2. *Basic justice* implies that all peoples are entitled to participate in the increasingly interdependent global economy in a way that ensures their freedom and dignity. When whole communities are effectively left out or excluded from equitable participation in the international order, basic justice is violated. We want a world that works fairly for all.

3. *Respect for human rights*, both political and economic, implies that international decisions, institutions and policies must be shaped by values that are more than economic. The creation of a global order in which these rights are secure for all must be a prime objective for all relevant actors on the international stage.

4. *The special place of the poor* in this moral perspective means that meeting the basic needs of the millions of deprived and hungry people in the world must be the No. 1 objective of international policy.

When those lines were written 10 years ago, they seemed totally unrealistic. There would not have been the will to do anything about them. They are more idealistic today. But that is all the more reason why they have to be reiterated.

Loss of Faith in Government

The third area that has taken on new dimensions in the last 10 years is the growing tendency to blame government for all our problems. It has become commonplace today to hear speeches, one after the other, about the ineptitude of government. The solution then to all problems is to have as little government as possible. One could say that this is the theme of the nineties. To win elections every politician has to give obeisance to those sentiments. The most divisive element in our political scene today is precisely the disagreements on the role of government. At first that division seemed to be along political party lines; today it is much more blurred.

Ten years ago the bishops did not feel they had to become involved in that debate. They reiterated the classical position in Catholic social teaching of a both/and position for government, emphasizing certain areas as the proper role of government and then citing the classical teaching about the use of subsidiarity in the execution of policies for social reform. But we bishops 10 years ago were very naive. We had not anticipated that money is power and that some forces would use that power to send out the message that this classical interpretation of the role of government was a "statist" position, even a naive form of socialism. That the bishops were positive on the role of government seemed to worry some because it went contrary to their political ideology, and thus they immediately tried to label the document as "leftist." Today there would be no way in which the bishops could avoid taking on this issue of the role of government since it dominates the political scene at this time.

It is noteworthy that even the self-styled libertarian Charles Murray gives the government some power in the regulation of the economy, namely, in the use of its antitrust powers. With the merging of large corporations to form big conglomerates, an ever-increasing phenomenon in our day, the question of antitrust legislation and the need to break up such large entities in order to have effective competition seems like a moot question. There exists no single authority able to do this on a world scale and we will have to rely on trade agreements, as ineffective as they seem to be at times.

The role of the state was laid out clearly by Pope John Paul II in *Centesimus Annus* (No. 40):

> It is the task of the State to provide for the defense and preservation of common goods such as the natural and human environments, which cannot be safe-guarded simply by market forces. Just as in the time of primitive capitalism the State had the duty of defending the basic rights of workers, so now, with the new capitalism, the State and all of society have the duty of defending those collective goods which, among others, constitute the essential framework for the legitimate pursuit of personal goals on the part of each individual.

In other places he remarks on the need for the free-market forces to be controlled by the State "to guarantee that the basic needs of the whole of society are satisfied" (No. 35). Even in the famous passage where he asks the question about whether those nations that had been in the Communist bloc should adopt capitalism, he answers cautiously, rejecting any form of capitalism "that is not circumscribed within a strong juridical framework that places it at the service of human freedom in its totality" (No. 42). This cautious response notes that other forces must be at work besides the free market and one of those forces is the needed corrections that only the power of the state can effect.

I wonder if the proponents of limited government in all economic affairs do not have to ask themselves about the effects that this rhetoric has had on other aspects of society where they consider government intervention, at times even strong intervention, as necessary. People do not live in a schizophrenic world. If government is so bad, people say, why should we not form our own militia? (an argument I hear in some of the rural parts of Wisconsin). This attitude also extends to all other regulations in society including moral behavior.

The bishops would avoid, I am sure, this libertarian strain in the debate today. They would not take seriously the neatly defined position of Charles Murray in his new short book, *What It Means to Be a Libertarian* (1997). In its negative tone toward government it is simply not in the tradition of Catholic social doctrine. That teaching has proposed a positive role for government and not just a minimalistic one. Nor would the bishops, in being true to the Catholic tradition, side with those who would see the role of government as total and decisive. They would keep to the middle-ground of stating those roles that are the rightful domain of government and then, using the principle of subsidiarity, outline how government is to help individuals, groups and social entities work toward solutions to social problems. They would not fall victim to the negative rhetoric against government these days, nor would they espouse concepts of higher centralization of power in government.

In this whole discussion of the role of government it would be necessary for the bishops to define more clearly what subsidiarity has meant in the Catholic social tradition. Some have used this concept naively to mean that the government stays out of all social concerns. Others have used it to support the power of the states over the Federal government. If these decentralizations had been the original meaning, then the word "subsidiarity" would not have been used by Pope Pius XI, because its basic insight is that the higher level of authority gives help; it does not wash its hands of all responsibility. The text most often cited is from *Quadragesimo Anno*, No. 79. I give it here in its totality since the first part of the passage is always omitted today (a practice that began with the encyclical *Mater et Magistra* of Pope John XXIII and has continued ever since):

> It is indeed true, as history clearly shows, that owing to the change in social conditions, much that was formerly done by small bodies can nowadays be accomplished only by large organizations. Nevertheless, it is a fundamental principle of social philosophy, fixed and unchangeable, that one should not withdraw from individuals and commit to the community what they can accomplish by their own enterprise and industry. So, too, it is an injustice and at the same time a grave evil and a disturbance of right order to transfer to the larger and higher collectivity functions which can be performed and provided for by lesser and subordinate bodies. Inasmuch as every social activity should, by its

very nature, prove a help to members of the body social, it should never destroy or absorb them.

The encyclical notes that there are some actions that can take place only on the highest of levels, given the present forms of our society. It would be necessary to outline these roles. Then the encyclical states that powers proper to individuals and groups should not be taken from them and given to the public sector. It would be well to outline these initiatives. Only finally does the principle relate to finding solutions to social ills. In that case, almost all agree that the local level is more qualified to find solutions to social problems, but only if they are of local origin and do not find their causes in other policies and programs that relate to the larger society. It does not imply either that all funding must also come from that local level. There are many problems, the solutions to which go beyond the means of the local community, and where help from outside would be needed.

The bishops would find in the words of Robert Kuttner the summation of their tradition at this point of history. In his recent book, *Everything for Sale: The Virtues and Limits of Markets* (1997), Kuttner wrote: "This book begins with the working hypothesis that a capitalist system is a superior form of economic organization, but even in a market economy there are realms of human life where markets are imperfect, inappropriate, or unattainable. Many forms of human motivation cannot be reduced to the market model of man."

Domestic Issues Still to Be Resolved

In this section I can only enumerate briefly the domestic issues the bishops would have to take into consideration if they were to took at the current scene in the United States. Almost all of these issues were noted by the bishops in their own anniversary document, *A Decade After "Economic Justice for All": Continuing Principles, Changing Context, New Challenges* (November 1995). That excellent document characterizes the present scene very well. I will only highlight a few issues that might be emphasized by the bishops if they were to write more extensively about the whole economic scene.

The bishops would probably place the rising disparity between poor and rich as the centerpiece of their domestic concerns. The statistics cited 10 years ago in No. 183 about economic inequality in our nation have become decidedly worse, not better. Everyone today is aware of the growing problem, everyone talks of the need to do something lest the social fabric of the nation be ripped apart; but there does not seem to be the will to take any corrective measures. It would be political suicide in our current climate to suggest any kind of program that would diminish this gap. If the bishops were to rewrite their letter, they would have to spend much time and effort on this issue and —if they spoke out strongly and prophetically—accept the consequences of being rejected or called all kinds of new or old names.

What the bishops wrote 10 years ago on the issues of employment and poverty is still very valid. I recall how we were assailed then by suggesting that the government might—if all other efforts in the private sector failed—become the employer of last resort. Yet I notice that this idea has become again a part of several of the welfare reform programs initiated by some of the most conservative governors.

So many of the issues faced 10 years ago are still with us. I can say that in rereading the sections on employment and on poverty they still made eminent sense. What might be missing now is the will again to take the big steps necessary to alleviate poverty, not just to reduce the number of people on welfare. The search for real jobs that bring sufficient wages and decent benefits is still often in vain. When this problem is compounded by the question of unemployment and poverty around the world—also of concern to all who believe in human solidarity—the proportions become unmanageable and tend to paralyze us.

Unfortunately, the concomitant issue of education that was dealt with in 1986 has not improved. Signs of hope are still not present.

No list would be complete without talking also about the immigration question and the connection between that challenge and Nafta and other such agreements. The bishops have spoken out on this issue in the last 10 years and thus the writers of a new pastoral letter would be able to use that track record.

Finally, I feel that the bishops today would also want to add a more lengthy section on labor and trade unionism. The principles of our Catholic social teaching on this issue are clear, but the present situation should induce us to look again at the realities of our labor force and its needs. Although business has been able to internationalize itself, labor has been less effective in doing so. Recently we have seen a revitalization of labor in the United States. Its connection with world labor movements will be most important as it faces up to a global economy. I feel sure bishops writing today would encourage that wider role for labor, since it is the area most highly affected by the globalization of the economy. My feeling is that if existing labor unions are not able to find strategies on how to meet the needs of the worker both here and abroad, some other force will rise up to deal with the global labor issues that are ever present among us and growing. I would only hope that the church would be a part of such an important wave of concerns.

CONCLUSION

I have sketched here, all too briefly, how I feel the bishops would approach rewriting the pastoral letter on the economy 10 years later. The globalization of the economy would be the lens under which the other factors would be examined. They would be forced to face up to the questions raised by that economy and plead for some basic principles to guide it as it moves toward the next millennium. All of the teaching that has been issued since then, be it from the Pope or from conferences of bishops around the world, would have to be studied. They would see that most of the domestic issues are the same as they were 10 years ago, but that the conditions are worse. They would be encouraged by what they wrote 10 years ago, but forced to go even deeper now in their analysis, because the economic situation of the world has moved so rapidly. The problems have grown more intractable, and the effects of wrong moves can be even more disastrous. I am sure the bishops would say that there is now more need for guiding principles than there was 10 years ago.

Probably bishops who hear or read my words will be thinking: But should not the lay people be doing this job? Where are the universities? They would be right. It is a project now for all of us.

18

RACISM: A TARNISHED REFLECTION OF OURSELVES[1]

Bishop James Griffin

I want to write to you about something which I believe disfigures the face of society, the church and individuals: racism.

Recent events in our world, our country and our local community remind us that despite our efforts and our progress, racism remains with us. This is true in spite of some advances over the last three or four decades to correct this unjust situation. We still see racism in inferior schooling for minority children, discriminatory treatment toward minority workers, and the unfair practices of business and industry. We hear it in racial slurs, belittling references to minorities and outright insults directed to persons because of their race.

Racism is a serious sin. It is a refusal to accept God's creative plan that all human beings are made in his image and likeness, that all persons have the same heavenly Father, regardless of their race or nationality. The teaching of Jesus Christ, "you shall love your neighbor as yourself," is intended to be inclusive, extending even to those whom we reject because of their ethnic or racial differences (see Luke 10:25-37). The Catholic Church proclaims that all races are children of God and brothers and sisters to one another. In doing this, she remains true to Gospel faith and Christian tradition.

This Gospel truth is echoed in our country's Declaration of Independence: "We hold these truths to be self-evident, that all men are created equal, that they are endowed by their Creator with certain

---

1. Pastoral letter of Bishop James Griffin, Columbus, Ohio, May 4, 1997.

unalienable rights, that among these are life, liberty and the pursuit of happiness."

This basic principle is spelled out in the Constitution and in repeated legislative enactments over the past 200 years. We can rightly say that racism is un-American and contrary to the laws of our nation. We must recognize that overt acts of racism are criminal.

We are all responsible for our society. We must each contribute in our own way to the molding of the society of which we are a part. We must also ensure the rights of all other members of society to do the same. Only when all people are free to influence the development of culture and society can that society become everything it can be and which we want it to be for the sake of the common good, for our own sakes and for future generations.

Blatant forms of racist practices can be readily known and condemned. It is the subtle forms that elude our perception. Before public acts occur, racism resides in the mind and heart. Prejudicial attitudes and feelings exist which at times are not so easily recognized. These can give rise to racist talk and racist activities, and ultimately to racist practices throughout our society.

Racism flows from personal attitudes and actions into the human world around us; it becomes a social evil. Our social institutions and structures are affected. None seems to escape: families and schools, public institutions and governmental programs, large corporations and small businesses, even our own church communities. As responsible members of our society, we are obliged to do our part to eradicate racism from this society—from the whole and from each of its component parts.

RACISM IN THE CHURCH

As a church, we must examine and confront the subtle forms of racism of which we are guilty. The Catholic Church in the United States is an overwhelmingly white church. As the bishops' Committee on Black Catholics stated, "History reveals that racism has played a powerful role in discouraging African Americans from the Catholic Church as a spiritual home." It is therefore vitally important that predominantly white parishes learn to worship and live as open invitations to people of all races. We need to change our hospitality habits in order to become a true gathering of believers. We must face the challenge of liberating ourselves from the bonds of racism. Racism, as a sin, harms not only the victim but the sinner too. We are held bound by our prejudices and our fears of letting go of control and power. Perhaps racism does not register as a "sin" in "my parish"—but it can be present. We must name and confess our prejudices in order to be freed from them. How does your parish welcome the stranger and celebrate diversity?

Those reading this letter who are Catholic must remember that we find our unity with Christ and one another in the eucharist. Each time I distribute holy communion to various congregations around the diocese, I am made aware of our unity in diversity. The faces of those receiving Christ are of all colors and yet all hunger after the same Lord. In this hunger is the key to our unity.

RACISM'S PERSONAL ROOTS

If we are to remove the sin and crime of racism from our midst, we must start with the self. All social sin begins in the choices of individuals to be unjust and is sustained by our blindness to those initial choices. As St. John says, "If we say we have no sin we deceive ourselves." We can say the same thing about prejudices: We all have them, though we may never have faced them honestly.

In order to overcome this blindness, I ask each of you to make a personal review of any prejudices you might hold. To confront our prejudices, we need to conduct a rigorous self-examination of our attitudes. With the teaching of the church on human dignity as our "compass," we also need another tool, a mirror in which to examine ourselves. I would suggest that every individual ask himself/herself the following questions as a kind of "morality mirror" in which to see his or her own prejudices:

- What prejudices do I now have? Can I identify the sources of those prejudices?

- What prejudices have I taken from my family and home life?

- What prejudices have I formed or accepted as a result of my experiences in life or from the media?

- How do my prejudices manifest themselves in my everyday living?

- How would I feel were I confronted by people who hold the same prejudices about me that I do about others?

- What one action can I take to begin to combat or remove the major prejudices in my life?

- What further action can I take to work on behalf of victims of racism, whether they be children, young people or adults?

This aspect of taking concrete action is especially important; if we can convince ourselves and others to act as if we truly believe in the equality and dignity of every person of every race, we will find that this action will change our belief. Consistently acting in a certain way begins to form beliefs—or, as may be the case, to "reform" beliefs—and changing our beliefs reforms our behavior.

Personal conversion and pastoral charity are necessary, but this conversion from prejudice must be linked to a sharing of power and influence with minority people. In this move to share power and influence, citizens in the majority race signal that racism is not to be tolerated. We cannot let economic fears deter us from acting justly. We cannot cling to power and control when doing so results in the perpetuation of racism and oppression.

In closing I want to address and challenge specific groups of citizens:

- To parents: I remind you that you are the first and best teachers of your children. By word, but even more by example, you form their moral intelligence. Be sure that respect for all sisters and brothers is part of the framework of your teaching. Seek ways to provide your children with positive experiences of many ethnic groups.

- To religious leaders: Be that prophetic voice to challenge the consciences and actions of your people on this issue of racism. Ask them to reflect seriously on what it means to be sisters and brothers, children of God. Pinpoint the real issues that your parish or congregation must address regarding racism.

- To government officials and community leaders: Do not allow the ugly head of racism to arise in our community. Above all, do not allow members of your staff to "trade" on this issue of racism for political gain.

- To business leaders: The "bottom line" cannot be the sole criterion of your profession. Business must be guided by ethics and principles, chief among which must be respect for every individual regardless of race and opportunity for every employee to rise to his or her full potential with no limits or exclusionary practices based on race.

- To teachers: You mold the future of our community. You have the best chance to eradicate the roots of racism from families and communities. You have the opportunity to plant the seeds of racial fairness in the hearts of our children. Please make the most of this opportunity.

- To all men and women of good will: The value of each of us is dependent on the value which we place on others. Once we make or allow the judgment that any other is expendable or to be limited in opportunity because of race, we open the door to the same fate befalling ourselves based on the same or other irrational criteria. Let us defend our own human dignity by defending the human dignity of every one of our sisters and brothers. Among other things, this means adopting an attitude of "zero tolerance" of racist comments or activity taking place even when you are not directly involved or affected. Do not turn your back in indifference or seek to take the easy way out.

To write of our shortcomings and to confess our failures is never easy or attractive, but this is the only way to face and eradicate racism in our midst. In this Easter season, I ask you to join me in prayer, reflection and action. I also ask you to carry with you and often refer to the "morality mirror" on this subject of racism which accompanies this letter. I close by reminding you of the final words of the pastoral letter on racism issued by the U.S. bishops in 1979. These same words were quoted in our subsequent pastoral, "For the Love of One Another" (1984):

> There must be no turning back along the road of justice, no sighing for bygone times of privilege, no nostalgia for simple solutions from another age. For we are children of the age to come, when the first shall be last and the last first, when blessed are they who serve Christ the Lord in all his brothers and sisters, especially those who are poor and suffer injustice.

19

TEN BUILDING BLOCKS OF CATHOLIC SOCIAL TEACHING

William J. Byron, S.J.

Principles, once internalized, lead to something. They prompt activity, impel motion, direct choices. A principled person always has a place to stand, knows where he or she is coming from and likely to end up. Principles always lead the person who possesses them somewhere, for some purpose, to do something, or choose not to.

In June, the National Conference of Catholic Bishops issued *Sharing Catholic Social Teaching: Challenges and Directions—Reflections of the U.S. Catholic Bishops,* a document intended to call the attention of all U.S. Catholics to the existence of Catholic social principles—a body of doctrine with which, the bishops say, "far too many Catholics are not familiar." In fact, they add, "many Catholics do not adequately understand that the social teaching of the Church is an essential part of Catholic faith." Strong words.

A companion document, "Summary Report of the Task Force on Catholic Social Teaching and Catholic Education," is included in the same booklet that contains the bishops' reflections on this "serious challenge for all Catholics." Along with about 30 others—educators from all levels, scholars, publishers, social ministry professionals—I served on the task force that produced the report.

The task force was convened in 1995 by Archbishop John R. Roach, the retired archbishop of St. Paul–Minneapolis. Often during our periodic meetings over the course of two years, it occurred to me that one (admittedly only one) reason why the body of Catholic social teaching is underappreciated, undercommunicated and not sufficiently understood is that the principles on which the doctrine is based are not clearly articulated and conveniently condensed. They are not "packaged" for catechetical purposes like the Ten Commandments and the seven sacraments. While many Catholics can come up with the eight Beatitudes and some would be willing to take a stab at listing the four cardinal virtues, few, if any, have a ready reply to the catechetical question the bishops want to raise: What are those Catholic social principles that are to be accepted as an essential part of the faith? The next question, of course, looks to how they can best be personally appropriated—internalized—so that they can lead to action.

On the 10th anniversary of their 1986 pastoral letter "Economic Justice for All," the bishops issued a 10-point summary of their teaching on the applicability of Catholic social principles to the economy. We on the task force had that summary in mind as we considered the broader issue of the applicability of Catholic social thought to a range of issues that go beyond the economic to include family, religious, social, political, technological, recreational and cultural considerations. It would be a mistake, of course, to confine Catholic social teaching to the economic sphere.

How many Catholic social principles are there? Combing through the documents mentioned above, I have come up with 10. They are not listed by number in these documents. In one instance, I have split into two principles a single theme articulated by the bishops. There is nothing at all official about my count. Some future *Catechism of the Catholic Church* may list more or fewer than these 10, if compilers of that future teaching aid find that Catholic social teaching is suitable for framing in such a fashion. In any case, I offer my list of 10 for three reasons: (1) Some reasonably complete list is needed if the ignorance cited by the bishops is going to be addressed; (2) any list can serve to invite the hand of both editors and teachers to smooth out the sentences for clarity and ease of memorization; and (3) any widely circulated list will stimulate further thought on the part of scholars and activists as to what belongs in a set of principles that can serve as a table of contents for the larger body of Catholic social teaching.

So, using these documents as my source, I here present 10 principles of Catholic social teaching, which should not be seen as a rewriting of the documents, but just editing and reformatting.

1. The Principle of Human Dignity

"Every human being is created in the image of God and redeemed by Jesus Christ, and therefore is invaluable and worthy of respect as a member of the human family" (*Reflections*, p. 1).

This is the bedrock principle of Catholic social teaching. Every person—regardless of race, sex, age, national origin, religion, sexual orientation, employment or economic status, health, intelligence, achievement or any other differentiating characteristic—is worthy of respect. It is not what you do or what you have that gives you a claim on respect; it is simply being human that establishes your dignity. Given that dignity, the human person is, in the Catholic view, never a means, always an end.

The body of Catholic social teaching opens with the human person, but it does not close there. Individuals have dignity; individualism has no place in Catholic social thought. The principle of human dignity gives the human person a claim on membership in a community, the human family.

2. The Principle of Respect for Human Life

"Every person, from the moment of conception to natural death, has inherent dignity and a right to life consistent with that dignity" (*Reflections*, pp. 1–2).

Human life at every stage of development and decline is precious and therefore worthy of protection and respect. It is always wrong directly to attack innocent human life. The Catholic tradition sees the sacredness of human life as part of any moral vision for a just and good society.

3. The Principle of Association

"[O]ur tradition proclaims that the person is not only sacred but also social. How we organize our society—in economics and politics, in law and policy—directly affects human dignity and the capacity of individuals to grow in community" (*Reflections*, p. 4).

The centerpiece of society is the family; family stability must always be protected and never undermined. By association with others—in families and in other social institutions that foster growth, protect dignity and promote the common good—human persons achieve their fulfillment.

4. The Principle of Participation

"We believe people have a right and a duty to participate in society, seeking together the common good and well-being of all, especially the poor and vulnerable" (*Reflections*, p. 5).

Without participation, the benefits available to an individual through any social institution cannot be realized. The human person has a right not to be shut out from participating in those institutions that are necessary for human fulfillment.

This principle applies in a special way to conditions associated with work. "Work is more than a way to make a living; it is a form of continuing participation in God's creation. If the dignity of work is to be protected, then the basic rights of workers must be respected—the right to productive work, to decent and fair wages, to organize and join unions, to private property, and to economic initiative" (*Reflections*, p. 5).

5. The Principle of Preferential Protection for the Poor and Vulnerable

"In a society marred by deepening divisions between rich and poor, our tradition recalls the story of the last judgment (Mt. 25:31-46) and instructs us to put the needs of the poor and vulnerable first" (*Reflections*, p. 5).

Why is this so? Because the common good—the good of society as a whole—requires it. The opposite of rich and powerful is poor and powerless. If the good of all, the common good, is to prevail, preferential protection must move toward those affected adversely by the absence of power and the presence of privation. Otherwise the balance needed to keep society in one piece will be broken to the detriment of the whole.

6. The Principle of Solidarity

"Catholic social teaching proclaims that we are our brothers' and sisters' keepers, wherever they live. We are one human family. . . . Learning to practice the virtue of solidarity means learning that 'loving our neighbor' has global dimensions in an interdependent world" (*Reflections*, p. 5).

The principle of solidarity functions as a moral category that leads to choices that will promote and protect the common good.

7. THE PRINCIPLE OF STEWARDSHIP

"The Catholic tradition insists that we show our respect for the Creator by our stewardship of creation" (*Reflections*, p. 6).

The steward is a manager, not an owner. In an era of rising consciousness about our physical environment, our tradition is calling us to a sense of moral responsibility for the protection of the environment —croplands, grasslands, woodlands, air, water, minerals and other natural deposits. Stewardship responsibilities also look toward our use of our personal talents, our attention to personal health and our use of personal property.

8. THE PRINCIPLE OF SUBSIDIARITY

This principle deals chiefly with "the responsibilities and limits of government, and the essential roles of voluntary associations" (*Reflections*, p. 6).

The principle of subsidiarity puts a proper limit on government by insisting that no higher level of organization should perform any function that can be handled efficiently and effectively at a lower level of organization by human persons who, individually or in groups, are closer to the problems and closer to the ground. Oppressive governments are always in violation of the principle of subsidiarity; overactive governments frequently violate this principle.

All eight of these principles were culled from the relatively brief "Reflections of the U.S. Catholic Bishops," as the second subtitle of *Sharing Catholic Social Teaching* describes this published product of the N.C.C.B. As I read on through the summary of the task force report, I found an articulation of two additional principles, which follow.

9. THE PRINCIPLE OF HUMAN EQUALITY

"Equality of all persons comes from their essential dignity. . . . While differences in talents are a part of God's plan, social and cultural discrimination in fundamental rights . . . are not compatible with God's design" ("Summary," pp. 23–4).

Treating equals equally is one way of defining justice, also understood classically as rendering to each person his or her due. Underlying the notion of equality is the simple principle of fairness; one of the earliest ethical stirrings felt in the developing human person is a sense of what is "fair" and what is not.

10. THE PRINCIPLE OF THE COMMON GOOD

"The common good is understood as the social conditions that allow people to reach their full human potential and to realize their human dignity" ("Summary," p. 25).

The social conditions the bishops have in mind presuppose "respect for the person," "the social well-being and development of the group" and the maintenance by public authority of "peace and security." Today, "in an age of global interdependence," the principle of the common good points to the "need for international structures that can promote the just development of the human family across regional and national lines."

What constitutes the common good is always going to be a matter for debate. The absence of any concern for or sensitivity to the common good is a sure sign of a society in need of help. As a sense of community is eroded, concern for the common good declines. A proper communitarian concern is the antidote to unbridled individualism, which, like unrestrained selfishness in personal relations, can destroy balance, harmony and peace within and among groups, neighborhoods, regions and nations.

It would not be inconsistent with either the *Reflections* or the "Summary" to articulate a separate principle of justice and another principle that affirms both the right to private property and what the "Summary" calls the "universal destination of goods," by which is meant that the goods of this world are intended by God for the benefit of everyone. But these principles are implied in those already listed; I think I'll stop counting at 10. The door remains wide open for additional themes, theses or what I have been calling simply "principles."

I am often asked what the difference is between a value and a principle. The terms are frequently used interchangeably. I like the "leads-to-something" implication of principle, while acknowledging that values, once internalized, will prompt people to act consistently with what they cherish and consider to be valuable—i.e., with what they judge to be worth their time, treasure and talent. Neither principles nor values lead anywhere if they remain abstract, embalmed in print, or are not internalized by human persons and carried in human hearts. Encouraging internalization of these principles is a pedagogical challenge that could be the subject of another article.

By including Catholic social teaching among the essentials of the faith, the bishops are affirming the existence of *credenda* (things to be believed) that become, in the believer, a basis for the *agenda* (things to be done) the believer must follow. Thus Catholic social action flows from Catholic social doctrine. How to bring the social portion of the doctrine of the faith to the attention of believers is the challenge the bishops have now put once again before Catholic pastors and educators at every level.

By the arrangement I've attempted here, this agenda rests on 10 building blocks:

- Human Person
- Human Life
- Association
- Participation
- Preference for the Poor
- Solidarity
- Stewardship
- Subsidiarity
- Equality
- Common Good

People who enjoy coming up with acronyms could rearrange the order to construct an easily remembered set of capital letters. Whatever the order and regardless of the labels, this set of principles might constitute topics for an adult education lecture series, segments for a semester-long course, chapters in a textbook, offices or sections in a research center or simply 10 "bins" for gathering the collected wisdom drawn from Scripture; patristic literature; Scholastic, conciliar and papal teaching; church history; systematic, moral and pastoral theology, and the ever-developing body of social reflection coming from episcopal conferences and other sources.

Not to be overlooked is the possibility of 10 biographical essays focusing on persons who embodied one or more of these principles in a significant way—Dorothy Day, Cardinal Joseph Bernardin, Mother Teresa, for instance. Also possible would be a collection of excerpts, organized under these 10 headings, from Chrysostom, Ambrose, Aquinas and other great social voices from the Catholic past. If they are to be taught, the principles need a human face; the lessons have to be conveyed in words and images that move the heart.

These 10 organizational categories can accommodate every conceivable social issue; they can provide any social problem with an analytical home. Analysis and reflection targeted on this material can become the base for moral instruction and formation of conscience. And that, of course, is the whole point of bringing Catholic education and Catholic social teaching together into the new working partnership hoped for by the National Conference of Catholic Bishops.

Meanwhile, the interested inquirer can find references for further reading in the back of the N.C.C.B. booklet, or one could simply consult the index in the new *Catechism of the Catholic Church* for leads to fuller explanations of Catholic social teaching. And if anyone wonders why the Catholic bishops reflect and write occasionally about war, peace, nuclear weapons, the economy, abortion, euthanasia, health insurance and a wide range of other topics that have a clear social and moral dimension, these principles provide the necessary interpretative framework for understanding the significance of the bishops' pastoral letters. They cannot be dismissed out of hand as political tracts; they must be held in respect as important instruments for teaching the Catholic faith.

20

THE CRISIS OF AMERICAN DEMOCRACY: A CATHOLIC PERSPECTIVE

Kenneth R. Himes, O.F.M.

More than a few social commentators have remarked that the present state of American democracy is not especially good. Whether it be low voter turnouts, the incivility of public debate, the fragility of our sense of community, or a dozen other items, the general sense is that we, as a people, could be doing better than we presently are in how we govern ourselves. In this essay, I intend to make the case that the Christian churches have a potentially important role in revitalizing an American democracy which is in crisis. I survey three aspects of the crisis before our nation and comment on how the resources of the Christian community might suggest a response to each element of the crisis. The three aspects or elements are: 1) the assault on the state, 2) the breakdown of the institutions which constitute civil society, and 3) the alienation of citizens from the political process. In the first half of this essay, I describe each of the three elements of the present crisis, and then in the second section, I inquire into what resources within the Christian community might assist in addressing the crisis.[1]

I do not mean to suggest that these three elements capture all that is problematic with our democracy. But each of the difficulties is serious and each requires our attention. Nor do I wish to suggest that Christians have all the answers to our nation's problems or that other religious communities do not have something constructive to offer as well

1. The original version of this essay was delivered as the annual McKeever Lecture while the author held the Paul McKeever Chair of Moral Theology at St. John's University (Jamaica, NY) during the 1996–97 academic year.

to the crisis of American democracy. The restriction of my remarks to the Christian tradition, and in particular Catholicism, is simply due to the fact that it is the tradition within which I stand. Furthermore, let me be clear about my claim that there are resources of great potential within the Christian community to address these crises. Whether the potential will be realized one can only hope, not guarantee.

Part I

The Assault on the State

In his essay *Our Enemy, the State,* first published in 1935, Albert Jay Nock stated his thesis directly: "The State is no proper agency for human welfare." While largely ignored during the New Deal years in which he wrote, Nock's outlook has gained adherents of late. This should not be a surprise, for Nock's anti-statism has deep roots in America's collective psyche. His is a thesis which gathers a fair amount of support today. It is not only extremists, such as the "Montana Freemen" or the "Michigan Militia," who rally around such a viewpoint. Within the offices of Washington think tanks such as the Cato Institute or Congressional offices of certain House Republicans, there is much sympathy for the opinion that the state is a threat to freedom, common sense, and human happiness.

A splendid book, *They Only Look Dead,* by E. J. Dionne, Jr., convincingly makes the case that a substantial segment of the Republican Party, not the Christian right but the libertarian wing of the party, has set itself the goal of dismantling much of what the federal government has done since the turn of the century. "After years of circumlocution and evasion, the Republicans have set out to overturn not only the Great Society but also the New Deal and the Progressive tradition."[2] This boldness of purpose, encouraged by the Republican takeover of both houses of Congress in 1994, brought an energy and clarity to the GOP.

Behind the libertarian agenda is a conviction that the federal government "is not only essentially inefficient but also inherently oppressive."[3] To understand how radical is this critique of the state one need only reflect upon the present House Majority Leader's equation of Franklin Roosevelt, John Kennedy, and Lyndon Johnson with Joseph Stalin and Mao Zedong.[4] In such a perspective there is no essential

2. E. J. Dionne, Jr., *They Only Look Dead* (NY: Simon and Schuster, 1996) 11.
3. Ibid., 286.
4. "Behind our New Deals and New Frontiers and Great Societies you will find, with a difference only in power and nerve, the same sort of person who gave the world its

difference between a democratically elected government and dictator-ship. If it is government, any government, it is a threat; and to pre-serve freedom, government must be reduced to its smallest possible size. The libertarian philosophy views just about all acts of govern-ment as steps along the path to tyranny. From within this framework, environmental regulations do not preserve clean air and water; they interfere with entrepreneurial freedom. Occupational safety regula-tions are not protections of employees from hazardous work-condi-tions; they are restrictions upon the freedom of contract. Taxes for Medicaid are not means of caring for the indigent sick; they are seizures of private property.

Leaders of this movement are forthright in their love of free mar-kets and their distaste for government. Again, Representative Armey puts his position bluntly: "the market is rational and the government is dumb."[5] One can only conclude from such an unnuanced statement that for Armey, "it is rational to accept problems created by unemploy-ment, low wages, business cycles, pollution and simple human failings; and dumb to use government to try to lessen the human costs associ-ated with them."[6] Libertarian Republicans (and this is the group from which most of the party leadership hails) have formed what conserva-tive activist Grover Norquist has called the "leave us alone" coalition.[7] Government is simply a nuisance and the less of it the better. Progress comes through the working of the free market, and whenever the state interferes in the market, human freedom and dignity are threatened.

The Breakdown of Civil Society

In February 1995 the senior senator of New Jersey, Bill Bradley, gave a speech at the Washington Press Club. He began by talking about a dinner he attended two nights earlier. It was a dinner to honor Jack Danforth, the recently retired senator from Missouri. Bradley noted that Danforth decided voluntarily to leave government to tackle one of the nation's most significant problems, the plight of inner-city youth, and he chose to work with religious organizations for the solution.

Bradley then went on to reflect upon the importance of civil so-ciety and the need to revitalize it. He described civil society this way:

Five Year Plans and Great Leaps Forward—the Soviet and Chinese counterparts." Dick Armey, *The Freedom Revolution* (Washington, D.C.: Regnery Publishing, 1995) 15–16, as quoted by Dionne, 286.

5. Armey, 316, as quoted by Dionne, 290.

6. Dionne, 290–91.

7. As quoted by Dionne, 156.

> Civil society is the place where Americans make their home, sustain their marriages, raise their families, hang out with their friends, meet their neighbors, educate their children, worship their god. It is the churches, schools, fraternities, community centers, labor unions, synagogues, sports leagues, PTAs, libraries and barber shops. It is where opinions are expressed and refined, where views are exchanged and agreements made, where a sense of common purpose and consensus are forged. . . . Civil society . . . is the sphere of our most basic humanity—the personal, everyday realm that is governed by values such as responsibility, trust, fraternity, solidarity and love.[8]

The failure of the ideologies of the dominant political parties, according to Bradley, is that they fail to see that government (in the case of the Democrats) and the market (in the case of the Republicans) are not enough to make a civilization. There must be a healthy, robust civic sector—a public space where human communities can flourish.

Laced throughout Bradley's remarks was a sense that the social fabric of American life is unraveling. Voluntary associations are dying and the sense of community is strained. There is among people a widespread feeling, which cuts across lines of class, race and geography, that the everyday world of family, neighborhood, religious community, and voluntary organization is under siege. Perhaps, said Bradley, that is one reason why the TV show "Cheers" was so beloved. It was the place, as the opening song put it, "where everybody knows your name, and they're always glad you came." It is an image of a personal and communal life we would like to have, yet far too many of us do not experience this dimension of local community hinted at by the popular sitcom.

This talk of local groups and community may be dismissed as corny and sentimental by the national political elites, since such concerns are all small-time for these folks. But that is one more aspect of the problem, claimed Bradley. The worlds of big business and national politics have de-legitimated local life. The everyday domain of voluntary associations and community organizations seems peripheral to the market and government where the talk is of billions of dollars and millions of people, and, significantly, the talk takes place on television. The national and international megastructures of politics and business have led us to discount the spiritual, the cultural, and

8. Bill Bradley, "America's Challenge: Revitalizing Our National Community," Speech at The National Press Club (February 9, 1995) 2. I am using the text provided by the Senator's office. A slightly modified version of the speech appeared with the same title in *National Civic Review* 84 (Spring, 1995) 94–100.

the social known at the local level. Yet, it is upon these too often neglected things, the structures of civic life, that society rests.

Bradley is too reflective a man simply to dismiss the larger world
of national government and business, but he wants these realms to
support and enable local institutions, not undermine them. At the national level there are things which should be done to facilitate the renewal of civil society, but neither government nor big business can
create civil society. We can have laws which "insist that fathers support their children financially, but fathers have to see the importance
of spending time with their children." Businesses can work out ways
of providing more adequate parental leave, "but parents have to use
that time to raise their children." Mothers and fathers can be given information and tools "to influence the story-telling of the mass media,
but they ultimately must exercise that control." Congress can even
clean up campaign financing to reduce the impact of special interests
and money, but people have to study the issues and come out to vote.[9]

At about the same time as Bradley's speech, an article entitled
"Bowling Alone" by the Harvard political scientist Robert Putnam
was published. Putnam puzzled over reports that 80 million Americans bowled at least once in 1993, a ten percent increase over 1980,
but that league bowling had declined forty percent in the same period.[10] Putnam went on to make the point that the decline in communal activity at the bowling alley is not an isolated trend. Membership
in a wide variety of community organizations has been dropping in
recent decades. Labor unions, parent-teacher associations, women's
clubs, fraternal organizations, all have declined. The Red Cross and
the Boy Scouts have found it harder to recruit volunteers. Surveys
show fewer people having friendships among their close neighbors.

Putnam presents such data, and much more in his other writings,[11]
as evidence for the decline of what he calls "social capital." "By anal-

9. Ibid., 6.

10. Robert Putnam, "Bowling Alone," *Journal of Democracy* 6 (1995) 65–78.

11. Other recent essays by Putnam in which he explores the issue of social capital
and its decline are: "The Prosperous Community," *The American Prospect* #13 (1993) 35–
42; "What Makes Democracy Work?" *National Civic Review* 82 (1993) 101–107; "Bowling
Alone Revisited," *The Responsive Community* 5 (1995) 18–33; "Tuning In, Tuning Out: The
Strange Disappearance of Social Capital in America," *PS: Political Science and Politics* 28
(1995) 664–683. This last essay provides a detailed empirical argument using a number
of research studies. The same essay appears in a slightly revised format in *The American
Prospect* #24 (1996) 34–48 and is followed by a series of critical reactions found in issues
#25 and 26 of the journal, all under the heading "Unsolved Mysteries: The Tocqueville
Files."

ogy with notions of physical capital and human capital—tools and training that enhance individual productivity," the term social capital "refers to features of social organization, such as networks, norms, and trust that facilitate coordination and cooperation for mutual benefit."[12] Its decline has paralleled a decline in our trust of public institutions and one another. Between 1960 and 1993 the proportion of Americans who said most people can be trusted fell by more than a third. Upon reflection this is not a surprising fact. For the lack of interaction between people, the failure to bring people together to work for common goals, keeps us strangers to one another. When people are strangers, there is a tendency not to trust them but to be suspicious. By contrast, studies also show that members of civic associations are more likely than non-members to participate in politics, spend time with neighbors, and to express social trust.

There are many reasons for the decline in neighborliness, in volunteer activity, in civic-mindedness. More women work outside the home; both men and women work longer hours; television holds people in the living room; partisan politics repels people by its crudity and disappoints them by its ineffectiveness. Putnam's thesis, however, remains: without a good supply of "social capital," the institutions of self-government can easily break down. True, membership in some national organizations—the NRA, the AARP, and environmental groups—is up. But writing a check and having one's name on a mailing list are not substitutes for working through a problem with fellow citizens. There is also the proliferation of self-help groups in recent decades, but "some small groups merely provide occasions for individuals to focus on themselves in the presence of others."[13] Such groups, while certainly useful and of value, cannot substitute for families, neighborhoods, and broader community commitments. Putnam's conclusion is a warning: unless more Americans start working with each other on shared civic enterprises, and thereby learning to trust each other, the disintegration of public life will continue and the formal governmental institutions of the nation will undergo a credibility crisis.

Other voices could be added to those I have cited, but my point is simple: there is in our society today a widely shared and deeply felt sense that fundamental institutions of civil society are weakening, in

---

12. "The Prosperous Community," 35–36.

13. Robert Wuthnow, *Sharing the Journey: Support Groups and America's New Quest for Community* (New York: The Free Press, 1994) 45, as quoted in Putnam, "Bowling Alone," 72.

some cases are already in serious decline, and this entails a significant threat to the viability of the democratic experiment in the United States.[14]

Political Alienation

One of the clear signs of the times is the degree of political alienation which exists in our nation. The problem is manifested in a variety of ways. One symptom is the number of Americans who care little about, and have significant gaps in their knowledge of, how democratic politics works. Study after study provides evidence of the general ignorance that exists about who one's representative in Congress is, how a bill becomes a law, or what major legislation has been passed by Congress in a given year.

We know some of the causes of the alienation. The dominance of money in the process points to the degree that politicians serve contributors not constituents. There is the polarization of the body politic, divided by ideological partisans who develop policies meant not to secure the common good but rather to capture a segment of the electorate. We have a politics of trivialization which makes public life into a soap opera. For example, we know more about the private lives and finances of our leaders and less and less about the substance of issues—welfare reform, health care, affirmative action. In addition, John Carr of the U.S. Catholic Conference has spoken of the politics of gesture and gimmick: "three strikes and you're out" as a judicial policy; balanced budget amendments without budget planning as economic policy; two-year cutoffs of welfare assistance without strategies for job creation as social policy. There is also what E. J. Dionne has called, the "politics of annihilation"[15]—namely, it is no longer sufficient merely to have more votes than one's opponent. Now one must try to destroy the moral standing and reputation of an adversary. Think of the attacks on Clarence Thomas from the left or some of the

---

14. Additional recent works which are important for the role of civil society and American democracy are Robert Bellah et al., *The Good Society* (New York: Alfred Knopf, 1991); Peter Berger and Richard Neuhaus, *To Empower People* (Washington, D.C.: American Enterprise Institute, 1977); Jean Bethke Elshtain, *Democracy on Trial* (New York: Basic Books, 1995); Christopher Lasch, *The Revolt of the Elites and the Betrayal of Democracy* (New York: W. W. Norton and Company, 1995); Adam Seligman, *The Idea of Civil Society* (Princeton: Princeton University Press, 1992); Sidney Verba et al., *Voice and Equality* (Cambridge: Harvard University Press, 1996); Alan Wolfe, *Whose Keeper?* (Berkeley: University of California Press, 1989).

15. Dionne, 20–21.

things which have been said about the Clintons on the right. And we have the political tactic of offering false choices: big government versus small government—as if we must have one or the other, when what we need is effective government, which may require activism in some areas and non-intervention in others.

The result is that many people have gotten so used to trashing political institutions and public officials that we have no confidence in the art of politics. People do not vote, do not want to pay taxes for public services, and do not understand the legislation being passed in their name. The media have only heightened this alienation, to the point where it is evident that journalists distort the news not so much by being liberal or conservative but by being cynical. They teach us to be resigned to our political situation and skeptical of all public figures, thus encouraging further alienation from political life.

All this has led to the rise of what might be called the politics of anger. We lash out at crime, or become irritable about our economic anxiety, or complain about "them," whoever they are. We fail to understand the larger cultural and structural forces at work in the society. Perhaps nothing illustrates the politics of anger so clearly as the phenomenon of talk radio. The Rush Limbaughs of the airwaves preside over shows filled with complaint, anger, and scornful humor. There is little that is good-natured about these shows. In some places talk radio is championed as the new democracy, but actually it is passive and does not introduce people to the real world of pluralism, compromise, political feasibility, and tolerance. Talk radio is merely a platform to emote in public, to let off steam. It seems closer to primal scream therapy than democracy. Involvement in public life is not the result of such an exercise. Instead, the result is the reinforcement of anger and prejudice due to the homogeneity of the listening audience.

For too long the elites in our society thought apathy and ignorance were unfortunate and only hurt the apathetic and ignorant. Despite it all, American democracy would go about its business, to be taken care of by those who were politically engaged. Today we are more willing to consider that apathy and ignorance have fed the free-floating anxiety and anger which hurt the nation as a whole and which make democracy increasingly difficult to maintain. What is beginning to dawn on people is that the solution to this problem is not more government, as some liberals would have it, nor leaner government, as conservatives would have it. For there is a limit to what any government can do to revitalize society, especially when many see government as the problem in the first place.

Ultimately, democracy must come from the ground up. It cannot be imposed by the desire of an elite group or created from outside a society. Is this not the lesson learned in those nations where democracy was thought of as simply a matter of holding elections without attending to the formation of a body politic capable of public discourse, political participation, and self-governance? The struggles we see in places as diverse as Russia, Algeria, Guatemala, Liberia, and the former Yugoslavia all point to the simple fact that it is impossible to have a democracy without a critical mass of democrats. As a major study recently completed on civic voluntarism maintains, "Citizen participation is at the heart of democracy. . . . Political participation provides the mechanism by which citizens can communicate information about their interests, preferences, and needs and generate pressure to respond."[16] Absent such widespread participation, democracy becomes a hollow exercise, legitimating the disproportionate power of a minority over the institutions of self-rule. Government, in turn, becomes not a mechanism to coordinate the activities of society, but rather a distant force over which apathetic and ignorant citizens have little control and which they resent profoundly.

Part II

In the second half of this essay, I suggest a response to each of the elements of our democratic crisis: the assault on the state, the breakdown of civil society, and the extent of our political alienation. Although each part of the response will be treated separately, interconnections exist among the responses, just as there are interconnections among the elements of the crisis described above.

The Nature and Purpose of the State

In Catholic social teaching, as with many other traditions of Christian social thought, the nature of the state is understood within the broad context of political anthropology and the vision of society. At the very heart of the Catholic social tradition is the conviction that the person is defined relationally—by the relationships he or she has with God, other persons, other creatures. Not only the relationship with God but our relationship with the rest of creation and living creatures underscores the conviction that at the heart of an appropriate under-

---

16. Sidney Verba, Kay Lehman Schlozman, Henry Brady, *Voice and Equality* (Cambridge: Harvard University Press, 1996) 1.

standing of personhood is relationality. "Sociality is as essential to human nature as rationality."[17] The isolated individual is an abstraction. Thus, society is not simply a human creation, but rather it is divinely ordained, for without society the person could not satisfy basic human needs.

Humanity's relationship with God is grounded in the belief that each person is created in the divine image. Thus, there is a fundamental personal dignity that must be respected. This understanding of the human—as having a unique and personal dignity due to the *imago Dei* and as being fundamentally social—sets the social teaching of many churches on a path that would oppose the two great rival political theories of the nineteenth century, liberal individualism and Marxist collectivism.

Each of the two emphases—personal uniqueness and sociality—are important. At the same time that it upholds the dignity and uniqueness of the individual, the Christian tradition understands that the perfection of the self is realized only in community. Human beings achieve their perfection through involvement in a dense web of overlapping relationships that create a variety of communal experiences for the person. As a result, liberalism's emphasis on the unencumbered individual freely calculating the benefit of entering into a social contract is judged to be neither empirically accurate nor morally desirable. Thus, for example, within the perspective of Catholicism, the classical liberal model of society as a contract among independent individuals is opposed on behalf of a viewpoint which emphasizes reciprocity and mutuality.[18]

Marxism's temptation to a collectivist vision is also judged unworthy. While never denying the communal nature of the person, there is the emphasis on the dignity and uniqueness of the person in Christian social teaching. Treating humankind as one great mass of people, without attention to the uniqueness of personal existence, is not an acceptable alternative to the failings of liberal theory. The vision of Christianity requires that the individual person not become a mere numerical concept, but rather be given attention within his or her concrete situation, thereby demanding a healthy respect for the particular relationships and communities which nourish the unique human personality.

---

17. Henri Rommen, *The State in Catholic Social Thought* (St. Louis: Herder Book Co., 1945) 138.
  18. Ibid., 123–28.

Speaking of the Catholic tradition, one scholar has stated that at the heart of that tradition is a "theologically inspired communitarian ethic."[19] Communitarianism sees society neither as one great collective nor as a voluntary choice by those rationally maximizing self-interest. Rather, the human person was made for community, and society is a community of communities organically related to one another. It is through participation within a variety of communities that the human person flourishes.

The understanding of the state in this framework is an outgrowth of the communitarian vision of the human person and society. The state is related to the social nature of the person, for it is the institution which gives shape and form to the virtue of solidarity; that is, the state provides public order for the multiplicity of social groupings— families, professional associations, religious communities, economic corporations, and so forth. From this perspective, the state "proceeds by inner moral necessity from the social nature" of the person as a means of developing a rich social life of mutuality and cooperation which, in turn, permits the full realization of individual personality.[20] Church teaching claims that the state's purpose is to protect and promote the common good. This responsibility, the very reason for the state's existence, is ordained by God who has created humankind in such a way that persons are social; therefore, we have an obligation to contribute to the common good, and this good requires a political institution to protect and promote that goal.

Such an understanding of the state's purpose and its consequences is readily distinguished from the classical liberal position, where the duty to contribute to a common end is dimly perceived, since the state's role is interpreted as merely a convenience which facilitates the individual pursuit of self-interest.[21] In this liberal framework, it is hard to allow any positive role for the state interfering in the economic sphere, beyond that of enforcing contractual obligations of commutative justice. In contrast, the communitarian tradition, typical of many Christian churches, emphasizes distributive, legal, and social justice. The first addresses the person's rights to share in the goods of the community; the second addresses the duties of the person to the community; and social justice requires that societal institutions be

19. Michael Schuck, *That They Be One* (Washington, D.C.: Georgetown University Press, 1991) 180.

20. Rommen, 137.

21. Pius XII, *The Major Addresses of Pope Pius XII*, vol. 2, ed. V. Yzermans (St. Paul: North Central Publishing, 1961) 125.

structured and organized in such a way that the demands of commutative, distributive, and legal justice can be adequately met.

Within Catholicism, it was Leo XIII who most obviously drew the line of demarcation between classical liberalism and a Christian communitarianism. This was done in two ways: first, he declared that justice was the foundational norm of the economic order, thereby ruling out the liberal exaltation of freedom in the market; and second, he insisted upon the right of the state to intervene in the economic order. Leo's concern was the failure of governments to act responsibly in the face of threats to the common good.[22] His argument in *Rerum Novarum* was rather sweeping, calling upon the state "in general to do everything necessary for the general welfare which could not be handled as well by private interests."[23] In particular, the state bears a responsibility to care for those who are most in need. As Leo wrote: "When there is a question of protecting the rights of individuals, the poor and helpless have a claim to special consideration."[24]

As the papal commentators Jean-Yves Calvez and Jacques Perrin suggest, the right to intervene is not something newly minted and added to the Catholic theory of the state. Rather, the right flows from the very nature of the state: "The principle of this intervention is that the prosperity of the community and its members is an immediate part of the end which the state ought to be seeking."[25] That is, the end of the state is the common good of which economic prosperity is an integral part. So the state's intervention in the economic order is, in Leo's mind, in full accord with the Catholic theory of the state; indeed, it is a direct corollary of that theory.[26]

Such a view of the state places Catholicism alongside many other churches in their clear opposition to contemporary voices of libertarianism who attack the state and who see government as wrong and the market as right.[27] The present anti-state movement is posing a debate which has gone on before in our history: Should the government be permitted to intervene in economic life and temper the harsher

22. Richard Camp, *The Papal Ideology of Social Reform* (Leiden: E. J. Brill, 1969) 138.

23. Ibid., 141.

24. Leo XIII, *Rerum Novarum, Catholic Social Thought*, ed. D. O'Brien and T. Shannon (Maryknoll: Orbis Books, 1995) par, 29.

25. Jean-Yves Calvez and Jacques Perrin, *The Church and Social Justice* (Chicago: Henry Regnery, 1961) 319.

26. Ibid., 322.

27. See, for example, James A. Nash, "On the Goodness of Government," *Theology and Public Policy* 7:2 (1995) 3–25.

consequences of the free market, as well as to enhance economic opportunity? The libertarian answer to the question is to see the results
of the market as the natural and just outcome of free economic decisions. Christian social teaching offers an alternative view of government as the institution charged with protection of the temporal
common good, and this requires, not merely suggests, that the state
regulate those aspects of the economy where human dignity and
well-being are at risk.

This way of seeing government's role will be more appealing to
most Americans than the libertarian position, for while citizens do distrust government, they do not have great confidence in the unchecked
power of business corporations either. Americans desire limitations
on both the government and the market. That is why Pat Buchanan's
economic populism struck a chord within the electorate. Buchanan at-
tacked those companies which downsize while executives reap profits
with stock options; corporations that move factories from communities
with almost no advance notice; businesses that engage in union-bust-
ing or move to "right-to-work" states. People responded to his message
because the average American is no more blind to the faults of big business than he or she is to the problems of big government. But the libertarian position is incapable of adequately addressing the question of
reining in the power of corporations, for it opposes government intervention in the marketplace in principle. Christian social teaching, on
the other hand, believes there is a proper role for activist government
to expand economic opportunity, to protect individuals from the excesses of free-market economics, and to secure the common good of all.

Today, however, just as libertarians have found a home amidst the
GOP, there has been a "cult of governmentalism," creating a vast bureaucratic state that has undermined the local institutions of civil society, occupying space within the Democratic party. To address that
problem, another idea drawn from Christian social teaching can be
offered.

Civil Society and Subsidiarity

Because the common good is so multi-faceted, it cannot be assumed
that any one community can satisfy its achievement. While the goods
of political community are essential, they are insufficient to encompass
all that the common good entails. There remain the goods of family,
friendships, religion, and other key components of human life together.
To presuppose that one undifferentiated community of humanity is
adequate to realize the good of each person is to run the risk of creat-

ing what Pius XII called "the masses," whose "de-personalization" leads to the growth of the bureaucratic state.[28]

While the state is a highly prized form of community, the state cannot be understood in a totalitarian way. Here the contribution of liberalism to Christian social teaching must be acknowledged. The emphasis on individual liberty which liberalism has championed, and its concern for avoiding state encroachment upon legitimate areas of freedom, has had an impact on the teaching of the churches as seen by a growing appreciation for the limited constitutional state.[29] In the case of Catholicism, the lessons drawn from the experience of both the paternalistic states of eighteenth- and nineteenth-century European monarchies, as well as the totalitarian fascist and communist states of the twentieth century, have impressed upon the Vatican the benefits of liberal democracies. At least since the papacy of Pius XII the preference of Catholic social teaching is clear in this regard, joining it to the teachings of many other Christian churches in their earlier support for democratic political structures.

As previously noted, Leo XIII's defense of the state's right to intervene in economic life was straightforward, and no subsequent pope has disagreed with the argument laid out in *Rerum Novarum*. What has followed in later teaching is an examination of the extent of the state's right. Since Leo's argument was made in the face of liberal resistance to an activist state, it is understandable that his interest was to establish the right to intervene. It was left to later popes to articulate the limits of that right. Well known in this regard is Pius XI's formulation of the principle of subsidiarity. Subsidiarity, as explained in *Quadragesimo Anno*, can be easily paraphrased as "no bigger than necessary, no smaller than appropriate."

By the time of Pius XI, "the 'night watchman' state of the classical liberals was disappearing in Europe, but an apparition even more sinister, to him, had taken its place in some nations: this was the omnicompetent state."[30] Pius wished to avoid having Leo XIII's right to intervene turned into an apology for the state overwhelming all other forms of human association. He, therefore, invoked the idea of

---

28. Pius XII in Yzermans, 42.

29. An excellent overview of one church's attitude toward the modern democratic state can be found in Paul Sigmund, "Catholicism and Liberal Democracy," *Catholicism and Liberalism*, ed. R. B. Douglass and D. Hollenbach (New York: Cambridge University Press, 1994).

30. Camp, 145.

subsidiarity precisely as that norm which is meant to prohibit the re-
duction of the richness of human association to one form—the state.

Employment of subsidiarity distinguishes Catholic social teaching
from any sort of collectivist or totalitarian outlook, which permits the
state to dominate all other forms of communal life. Communitarianism offers strong support for a rich variety of associations giving life
and color to communal experience. Subsidiarity maintains that the
state's role is to help these smaller communities achieve their proper
aim whenever they are unable or unwilling to make their distinct
contribution to the overall well-being of the person and the larger
community. In effect, subsidiarity seeks to find the proper fit between
the task and the competence, so that groups are asked to do neither
more nor less than they should.

The aim of multiple associations, after all, is to permit persons to
realize the variety of goods which make for human flourishing by
fostering participation in an array of communal experiences. Subsidiarity regulates the institutions of society, especially the state, so
that participatory community is possible. Viewed in this way, subsidiarity is an instrumental norm meant to serve the foundational values of community and the common good which make for personal
well-being. These values necessitate a broad spectrum of communal
structures situated in the realm of civil society. Consequently, many
Christians will agree with E. J. Dionne's criticism of our present political choices as offered by the two major parties:

> By casting "government" and "the market" as the main mechanisms of
> social organization, the conventional political debate leaves out the most
> important institutions in people's lives—family, church, neighborhood,
> workplace organizations and a variety of other voluntary institutions
> ranging from sports clubs and youth groups to privately organized
> child-care centers and the loose fellowships created at taverns like
> Cheers of television fame.[31]

In a society as complex as ours, it is apparent that more than the
state is needed for realizing the common good; it is equally clear, however, that we do need the state. What is being debated vigorously
today is what level of state involvement is proper. In order to formulate an answer to that question, one must assess the forces which
threaten the basic goods esteemed by Christian social teaching. Surely,
the state can endanger those goods, but other forces may effectively

---

31. Dionne, 295–96.

block participation in communal life, thereby denying a person's ability to make a contribution to the common good. In this matter it is not possible to rely upon a single ideological premise to settle all cases.

The present Pope has noted that even in its well-intentioned activity the state may undercut the role of other communities, such as family, neighborhood, and voluntary associations. On this point he has been supported by thinkers like Robert Putnam who believe that more attention to the institutions of civil society is "a much-needed corrective to an exclusive emphasis on the formal institutions of government. . . ."[32] John Paul II warns that "the social assistance state leads to a loss of human energies and an inordinate increase of public agencies which are dominated more by bureaucratic ways of thinking than by concern for serving their clients." He goes on to say, "it would appear that needs are best understood and satisfied by people who are closest to them and who act as neighbors to those in need." His conclusion is that many people in need "can be helped effectively only by those who offer them genuine fraternal support, in addition to the necessary care."[33] Although critical of certain governmental practices within nations like our own, the Pope should not be read as anti-state. Instead, John Paul is advocating something similar to what social theorist Philip Selznick seeks as an alternative to the excesses of the bureaucratic welfare state:

> The alternative is not a rejection of government. . . . Rather, it is for the architects of the welfare state to transform their vision of how governments fulfill their responsibilities. Two strategies are appropriate. If the government will pay more attention to communal values and civil society, it will more clearly perceive and more adequately protect the needs of individual persons. And if it will adopt postbureaucratic modes of organization, the welfare state can become more limited, more accountable, and more humane.[34]

Evident throughout the contemporary papacy's formulation of the Christian social tradition is the persistence of the communitarian outlook. First, there is the charge that large bureaucratic structures are

32. Robert Putnam, "The Prosperous Community," 41.

33. John Paul II, *Centesimus Annus,* in O'Brien and Shannon, par. 48.

34. Philip Selznick, *The Moral Commonwealth* (Berkeley: University of California Press, 1992) 513. Putnam agrees: "Conservatives are right to emphasize the value of intermediary associations, but they misunderstand the potential synergy between private organization and the government. *Social capital is not a substitute for effective public policy but rather a prerequisite for it and, in part, a consequence of it.*" "The Prosperous Community," 42 (emphasis in original).

alienating and that governmental bureaucracy is no more humane than the bureaucracies of other large social structures. What is desirable is an approach to social action that is planned on a more human scale. A second communitarian theme is the value of locally based service agencies. It is quite possible that institutions which are closer to the grass-roots than large governmental offices are better able to deliver services which address the concerns of people. The third communitarian theme in recent teaching is that more than material needs must be addressed. People in any society do not live by bread alone, even though bread is necessary. The values cherished by humans include those which are discovered through the experience of being in relationship with others. Here the essential nature of human life as social and of society as an organic community of communities determine the appropriate response. Participation in a wide array of communities allows a person to experience social life through "interrelationships on many levels," and it offers an option to the person who is "often suffocated between two poles represented by the state and the marketplace."[35]

Again, subsidiarity is not to be equated with an anti-state stance, but it does require a strategy to maximize participation. Out of such opportunities for participation the reality of interdependence can be elevated to the experience of solidarity. Because of its size, the state may not provide the best way to structure solidarity in each case, although there is no reason to presume that non-governmental structures are always to be preferred. Required is that attention be paid to the institutions which make for a vibrant civil society, since such institutions not only serve people's needs but also bring vitality to political life, both keeping government in its place and making genuine democratic government possible by encouraging participation in public life.

Political Alienation and Political Participation

The third element of the crisis of American democracy is what I have referred to as political alienation. The decline of public civility, the absence of substantive political argument, the shallowness of electoral campaigns, the sense that politics is what professional politicians do, not what citizens of a democracy work at together—all these along with the apathy, ignorance, and anger among the population are evident in American democracy. It is not always clear just what is a symptom and what is a cause in the roster just recited, but the non-engagement of citizens with democratic politics is a serious problem for our nation.

35. John Paul II, par. 49.

A recent study on civic voluntarism and American politics offers some interesting lessons for Christians and all citizens. Sidney Verba, Kay Lehman Schlozman, and Henry Brady, the authors of the study, argue that political participation rests largely on two factors: motivation and capacity. They also list a third factor: networks of recruitment. People must want to be active, but they also need the resources which make participation possible. One of the authors' conclusions is that "both the motivation and the capacity to take part in politics have their roots in the fundamental non-political institutions with which individuals are associated during the course of their lives."[36] Among these fundamental institutions are family and school in the earliest years, and later on in life, one's job, various non-political organizations such as a sports club, and religious institutions.

I want to highlight two points. First, there is a clear connection between social life (that is, civil society) and political participation. Second, the authors believe the results of their study provide a deeper understanding than we have had up to now of the significant role which religion plays in American democracy.

The authors of the study propose three reasons why people do not take part in politics: "because they can't; because they don't want to; or because nobody asked."[37] "Can't" suggests a lack of resources; "don't want to" reflects an absence of motivation; and "nobody asked" implies a lack of recruitment. These three factors—motivation, resources, recruitment—together promote political participation and work against political alienation. Because political participation in the United States is a voluntary act, people must want to get involved. There are no sanctions or penalties imposed on those who do not participate. So motivation—which includes interest, adequate information, a belief in the efficacy of political action, and partisan intensity concerning an issue or candidate—is foundational. But overcoming apathy and ignorance is not enough; "it is not sufficient to know and care about politics."[38] Also required are resources for involvement. These include time, money, and civic skills. And third, there are networks of recruitment, those social locales—job sites, voluntary associations, churches—which provide the settings through which solicitations for activity come to us.

At a time when American democracy is in such a poor state, we need to remind ourselves that politics does not exist in a vacuum. It is

36. Verba et al., 3.
37. Ibid., 15.
38. Ibid., 354–55.

closely correlated to the condition of civil society, the existence and vitality of numerous non-political communities. Social institutions such as the family or workplace play a large role in stimulating political engagement and in recruiting voluntary activity. For example, "an argument about politics at the dinner table, a sermon on a public issue at church, a political discussion with a fellow worker or organization member" can motivate. We also know that "requests for political participation often arise in these settings from relatives or acquaintances made in school, in organizations or church, or on the job." Despite the fact that we live in an electronic age, "personal connections among acquaintances, friends, and relatives—often mediated through mutual institutional affiliations—are still crucial for political recruitment."[39]

Chairing a charity event, organizing a food pantry, planning an agenda for a meeting, giving a presentation before a study group—these actions, which are not directly political, foster skills that become easily transferable to political activity. What the authors show is "how ordinary and routine activity on the job, at church, or in an organization, activity that has nothing to do with politics or public issues, can develop organizational and communication skills that are relevant for politics and thus can facilitate political activity."[40] What is especially significant in the study's findings, and of interest to religious people, is the very important role played by the churches in providing the resource of civic skills for political participation. While the workplace offers more opportunities for such skill development than the churches, it does so in a way that promotes inequality. Usually certain kinds of jobs, frequently related to high educational background and financial remuneration, offer the best chances for learning civic skills. It is the churches that consistently provide the opportunity to acquire civic skills on a more equitable basis. Equal access for opportunities to learn civic skills is not stratified by income, education, race, gender, or ethnicity within the churches. This is not the case in the workplace or a variety of other social organizations. In sum, "religious institutions appear to have a powerful potential for enhancing the political resources available to citizens who would, otherwise, be resource-poor."[41]

A key word is "potential," since—and here is the not-so-good news for Catholics—of all the individual churches studied, it is the Catholic Church which has done the poorest job of teaching civic

39. Ibid., 17.
40. Ibid., 17–18.
41. Ibid., 320.

skills. Research shows a distinct difference between Protestant and Catholic Churches in the matter of training in civic skills. Despite the fact that the Catholic Church does offer opportunities for developing such skills in a more equitable way than non-religious institutions, it does so less effectively than its Protestant counterparts. Although not conclusive, the study suggests that the reason for this is the more hierarchical, more clerical style of ecclesiastical organization and leadership, as well as the sheer size of Catholic congregations, which do not encourage as much lay participation as other churches. Further exploration of this topic cannot be done here, but one lesson suggested by the data is that the internal life of a church has an impact on the effectiveness of its social mission.

Conclusion

Political alienation is a complex question, but it is one which cannot be ignored since further decline in political participation will impair the ability of the American people to be truly self-governing. The reversal of that trend is important and it is demonstrably certain that the Christian community has an important role to play in encouraging greater participation. But it is not only the churches which have this role, for what is clear is that many non-political institutions of civil society are important for fostering participation in democratic politics. Thus, subsidiarity will be a principle of a healthy society. And overcoming the alienation of citizens and restoring the vitality of civil society will, in turn, be essential ingredients in the effort to restore an appreciation for the irreplaceable, though limited, role of the state in securing the common good. It is fair to conclude that, among other resources for democratic renewal, the Christian churches, by their social teaching and institutional presence, can assist the American people in each step of the journey to make American democracy once again a government "of the people, by the people and for the people."